MAJESTY IN MISERY

2: THE JUDGMENT HALL

MAJESTY IN MISERY

2: THE JUDGMENT HALL

*Select Sermons on the
Passion of Christ from*

C. H. SPURGEON

THE BANNER OF TRUTH TRUST

THE BANNER OF TRUTH TRUST
3 Murrayfield Road, Edinburgh EH12 6EL, UK
P.O. Box 621, Carlisle, PA 17013, USA

*

© The Banner of Truth Trust 2005
ISBN 0 85151 915 6

*

Typeset in 11.5 /13 pt Sabon MT at the
Banner of Truth Trust, Edinburgh
Printed in the USA by
Versa Press, Inc.,
East Peoria, IL.

CONTENTS

FOLLOW TO THE JUDGMENT HALL;
  View the Lord of life arraigned.
O the wormwood and the gall!
  O the pangs His soul sustained!
Shun not suffering, shame, or loss:
  Learn of Him to bear the cross.
        James Montgomery, 1771–1854

B efore we enter the common hall of the soldiers, and gaze upon 'the sacred head once wounded', it will be well to consider who and what he was who was thus cruelly put to shame. Forget not the intrinsic excellence of his person; for he is the brightness of the Father's glory, and the express image of his person; he is in himself God over all, blessed for ever, the eternal Word by whom all things were made, and by whom all things consist. Though heir of all things, the Prince of the kings of the earth, he was despised and rejected of men, 'a man of sorrows and acquainted with grief'. . . .

What a descent his love to us compelled him to make! See how he fell to lift us from our fall! Do not also fail to re-member that at the very time when they were thus mocking him, he was still the Lord of all, and could have summoned twelve legions of angels to his rescue. There was majesty in his misery . . . Remember these things, and you will gaze upon him with enlightened eyes and tender hearts, and you will be able the more fully to enter into fellowship with him in his griefs. Remember whence he came, and it will the more astound you that he should have stooped so low. Remember what he was, and it will be the more marvellous that he should become our substitute.

                    C. H. SPURGEON, 1834–92

I

CHRIST BEFORE ANNAS ¹

Then the band and the captain and officers of the Jews took
Jesus and bound him and led him away to Annas first: for
he was father in law to Caiaphas, which was the high priest
that same year . . . The high priest then asked Jesus of his
disciples and of his doctrine. Jesus answered him, I spake
openly to the world; I ever taught in the synagogue, and in
the temple, whither the Jews always resort; and in secret
have I said nothing. Why askest thou me? ask them which
heard me, what I have said unto them: behold, they know
what I said. And when he had thus spoken, one of the
officers which stood by struck Jesus with the palm of his
hand, saying, Answerest thou the high priest so? Jesus
answered him, If I have spoken evil, bear witness of the evil:
but if well, why smitest thou me?
JOHN 18:12–13, 19–23

NOTE THE WORDS in verse 13: 'And led him away to Annas
first.' This man Annas has not become so famous as Pontius Pilate,
because his name did not happen to be mentioned in the Creed;
but, in some respects, he was even more guilty than the Roman
governor. He was one of those who handed over our Lord to Pilate,
and he is included in the judgment, 'he that delivered me unto thee
hath the greater sin.' It must not be forgotten that he was *first* in
trying the Saviour; let him have the full benefit of it: *'They led him
away to Annas first.'*

---

¹ Sermon No. 2,820. Preached at the Metropolitan Tabernacle on Thursday
evening, 26 October 1882.

Who was this man, to whose palace the Lord Jesus was first conducted? He was a man who had been high priest actually for a time, and had, for some fifty years, been regarded as high priest by the Jews, while members of his family, one after another, had in turns nominally held the office. The high-priesthood had been degraded from its permanence to become little more than an annual office, and hence the evangelist significantly says of Caiaphas that 'he was the high priest that same year.' But Annas would seem to have been secretly regarded by the Jews as the real high priest, and respect to him in that capacity was the more easily offered because, according to Josephus, five of his sons, and his son-in-law, Caiaphas, had succeeded him in the sacred office. To him, then, it was due that the victim of the priests should be first taken; he shall have this mark of distinction: 'they led him away to Annas first.' The Sacrifice of God, the Lamb of his Passover, the Scapegoat of the Lord's atonement, shall be brought before the priest, ere he be slain.

The house of Annas was united to that of Caiaphas, and it was proposed to detain the prisoner there till the Sanhedrin could be hastily convened for his trial. If he should be brought into the palace of Annas, the old man would be gratified by a sight of Jesus, and by conducting a preliminary examination, acting as deputy for his son-in-law. Without leaving his own house, he could thus indulge his malice, and have a finger in the business. Priestly hate is ever deep and unrelenting.

Today, none are such enemies of Christ's holy gospel as those who delight in priestcraft, and it is not without prophetic meaning that our Lord must be led, as a prisoner, first to a priest's house: 'They led him away to Annas first.' Not in the soldiers' barracks, nor in the governor's hall, but in the high priest's palace must Jesus meet with his first captivity: there it is that a Christ in bonds seems not altogether out of place.

> See how the patient Jesus stands,
> Insulted in His lowest case!
> Sinners have bound the Almighty's hands!
> And spit in their Creator's face!

Annas bore a very promising name, for it signifies *clement* or *merciful,* yet he was the man to begin the work of ensnaring the Lord Jesus in his speech, if he could be ensnared. He examined him first in a semi-private manner, that, by cunning questions, he might extract from him some ground of accusation. Under pretence of mercy, he turned inquisitor, and put his victim to the question. This priest, whose name was clemency, showed the usual tender mercies of the wicked, which are proverbially cruel. When Jesus is to be ill-treated in his servants, there is usually a pretence of pity and compassion. Persecutors are grieved to feel forced to be harsh; their tender spirits are wounded by being compelled to say a word against the Lord's people! Fain would they love them if they would not be so obstinate! With sweet language, they inflict bitter wounds; their words are softer than butter, but inwardly they are drawn swords.

If I read aright the character of this man Annas, he was one of the Saviour's bitterest enemies. He was a Sadducee. Is not this the 'liberal' side? Do we not reckon Pharisees to be the straitest sect of the Jews? Why he should have been so bitter against the Saviour, is pretty clear, since, if Pharisees, in their multiplication of ceremonies and self-righteousness, hate the Christ, so also do the Sadducees, in their unbelief and rejection of the great truths of revelation. Here, Ritualism and Rationalism go hand in hand, and the free-thinker, with all his profession of liberality, usually displays none of it toward the followers of the truth. The Broad Church is usually narrow enough when the doctrine of the cross is under discussion. Whether this Sadducee had an interest in the sales that were effected in the temple, and whether, as some suppose, he was greatly irritated, and touched in a very tender point, namely, in his pocket, when Jesus overthrew the tables of the money-changers, and the seats of them that sold doves, I cannot tell; but, certainly, for some reason or other, Annas was among the first of our Lord's persecutors, not only in order of time, but also in point of malice. The wealthy latitudinarian has a fierce enmity to the gospel of Christ Jesus, and will be found second to none in hunting down the adherents of Christ.

Did the military tribune and his cohort halt at the house of Annas because he had been at the bottom of the business and Pilate had ordered them, for the time, to do the will of the high priest and his father-in-law? Was this long-headed old gentleman the counsellor of the conspirators? Did the force of character, which kept him to the front for half a century, make him a leader at this junctures. Is it possible that they called at the house of Annas to hand over their victim, that Judas might receive the blood-money? At all events we hear no more of the traitor as being in the company of those who had seized upon his Lord.

At any rate, the Lord is led to Annas *first*, and we feel sure that there was a motive for that act. Annas, in some sense, had a priority in the peerage of enmity to Jesus; he was malignant, cruel, and unscrupulous enough to be premier in the ministry of persecutors. In all matters, there are first as well as last, and this man leads the van among the unjust judges of our Lord. He was a favourite of the first and most detestable of the Herods, and a friend of Pilate, the governor, and so, a fit ringleader in procuring the judicial murder of the innocent. All hope of justice was gone when the Holy One and the Just was delivered into those cruel and unrighteous hands. He was as determined as he was cold-blooded, and a lamb might as well look for favour from a wolf as Jesus expect candour from the old deputy high priest. For many a long year, he had held his own by flattering Herod, and the Roman, and the Jew; and he set about the work of mastering the Nazarene with cool determination and deep subtlety, hoping to pave the way for the men of the Sanhedrin who were even then being mustered to do the deed of blood on which their hearts were set.

In the house of this man, then, who is very properly called the high priest, having quite as good a right to the title as Caiaphas had, we see these two things. First, we see *our Lord under examination*; and, secondly, we see *our Lord wrongfully smitten*.

I. First, let us, tenderly, lovingly, adoringly, look at OUR DIVINE MASTER UNDER EXAMINATION.

My first remark is, that *this examination was informal, and extra judicial*. Jesus was not yet accused of anything; so far, no judge had taken his place upon the judgment-seat, neither were any witnesses called to give evidence against the prisoner. It was a sort of private examination, held with the view of extorting something from the captive, which might afterwards be used against him. You know how strongly and how properly our law forbids anything of the kind; and, though it may not have been contrary to Jewish law, it was certainly contrary to the eternal laws of right. A prisoner should not thus be questioned with the object of entangling him in his speech, and making him incriminate himself. If there is no charge formulated against him, let him go his way. If the entries on the charge-sheet are not completed, let him be remanded; but let him not be set before one of his most cruel foes to be questioned to his own hurt.

This is what was done in our Saviour's case when he was brought before Annas, and I think that I know many who treat him, at this time, quite as badly. They ask questions about him, and make enquiries concerning him; but they do not do it honestly and sincerely, or according to the rules of justice. You know how captious unbelievers often are, how they pick up any misquoted text, or half a text rent from its connection, and say that they are enquiring about Christ, when they are not doing it either judicially or as they would wish to be questioned were they themselves under examination. I fear that the bulk of those who cavil at the faith of Christ, do it not as honest men, and not as they would wish to have their own characters investigated. The last book which some of them think of reading is the New Testament, and the last thing that they try to understand is Christ's true character; and one of the last things that they will ever listen to is a full and fair statement of what his gospel really is. Still, to this day, the representatives of Annas are here, and there, and almost everywhere, questioning the followers of Christ, with the design of finding out something to jeer at, something which may be hawked about as a discrepancy, or held up as obsolete, and inconsistent with the spirit of this wonderful century, of which I hear so often that I am utterly sick of it, and long for the time when the nineteenth century shall go down to its ignoble grave.

Next, *this questioning of Christ was one-sided*: 'The high priest then asked Jesus of his disciples, and of his doctrine.' Why did he not ask him about himself – who and what he was, and enquire specially concerning his miracles, and his whole course of life? Why did not Annas enquire, 'Didst thou raise the dead? Didst thou open blind eyes? Didst thou heal the lepers? Didst thou go about doing good?' Oh, no! there was no question about any such things; they were all passed over as of no importance.

The questions began with the weakest point of all, or that which men have often regarded as the weakest; he 'asked Jesus of his disciples'. Can a leader help the follies and weaknesses of his followers? I suppose Annas put his question thus, 'Where are your disciples?' Ah! there was Peter down there in the hall, but Christ could not call him up to witness for him; John was probably somewhere in the background, but the rest had forsaken their Lord, and fled. Annas no doubt asked, 'Who are these disciples of thine? Where didst thou pick them up?' I daresay he knew that they were men of Galilee, mostly plain fishermen, and he meant to cast a slur upon Christ on that account. If he had known more about those disciples, he might have put a great many questions which would have reflected but little honour upon the religion of Jesus.

This is just as men do now, they ask concerning Christ's disciples. I do not deny that it is quite fair to enquire what is the influence of Christianity upon the men who believe it; but, oftentimes, that one point is thrust so prominently into the front that the wonders which Christ himself wrought are thrown into the background, and the investigation thus becomes one-sided. We are quite willing that Christ himself, and his work, all that has been, all that is to be, all his designs and purposes, should be examined; but, for the most part, men search for that which they think to be the weakest point of assault, and they say, 'Look at So-and-so, one of Christ's disciples; and look at So-and-so, one of his ministers. See what divisions there are in the churches'; and so forth. Yes; but, surely, if Christ be examined at all, he deserves to have a full and fair examination, it should not be upon one point alone. Blessed be his name, it matters not upon what point he is examined, He always has his answer ready, and a glorious one it is. If men were really willing to know the truth, they would take an all-round view of him, and look at him from this point and from that, and then judge him.

Further, *this examination was very disorderly*, for the high priest asked Christ 'of his disciples, and of his doctrine'. Now, logically, the enquiry should have been first concerning his doctrine, and then with respect to his disciples – first as to his teaching, and then as to the people influenced by it. But men like Annas put their questions anyhow – upside down, the first last and the last first – so that they may secure some accusation against Christ. Now, if any man will sit down quietly, and really study the life, and character, and teaching of Jesus of Nazareth, we shall be delighted to hear what he has to say about it; but let him study it in due order. Let him not pick out this, and leave out that, and put everything out of gear, so as to make a monster of him. Let him be looked at after the same manner as one would look at any other religious teacher, or as we might examine the character of any man brought before a court of law. I ask those, if there be any such now present, who have spoken harshly of our blessed Lord and Master, to do themselves the justice, and to do Christ the justice, to adopt another course, and to examine him as they would wish to be examined themselves, if their character and their designs were called in question.

Annas did not so, for *his examination of Christ was concerning his disciples and his doctrine*. With regard to his disciples, our Master said nothing. He had been saying much about them to his Father, and, in his almighty love and wisdom, he could have said much, there and then, concerning his disciples, if he had chosen to do so; but he did not and therein he proved his wisdom. All through the Scriptures, we find comparatively little said concerning God's people. The record is mostly of their faults and their failings. The reason for that is that this is not the day of their manifestation. That day comes on apace; and, 'when he shall appear, we shall be like him; for we shall see him as he is.' 'Then shall the righteous shine forth as the sun in the kingdom of their Father.' Annas thought that Christ's followers were a set of fanatics – ignorant, unskilled, worthless people, the lower orders. The catacombs tell us, as we read the rude inscriptions there, how few of those godly folk, of whom the world was not worthy, were men of education; the most of them were evidently plain, humble, common people. Our Lord Jesus Christ has no great reverence for earthly rank or grandeur; he loves the man, but cares little for the garb he wears; and of the poorest saints it is true that 'he is not ashamed to call them brethren'.

It is a mercy for us, who are on Christ's side, and who have been despised in consequence, that, in the resurrection, there will also be a resurrection of reputations as well as of bodies. There will be a bestowal of honour that has been denied here and of credit that has been refused on the earth. God has said it, so it must be true, 'Light is sown for the righteous', and their glad harvest time shall surely come; and then the glory will for ever blot out the shame and derision which may have been poured upon the faithful for the sake of Jesus Christ their Lord and Master. As yet, we will not ask him concerning his disciples; but that is the point that the adversary harps upon. Therefore, O ye disciples of Jesus, watch and pray, and seek to be like your Master! Pray to be kept from the evil which is in the world; and, as for the rest, if men despise you, count that as part of the bargain upon which you have entered, a bargain which shall, in due season, fill you with bliss eternal.

Annas also asked Christ concerning his doctrine – what it was that he taught to those who listened to him. I will not go into that matter, for I want to speak at some length upon the answer *which Christ gave to Annas*. He first protested that it was not fair for him to be thus questioned in private as to what he had said in public. The proper thing was to ask those who had heard him, For, said he, 'I spake openly to the world; I ever taught in the synagogue, and in the temple.' I chose the most public places for my teaching; I had no hole-and-corner gatherings, no little conventicle in which I urged my followers to sedition. No, 'I spake openly'. The heavens heard me. On the side of the hills, I proclaimed my message. By the seashore, I spake to all who gathered around me; multitudes were often present at my services; they know what I said, and they could bear witness concerning it if they were asked to do so.'

There was great openness about Christ. There was an utter absence of anything like the Jesuitical plan of saying one thing and meaning another, or using expressions that had double meaning in them. It is true that our Lord did not explain to the great mass of the people all that he said to them, for they were so stupid that they would not receive it; but, at the same time, there was nothing that his hearers really needed to know that he concealed from them. He carried his heart where all might read it; and even in his common teaching to the multitude, there was, if they had but had eyes to see it, all that he taught to his disciples in the most private place. There was no wish, on his part, to keep back any truth that ought to be made known to those who gathered to hear him.

I have heard it said that there are certain truths in God's Word which it is better for us not to preach. It is admitted that they are true, but it is alleged that they are not edifying. I will not agree to any such plan; this is just going back to old Rome's method. Whatsoever it has seemed good to God's wisdom to reveal, it is wise for God's servants to proclaim. Who are we that we are to judge between this truth and that and to say that this we are to preach, and that we are to withhold? This system would make us to be, after all, the judges of what Christ's gospel is to be. It must not be so among us, beloved; that would be assuming a responsibility which we are quite unable to bear. I believe that it is because the doctrines of grace have been too much kept from the pulpit, that the pews are getting so empty. Leave the doctrines of grace out of the preaching, and you have left the marrow and fatness out of it. What is there to make the people rush to your houses of prayer, and crowd them, if there be no preaching of the election of grace – no declaration of particular redemption, and effectual calling, no proclamation of the blessed final perseverance of the saints? If you leave these glorious truths out of your preaching, you have put on the table nothing but the horseradish and the parsley, but the joint of meat is conspicuous by its absence.

Some people say that these things are to be talked of among the saints, but must not be preached to sinners. Oh, say not so! Every doctrine of God's Word is good; every truth in the Bible is precious; and the omission of any one part of it, wilfully, and with design, may so impair the whole of our testimony that, instead of being, like Hermon, wet with dew, our ministry will be like the accursed Gilboa, upon which no dew descended. Whatsoever the Lord has taught to you by his Spirit, my brother, tell to others. According as you have opportunity, reveal to them what God has revealed to you; remember how Christ himself charged his disciples, 'What I tell you in darkness, that speak to in light; what ye hear in the ear, that preach ye upon the housetops.' And, today, the sublime and

9

majestic truths, which cluster around the sovereignty of God, are as much to be proclaimed as the softer, and tenderer, and apparently more winsome words which tell of infinite mercy to the chief of sinners. All truths are to be preached in due proportion; there is a time for this, and a time for that, and none must be omitted. There is a particular stone which is to be the key of the arch, and another which is to go on this side, another lower down, and yet another lower down still, and the omitting of any one stone, because it does not happen to be of what we reckon to the orthodox shape for usefulness, may spoil the whole bridge, and it may come down with a crash. Oh, that we may so build in our teaching, that our building will last throughout eternity! At the end of our ministry, may we be able to say, 'I have kept back nothing; all that Christ taught to me, I have taught to others, and so I have made full proof of my ministry.' Christ was able to appeal to those who had heard him, and who could tell what his testimony had been. May God give us grace to imitate him in this respect!

Our blessed Lord answered Annas by referring him to his public life and teaching. There was no need for any other defence. We cannot imagine anything more convincing. No eloquence of speech, or forcibleness of argument, could have so completely put the wily adversary out of the field. The inquisitor himself was so ashamed, and for the moment so confounded, that a zealous official struck Jesus with his open hand. The innocent, unabashed face of the persecuted Nazarene was thus smitten because his simple defence had silenced his cruel opponent. What a wonderful answer it was! How it commends his whole character to us, and makes him seem to be even more truly majestic than ever!

I am sure there is not one of us who would dare to say of our lives, at least not so unreservedly, what Jesus could truly say of his. Our Lord's life was emphatically lived among men. He was no recluse. From early morning to the last thing at night, he was associated with men; and, therefore, all that he did was done before the eyes of men. That 'fierce light that beats about a throne' ever beat about him. He was constantly being watched; every word that he uttered was remembered. Again and again, his enemies endeavoured to catch him in his speech. He could scarcely be allowed a moment's leisure, when he might unbosom himself, like one at his own fireside. He was always before the Argus-eyes of the ungodly world, who would see faults where there were none, and who, if there had been the least speck of blame, would have magnified it, and published it to the ends of the earth.

Moreover, our Lord was by no means a silent man. He spoke, and spoke often. Witness the Books that we have by way of record of that quiet life of his; and the things that he said and did were far more than those that are recorded, for John says, 'And there are also many other things which Jesus did, the which, if they should be written every one, I suppose that even the world itself could not contain the books that should be written.' Yet there was never any act or word of Christ's in which friend or foe could find a single speck of sin at all. He could even challenge Satan himself to find a flaw in his life: 'The prince of this world cometh, and hath nothing in me.'

His speech, too, was not only very frequent, but it was also very plain. He spoke so simply that even little children could understand him; I should think there was never one person in his audience who could truthfully say that he could not comprehend what the Preacher meant; and yet, though they could all tell what his meaning was, they could not honestly find fault with that meaning.

Another thing that is worthy of observation is that, frequently, he spoke under great provocation; yet he never lost his temper, nor spoke unadvisedly with his lips. You and I know that, if we ever lose our temper, we are apt to say all manner of unwise, and foolish, and wicked words; but our blessed Saviour never sinned in that way, however great was the provocation to which he was subjected. He was also often misrepresented; and our tendency is, when men speak falsely of us, to go beyond the bounds of truth or prudence in replying to them. Our Lord Jesus never did that. The pendulum of the great clock of his wonderful life never swung too far either one way or the other. You have not to correct any one saying of the Saviour by what he said at some other time; all his utterances are absolute truth, whether taken separately, or taken together. Even the false witnesses, who were bribed to bring accusations against him, altogether failed to find anything that could be laid to his charge.

It must not be forgotten, also, that our blessed Master frequently spoke in the midst of turmoil. He did not always have such a quiet, orderly assembly as we have when we gather for public worship; but he had to speak, often, amidst the clamour of the angry mob, and the opposition and even the maledictions of those who hated him. Yet, even under these trying circumstances, he spoke so that he could fearlessly challenge them all to find fault with anything that he had said in their hearing. Our Lord had spoken to all sorts of characters – bad, good, and indifferent – and there was especially one, who betrayed him, who had heard many of his most secret speeches. Judas had been with him in his retirement, and had listened to his words when only the favoured few had been present, yet there was no single sentence or syllable that even he could plead in extenuation of his great crime in betraying his Lord.

II. I have spoken, at such length, upon this first part of my subject that I have very little time left for the second portion, namely, OUR LORD JESUS WRONGFULLY SMITTEN: 'When he had thus spoken, one of the officers which stood by struck Jesus with the palm of his hand, saying, Answerest thou the high priest so?'

His answer was a very simple one, and a very proper one in all respects; yet, at the same time, it must have been a very stinging one if Annas was the kind of man that I think he was, for our Saviour seemed to say, (you may read it between the lines,) '*I* am not plotting in secret against another man's life. *I* have not talked with another man with the object of entangling him in his speech. *I* have not been a conspirator, but I have spoken publicly in the synagogues, and taught in the temple, in the very centre of the place of concourse; but, in secret have I said nothing.' This must have been a very sharp rebuke to Annas, if any conscience was left in the wretched man; so one of the abjects that stood around the hierarch smote Christ, and said, 'Answerest thou the high priest so?'

Now, in the first instance, Christ met with the opposition of so-called enquiry; but here he had the vulgar opposition of persecution. Alas! there are still many, who never enquire about Christ at all, but they decide against him, and then they begin to persecute wife, child, friend, neighbour, or whoever it may be that is on

Christ's side; and, often, they strike him as this officer struck our Lord. This was a most cowardly act, for Christ was bound and helpless. Yet we have the same sort of conduct in our own day. It does seem to me a wretched thing that, if some people choose to go through the streets singing hymns, they shall be pelted with stones and mud while their own hands are bound. They cannot turn round, and fight their assailants, for their Christianity has tied their hands, and the cruel mobs know it. If these men want to fight, why do they not find some fellows, like themselves, walking through the streets, and attack them, and then see what will come of it? They are afraid to do that; for, to this day, persecution is always against men whose hands are bound. If our religion taught us to answer sharply, and to give cuff for cuff, and kick for kick, it would be all fair; but when we are commanded not to resist evil, and our very faithfulness to Christ prevents our replying to the foul language that is used against us, it is brutally cruel that we should be thus persecuted. Read all history through, and see whether some have not degraded themselves utterly beneath contempt by burning men who would not have touched a hair of their heads – and putting to death poor men and women who could not have done them any injury, and who never wished to do so. That is the story of Christ and his followers all the way through – first, to be questioned by people who do not want to know the truth; and, next, to be persecuted by people who really have not anything to say against them.

To the man who thus wrongfully smote him, our Saviour said, 'If I have spoken evil, bear witness of the evil: but if well, why smitest thou me?' We also may say to those who wantonly smite Christ's followers. 'Why do ye so? Has Christianity done any harm to manhood in general, or to you in particular?' What has been the force that has broken the power of tyrants? At the bottom, in many countries, it has been the Word of God that has made men free. In our own times, what ended the slave trade, and set the Negro free? What is it that, today, is the most potent force against the drunkenness of our land? Surely, nothing but the gospel of Jesus Christ. Have we, as Christians, any aim, in all the world, of which anyone can accuse us? Are we doing mischief to our fellow-men? Do we teach drunkenness, or lust, or oppression? Do you hear from

13

us anything about robbing you of your birthright, or injuring you in any way whatsoever? Nay, you know that it is not so. Our war is for peace. Every blow that we strike is against blows. If we have to denounce anything, we do most of all denounce denunciation; and if we are bitter at all, most of all are we bitter against bitterness, and envy, and malice, and all uncharitableness.

Oh, that we could always give to our persecutors such an answer as our blessed Master gave, to the officer who smote him, 'If I have spoken evil, bear witness of the evil: but if well, why smitest thou me?' There are times when we dare not say that, but we would rather say, 'If I have spoken evil, do not recall it, do not bring it to my recollection. If I have spoken evil, try to forget it; or, at least, if thou rememberest it, repeat it not to another, for I am afraid that I may have said much that might stain my profess sign, and grieve my God.' I think that, if we had our choice as to whether we would be smitten on the face, or have our own words brought up as witnesses against us, we should each one, say, 'If I have spoken evil, do not bear witness of the evil; but much rather smite me than bear witness against me.'

Yet it is not always so; there are times when, in conscious integrity, or concerning certain words or acts of ours, we can challenge any man to find fault with us; but, taking the whole range of our lives, in public and in private, most of us would be loath to ask for such a test as that. When our adversaries persecute us, we might say to them, 'Ah! did you really know all that we have been, you would not so much persecute us for our goodness, but punish us for our badness.' When I have been slandered, I have often said to myself, 'Ah! they have spoken a lie against me; but, if they had known me better, they might have said quite as bad a thing as that, and yet have only spoken what was true.' There is not one man living, who is in his right senses, who would like to have all his thoughts written down, or all his words and acts recorded. We have often wished that half our words could be blotted out with our tears, and then the other half would have to be washed with blood before we could ourselves endure it, and much less could our Lord endure it without the application of that precious blood of Jesus, that cleanseth from all sin.

Now, I think that all this, of which I have been speaking to you, ought very much to endear the Master to us; and it will do so if we remember and believe that God 'hath made him to be sin for us, who knew no sin, that we might be made the righteousness of God in him.' Here is a Lamb, that is fit for sacrifice. The high priest and all his officers may examine it as much as they please; they will find that it is perfect. There is not a blemish in it. There is no redundance, and there is no omission. There is neither speck nor spot of sin in Christ; we cannot find any fault in him. Whether we look at him within or without, in his youth, or in his childhood, or in his manhood – in his life or in his death – in his speech or in his silence, in his feelings, or in his thoughts, or in his acts – he is good, and only good, and blessed be his holy name forever and ever! Amen.

2

CHRIST IN BONDS[1]

Now Annas had sent him bound unto Caiaphas the high
priest. [The *Revised Version* says, Annas therefore sent
him bound unto Caiaphas the high priest.]
JOHN 18:24

OUR ONLY SUBJECT, on this occasion, is, CHRIST IN BONDS
– the Son of God as an Ambassador in bonds, a King in chains –
the God-man sent, bound, to take his trial in the court of the high
priest, Caiaphas.

It seems to me that this binding of our Lord shows, first, something of fear on the part of his captors. Why did they bind him?
He would not attack them; he had no desire to escape out of
their hands; yet, probably, they thought that he might break loose
from them, or in some way outwit them. Alas! that men should
ever have been thus afraid of him who came alone from heaven,
neither bearing arms nor wearing armour – who came to injure
none, nor even to protect himself against the hurts that any might
inflict upon him – at first, lying as a babe in a manger, and all
his life long exhibiting rather the weakness of manhood than its
strength; yet were his adversaries often afraid of him. So is it still;
there is a latent, secret conviction in the minds of men that the
Christ is greater than he seems to be. Even when they attack him
with their infidel weapons, they never seem to be satisfied with
their own arguments, and they are continually seeking fresh ones.
To this very day, the ungodly are afraid of Christ, and, often,
their raging against him resembles the noise made by the boy

---

[1] Sermon No. 2,822. Preached at the Metropolitan Tabernacle on Thursday
evening, 2 November 1882.

who, when hurrying through the graveyard, whistles to keep his courage up.

They also bound Christ, no doubt, to increase the shame of his condition. Our Saviour said to those who came to arrest him in the garden, 'Are ye come out as against a thief, with swords, and with staves to take me?' And now they bound him fast as though he were a thief – perhaps tied his hands, with tight cords, behind his back, to show that they regarded him as a felon, and that they were not taking him into a civil court where some case of law might be pending, but they already condemned him by the very act of binding him. They treated him as if he were already sentenced, and were not worthy to stand, a free man, and plead for himself before the judgment-seat. Oh, what a shame that the Lord of life and glory should be bound – that he, whom angels delight to worship, that he who is the very sun of their heaven, should yet be bound as though he were a malefactor, and be sent away to be tried for his life!

We may also look at this matter of the binding of the Saviour as an increase of his pain. I suppose none of you have ever been bound as our Lord was at that time; if you had been, you would know the discomfort and pain which must attend such action. John tells us that, in Gethsemane, 'the band and the captain and officers of the Jews took Jesus, and bound him.' He had scarcely risen from his knees, and the bloody sweat was like fresh ruby dew upon him, yet these men 'bound him, and led him away to Annas first'. I do not find any indication that his bonds were unloosed by Annas, or that he had even a moment's relief or relaxation granted to him; but, with the cruel ropes still binding him fast, he was sent across the great hall into the other wing of the palace in which Caiaphas resided: 'Annas sent him bound unto Caiaphas.' Then this, surely, must have been done in very wantonness of malice. I have already said that they seemed to have some sort of fear that their captive would, after all, escape from them; yet they might, readily enough, have banished that fear from their minds. There was no need to bind HIM. O cruel persecutors, look into his face! If you are resolved to lead him away to his death, you may lead him like a sheep goes to the slaughter. He will not even open his mouth to upbraid you. There was no need to put any bonds upon One so gentle as he was. Out of very wantonness, I say, they must have done it, that they might express their hatred by every conceivable method, both in the little details, and in the great end at which they were aiming all the while, namely, to put him to a most painful death. Ah, me! how shamefully was our blessed Master maltreated in this inhospitable world! Men had often been regicides, and we need not wonder at that when we think what tyrants they were who were thus slain; but these men were turning into deicides, putting to death the Son of God himself; and, ere they did it, they heaped upon him every mark of scorn and dishonour that was possible, that they might cause him to die with opprobrium as well as with pain.

You, who love your Saviour, will think with tender sympathy of how he was bound by these wicked men; my special object is, to try to find out what are the lessons which we may learn from the bonds of Christ.

I. The first lesson is this. From the binding of our dear Redeemer, I learn a lesson concerning sin. THE BONDS OF CHRIST TEACH US WHAT SIN WOULD DO TO GOD IF IT COULD.

The unregenerate heart, in its enmity against God, would treat him exactly as the men of nineteen hundred years ago served the Son of God. What was done to Jesus is just what man would do, if he could, to the Lord God of heaven and earth himself. 'What!' say you, 'would men bind God?' Ah, sirs! they would do much more than that if they could, but they would certainly do that. They would annihilate God if they could, for 'the fool hath said in his heart, "No God"' – that is to say, 'No God for me!' He would kill God if it were possible. There would be no gladder news to many men, who are living today, than for them to be informed, with absolute certainty, that there was no God at all; all their fears would be at once silenced by such tidings. As for us, who love and trust him, all our joys would be gone, and our worst fears would be realized, if God were gone; but, as for the ungodly, it would be the gladdest news that ever was rung out from church steeple if they could be assured that God was dead. They would kill him if they could; but, as they cannot kill him; they seek to bind him.

Observe how they try to do this *by denying his power.* There are many men, who say that they believe in God, yet what sort of God is it in whom they believe? It is a God who is fettered by his own laws. 'Here is the world,' they say, 'but let not anyone suppose that God has anything to do with the world.' They seem to have a theory that somehow or other, it got wound up, like a great clock, and it has been going on ever since. God has not even been to see it; indeed, the probability is that he cannot see. Their god does not see, and does not know anything; he is not the living God. They pretend to pay him the compliment of saying that there may be some great first cause; they do not know even that for certain, because they do not know anything. We live in an age in which the man, who professes to be a learned man, calls himself 'an agnostic' – a Greek word which, in the Latin, signifies 'an ignoramus'. That is, when you get to be a very clever man, then you become an ignoramus, knowing nothing at all. Such people go crowing, all over the world, that they do not know anything at all; they do not know whether there is any God at all, or if there is a God, they do not know that he has anything to do with the world. They say that it is going on just on its own account. God may set worlds going if he pleases, but he has nothing do with them afterwards.

Ah, beloved! but the truth is, that God's laws are simply the ways in which he acts. There is no force in the world apart from God. All the potency of attraction is simply because God still lives, and pours his energy into the matter that attracts. Every moment, it is God who works in all things according to the good pleasure of his own will. Omnipotence is, in fact, the source of all the potency that there is in the universe. God is everywhere; and, instead of being banished from the world, and the world going on without him, if God were not here, this planet, and the sun, and moon, and stars, would retire into their native nothingness, as a moment's foam subsides into the wave that bears it, and is gone for ever. God alone is. All the rest – call them what you please – are appearances that come out of his ever-existing power. God is. The other things may be or may not be; but God is. Well did David write, under the Spirit's inspiration, 'God hath spoken once; twice have I heard this: that power belongeth unto God.' But that is not the kind of God that the ungodly want; they want one whose hands they can bind so as to make him powerless.

Especially will they do this *with regard to providence*. 'Look,' say they; 'you Christian people pray, and you are foolish enough to believe that, because you pray, God hears you, and sends you the blessings that you ask for.' It is assumed that we are fools; but, I think, it is a mere assumption. Probably, these gentlemen, who are so generous in disposing of their epithets, may be giving away what really belongs to themselves We are fools; so they say – these men of culture, the thinking people; at least, they are the people who call themselves by these high-sounding names, and having done so, then, to prove that their culture has made perfect gentle-men of them, they call all the rest of us, and especially all Christians, fools. Well, we are not anxious to contend with them as to that matter, and we are quite satisfied to take the position that we do take, and to be called fools, because we believe that God does hear and answer our petitions. Even when these people are willing to own that there is a God in providence at all, he is hand-tied, so that he can do nothing. Well, as far as I am concerned, I would as soon believe in a god made out of the mud of the Ganges, or in the fetish of the Hottentot, as bow my knee to a god who could not hear, and could not answer me.

Some unbelievers talk of a God who is hand bound *so far as the punishment of sin is concerned*. 'Men will die like dogs'; so some of these doggish men say, 'God will not punish sin'; so say some sinners, who imagine that they have prepared a dunghill for them-selves to fall upon whenever God shall fling them out of window as utterly worthless. They imbibe ideas that are contrary to the truth about the Most High in order that they may be able to sin with impunity. But, whatever they may think or say, let us rest assured that there is a God, and that he is a God before whom every one of us must appear to give an account of the deeds done in the body, whether they be good or whether they be evil. We may be quite certain that, although, in his longsuffering, he may patiently wait a while before punishing iniquity, yet his hand is not bound, and he will lift it ere long; and when he raises it to smite the man who has broken his laws, he will do it so effectually that the sinner shall know that, verily, there is a God who will not pass by transgression, or wink at sin, when it remains unrepented of. Let us, then, be ever happy to bear our testimony that God cannot be bound, but let us always expect to see unconverted men, in one way or another, attempting to bind the hands of the Most High as these sinners in Jerusalem bound the Christ of God.

Some people think that God ought to do this, and he ought not to do that; and the moment you begin to reason with them, they do not refer to what the Scripture says, but they have a preconceived notion as to what ought to be done or not done. That is to say, you would tie his hands, so that *he must do what you judge to be right;* but, if he judges any particular course to be right, and it does not meet your taste, then, straightway, you will either have no God at all, or else a god that shall be handcuffed by your reason, and held in bonds to do your bidding. In the person of our blessed Master brought from Gethsemane with his hands tightly bound, we see an exact picture of what wicked men would always do with God if they could, and what they actually do to him, spiritually, in their own minds and hearts. God save us from being guilty of such a sin as that! Oh, that the precious blood of our Lord Jesus Christ may cleanse that sin away if it lies as a load upon the conscience of anyone whom I am now addressing!

II. Secondly, we have here A LESSON OF LOVE.

Our Lord Jesus was sent away, bound, by Annas to Caiaphas; but, before they bound him, there were other bands upon him. *Christ was bound by the cords of love;* and who but himself had bound him thus? Of old, or ever the earth was, his prescient eye foresaw all his people, and their sin, and he loved them, and he gave himself to them then, in the eternal purpose; and often did he look, through the vista of the ages, upon the men and women who were yet to be born, and, with a near and dear love to each one of them, he pledged himself that, for them, he would bear the shame, and the spitting, and that he would even die in their room and stead, that he might redeem them unto himself. So, when I see our Divine Master thus led to the judgment-seat, I grieve over the bonds of cord with which men tied him, but my heart exults over these invisible bands with which he bound himself by purpose, by covenant, by oath, by infinite, immutable love, that he would give himself to be a ransom for his people.

Then, following upon those cords of love, if you look closely, you will see his love again displayed in that *he was bound with our bonds*. We, dear friends, had sinned against God, and so had incurred the sentence of infallible justice, and now that sentence must fall upon him. We ought to have been bound, but Christ was bound instead of us. If you and I had been bound with despair, and hopelessly led away to that prison from which none shall ever escape; if this had been the moment when we were commencing to feel the torments of the hell which our sins deserve, what could we have said? But, lo! in our room, and place, and stead, Jesus is led away to bear the wrath of heaven. He must not lift his hand in his own defence, or raise his finger for his own comfort, for he is bearing –

> That we might never bear,
> His Father's righteous ire.

III. But now, thirdly, learn hence A LESSON OF GREAT PRIVILEGE.

Our Lord Jesus Christ was bound, and there flows from that fact its opposite, *then, his, people are all free*. When Christ was made a curse for us, he became a blessing to us. When Christ was made sin for us, we were made the righteousness of God in him. When he died, then we lived. And so, as he was bound, we are set free. The type of that exchange of prisoners is seen in the fact that Barabbas was set free when the Lord Jesus Christ was given up to be crucified; and still more in his plea for his disciples in the garden, 'If therefore ye seek me, let these go their way.' It is with wondrous joy in our hearts that we sing –

> We were sore in bondage bound,
> But our Jesus set us free.

Do we, think you, dear friends, use our liberty as we should? Do we not, sometimes, pray to God as if we were tongue-tied, and had the bonds upon our tongue? Do we not go to the great coffers full of grace, and, instead of helping ourselves, as we have the right to do, we stand there as if our hands were bound, and we could not take a single pennyworth of the abundant fullness that is laid up there for us? Sometimes, when there is work to be done for Christ, we feel as if we were in bonds. We dare not stretch out our hands, we are afraid to do so; yet Jesus has set us free. O believer, why dost thou go about as if thou still didst wear the fetters on thy feet? Why dost thou stand like one who is still in bonds? Thy freedom is sure freedom, and it is righteous freedom. Christ, the great Emancipator, has made thee free, and thou art 'free indeed'. Enjoy thy liberty; enjoy access to God; enjoy the privilege of claiming the promises which God has given to you. Enjoy the exercise of the power with which God has endowed you, enjoy the holy anointing with which the Lord has prepared you for his service. Do not sit and mope like a bird in a cage, when you are free to soar away. I can conceive of a bird, that has been in a cage for years; the cage may be all taken away – every wire of it; and yet the poor thing has been so accustomed to sit on that perch inside the cage, that it takes no notice of the fact that its prison-house is gone, and there it sits and mopes still. Away with thee, sweet songster! The green fields and the blue sky are all thine own. Stretch thy wings, and soar away above the clouds, and sing the carol of thy freedom as though thou wouldst make it reach the ears of the angels. So let it be with your spirit, and with mine, beloved. Christ has set us free; therefore, let us not go back into bondage, or sit still as though we were in prison, but let us rejoice in our liberty this very hour, and let us do so all our days.

IV. The fourth lesson, from the binding of Christ, is A LESSON OF OBLIGATION.

This may seem like a paradox in contrast with the previous lesson, yet is it equally true. Beloved, was Jesus bound for you and for me? *Then, let us be bound for him and to him.* I rejoice in the sweet inability that results from perfect love to Christ. 'Inability?' you ask. Yes, I mean inability. The true child of God 'cannot sin, because he is born of God.' There are many other things that he cannot do; he cannot forsake his Lord, for he says, with Peter, 'Lord, to whom shall we go? Thou hast the words of eternal life.' He cannot forget his obligations; he cannot withhold his time, his strength, his substance, from his Lord; he cannot become an earthworm and a money-grabber. He cannot wed his soul to any other, for Christ has espoused him to himself as a chaste virgin. There are times when the child of God says, with Nehemiah, 'Should such a man as I flee?' Or, 'How can such a privileged individual as I am indulge in such-and-such a sin?' The ungodly sometimes jeer at us, and say, 'Ah, you cannot do so-and-so! We can.' And we reply, 'We have lost no power that we ever wish to have, and we have gained the power of concentrating all our force upon righteousness and truth; and, now, our heart is bound too fast to Christ for us to go after your idols. Our eyes are now so taken up with the sight of our Saviour that we cannot see any charms in the things with which you would bewitch us. Our memory is now so full of Christ that we have no desire to pollute the precious stores that lie therein by memories of sin.'

Henceforth, we are crucified with Christ, and that brings to us a blessed inability in which we greatly rejoice. Our heart may stir, perhaps, a little, but our hands and feet are fastened to the wood, and cannot move. Oh, blessed is the inability when, at last, neither heart can love, nor brain can think, nor hand can do, nor even imagination can conceive anything that goes beyond the sweet circle of a complete consecration to the Lord, and absolute dedication to his service! Come, then, ye angels of the Lord, and bind us to him! Let this be the prayer of every believer, 'Bind the sacrifice with cords, even unto the horns of the altar.' Let nothing ever tempt us away from our Lord. Ye may count the cost of all Egypt's treasure, and then let it go; and it shall vanish like a dream, for there is nothing in it.

> Solid joys and lasting treasure,
> None but Zion's children know –

and these shall remain with you who are bound to Christ, with him to live, and for him to die, if need be. So, whenever we see Christ in bonds, let us pray that we also may wear his bonds, and be just as much bound as he was. 'O God!' let every Christian say, 'I am thy servant, and the son of thine handmaid. Thou hast loosed my bonds, now bind me to thyself and to thy blessed service once for all.'

V. The last lesson is one which I pray that we may all of us learn, whether we are saints or sinners; it is A LESSON OF WARNING.

Dear friends, I have tried to picture, though I have done it in a very feeble way, Christ being bound with cords; and now I want very solemnly to say to all of you, Do not you bind Christ with cords. Beware, you who are unconverted, that you never bind Christ. You may do so *by not reading his Word*. You have a Bible at home, but you never read it; it is clasped, laid away in a drawer with your best pocket handkerchiefs. Is it not so? That is another picture of Christ in bonds – a poor shut-up Bible, that is never allowed to speak with you – nay, not even to have half a word with you, for you are in such a hurry about other things that you cannot listen to it. Untie the cords; let it have its liberty. Commune with it sometimes. Let the heart of God in the Bible speak to your own heart. If you do not, that clasped Bible – that shut-up Bible – that precious Book hidden away in the drawer – is Christ in prison; and, one day, when you little expect it, you will hear Christ say, 'Inasmuch as ye did this to the greatest of all my witnesses, ye did it unto me.' You kept Moses, and Isaiah, and Jeremiah, and all the prophets, in prison; and all the apostles, and the Master himself, you bound with cords, and you would not hear a word that they had to say. Let not that be true of any one of you, dear friends.

There are others *who will not go to hear the Word*. They do not attend any place of worship. They may have dropped in here for once; but, as a rule, they never go anywhere to worship God. Here, in London, people live in the street where there is a soul-saving ministry, yet many of them never cross the threshold of the house of prayer. In some streets, not one in a hundred ever darkens the doors of the place where God's people gather for worship. Is not that tying Christ's hands? How can the gospel get to people who will not hear it – absolutely refuse to listen to it? They are really gagging our blessed Master, and that is even worse than binding him with cords. They thrust a gag between his teeth, and make him hold his tongue so far as they are concerned. Some of them, if they could, would gag the messenger as well as his Master, for they want him not. 'Trouble us not,' they say. 'Art thou come to torment us before the time?' And so they bind Christ, and send him away, just as Annas sent him bound to Caiaphas.

Some there are, who both read the Bible, and go to hear the gospel, but they tie Christ up, all the same, *by prejudice.* Some people can never get a blessing, through certain ministers, because they have made up their minds that they will not be profited by them. You know how they come, with some preconceived notion; and though an angel from heaven were to speak, they would pick holes in whatever he might say, because of the prejudice which exists in their mind. Probably, they can give no better reason for their antagonism than the person gave who did not like Dr Fell –

> I do not like you, Dr Fell,
> The reason why, I cannot tell;
> But this I know, and know full well,
> I do not like you, Dr Fell.

I have known men bind Christ in another way, *by delaying their decision.* They have heard a sermon, and have felt its power, their soul has been impressed by it; but their chief idea has been to try to escape from Christ, or to bind his hands, if possible. I think I have told you before that, once, when I was preaching in the country, the gentleman, with whom I stayed, suddenly got up, towards the end of the sermon, and went out; and a dear friend, who had gone with me, followed him outside, and asked him, 'What brought you out here?' He replied, 'If I had stopped there another five minutes, I should have got converted. Mr Spurgeon seems to treat me just as if I were made of India rubber; he squeezes me into any shape he likes, so I was obliged to come out.' 'But,' my friend said, 'might it not have been a great blessing to you if you had been converted?' 'Well, no,' he replied; 'at least, not just now. I have some things in prospect that I really could not miss, so I cannot afford to be converted just now.' There are others, who do not act quite like that, but the result is the same. They say, by their actions, if not in so many words, 'Now, Lord, I am going to tie you up for a little while. I mean to give heed to you by-and-by; I hope your blessed hand will be laid upon me for my salvation, but not just now, please – not just now.' Such people always use silken cords, but the binding is just as effective and it would be if they took an ugly pair of handcuffs, such as a policeman pulls out for a thief. The man says, 'Permit me just to tie your hands for a little while – another month, perhaps – possibly another year.' Oh, that accursed procrastination! How many have been ruined to all eternity by it? It is the bond that binds the hand of Christ the Saviour, who says, 'Now is the day of salvation.'

Other men bind the hands of Christ *by seeking pleasure in sin*. After having been impressed under a sermon, they go straight away to some ungodly meeting-place – a public-house, perhaps; or, on the morrow, they go into society where every serious thought will, in all probability, be stamped out as men stamp out a fire; and what is this but binding the hands of Christ? I know some – I tremble as I think of them – who persistently do that which they know will prevent them from ever feeling the power of the Word of God. Oh, that, by some means, they could be wrenched out of their present position, and be carried right away where truth might influence them, that so they might be led to Jesus' feet! I think I hear someone say, 'That is a shocking way to bind Christ's hands.' Then mind, my friend, that you do not yourself fall into that sin.

Now, in closing, I want to speak to the Lord's own people just for a minute or two.

Do you not think, beloved, that you and I have sometimes tied Christ's hands? You remember reading this sentence, 'He could not do many mighty works there.' His hands were tied; but what tied them? Finish the quotation: *'because of their unbelief'*. Are there not many churches where they have tied the hands of Christ because they do not believe he can do any mighty works there? If the Lord Jesus Christ were to convert three thousand people, at one time, under their pastor's preaching, what do you think the deacons and elders of that church would probably say? 'Well, we never thought that we should see such excitement as this here; to think that it should have come into our place of worship! We must be very careful now. No doubt these people will be wanting to join the church. We shall have to summer them, and winter them, and try them a good deal; we do not like such excitement.' Ah, sirs, you need not trouble yourselves with any such expectation! God is not likely to give such a blessing to you; he never sends his children where they are not wanted; and, as a rule, until he prepares his people to receive the blessing, the blessing will not come.

Do you not think, also, that *a minister may very easily tie the hands of Christ?* I am afraid I have done so, sometimes, without meaning it. Suppose I were to preach some very fine sermons – I do not do that, mark you – but just suppose I were to preach some very fine sermons that went right over people's heads, and a good old woman were to say, 'I would not have the presumption to understand it, but it is very wonderful', do you not think that I should be tying Christ's hands with garlands of flowers? And may we not come into the pulpit, and talk a lot of theological jargon, and use words which are appropriate to us in the classroom, but quite misunderstood, or never understood at all, by the mass of the people? Is not that tying Christ's hands? And when a preacher is what they call very 'heavy' – by which is not meant that he is weighty – but dull; or when he is very cold and heartless, and preaches as if he were working by the piece, and would be glad to get it all over – when that is the case, do you not think that Christ's hands are tied? Have you never heard sermons of which you might fairly say, 'Well, if God were to convert anybody by that discourse, it certainly would be a miraculous kind of miracle – something altogether out of the common way of miracles, for he would be using an implement that was positively calculated to produce just the opposite effect, and making it accomplish his purposes of grace'? I have heard such sermons, now and then, to my great sorrow. And you Sunday-school teachers must take care that you do not so teach as really to be hindrances to your scholars rather than helps, for that is to tie the hands of Christ, and to lead him into your class, like Samson bound, rather to make sport for Philistines than to get honour to himself. May we all have the grace given to us to avoid such an evil as that!

And do you not think, dear friends, that we, who do love Christ, bind his hands *when we are cowardly and retiring, and never say a word for him?* How can the gospel save sinners if it is never spoken to them? If you never introduce Christ to your companions – never put a little book on your friend's table – never try to say just a word about the Saviour to him, is not that tying Christ's hands? The next thing to having no Christ at all is for the church to be silent concerning him. It is an awful thing to contemplate what it would be if there were no Saviour; but what improvement is it if there be a Saviour, but men never hear of him? Come, you very retiring people, do not excuse yourselves any longer. 'Oh, but!' says one, 'I always was of a very retiring disposition.' So was that soldier, who was shot for running away in the day of battle; he was guilty of cowardice, and was put to death for it. If you have been, up to the present time, binding the Master by your retiring spirit, you should at once come forward, and declare what Christ has done for you, that, with unbound hands, he may do the like for others.

And do you not think that, *whenever we are inconsistent in our conduct* – especially in the family – we tie the hands of Christ? There is a father praying for his children that they may live before God. Five minutes after, listen to him. Why, his boys hate the sight of him! He is such a tyrant to them that they cannot endure him. There is a mother, too, who is praying God to save her daughters. She goes upstairs, and pleads very earnestly for them; yet she comes down, and lets them have whatever they like to ask, and never says a word by way of checking them in their evil courses. She acts like a female Eli to every one of them; is not she tying the hands of Christ? What can she expect but that God, who works according to rules, will be more likely to let her unkind kindness influence her girls for evil, than to answer her prayers for their conversion? Let us be holy, dear friends, for then we shall, by faith, see the holy God freely moving and working among us, and doing great deeds to his own glory. So may he do, for our Lord Jesus Christ's sake! Amen.

3

MAJESTY IN MISERY[1]

And the men that held Jesus mocked him, and smote him.
And when they had blindfolded him, they struck him on
the face, and asked him saying, Prophesy, who is it that
smote thee? And many other things blasphemously
spake they against him.
LUKE 22:63–65

I SUPPOSE that all this cruelty took place while our Lord was
before Caiaphas, in the dead of night, before the Sanhedrin had
been fully gathered together to hold their trial at daybreak. His
enemies were in so great a hurry to condemn him that, as soon as
he arrived at the high priest's house, they must needs have a kind
of preliminary examination that they might try the tack upon
which they meant to sail in endeavouring to procure a conviction
against him. After he had been thus, in an informal and illegal
way, condemned without any proper trial, they left him in the
custody of their officers until, early in the morning, they should
have summoned the rest of their companions, so as again to go
through the farce of trying him whom they knew to be innocent.

While these officials had Christ in their keeping, they might at
least have left him in peace and quietness. According to the rules
of all civilized nations, a prisoner detained in custody should be
guarded from insult and ill-treatment while in that condition.
Whatever his ultimate punishment may be, after he has been tried,
and found guilty, while he is as yet uncondemned, he is reckoned

[1] Sermon No. 2,825. Preached at the Metropolitan Tabernacle on Sunday evening,
7 October 1883.

to be under the protection of the state that has arrested him, and he ought not to be subjected to insult or injury. But here, as if they had been so many savages, the judges of our Lord abandoned him to those abjects whom they employed to do their foul work, and those wretched creatures treated him with mingled cruelty and scorn: 'The men that held Jesus mocked him, and smote him.' Could they not have allowed him a little time of rest? The traces of the bloody sweat must still have been upon him. They could see, by the emaciation of his person, that he was, as it had been long before foretold that he would be, 'a man of sorrows, and acquainted with grief'. He must already have been ready to faint under the rough usage which had been meted out to him both before and at his preliminary trials before Annas and Caiaphas. His tormentors must have seen how exhausted he was, yet they had no pity for him in their hard, unfeeling hearts, and they allowed him no respite, and gave him no opportunity to prepare himself to answer the charges that were about to be brought against him. There were none found to vindicate his character, or to plead his cause; but the intervals between the informal and the more formal trials were spent in mockery and in scorn.

These men were gross cowards. I am sure that they must have been, because they were so cruel, for cruelty is one of the badges of cowardice wherever you find it. These are the very men who, in the garden, 'went backward, and fell to the ground', when Christ did but say, 'I am he', in answer to their declaration that they were seeking 'Jesus of Nazareth'. They went out, with swords and staves, to take him prisoner, yet they fell to the ground when he did but speak a word or two to them; but now that they had him in their power, and perceived that he was, apparently, not inclined to exert the divine energy with which he was endowed, but that he was as submissive as a sheep before her shearers, they determined to be as cruel as they could to him. God grant that the sin of cruelty to anything that lives may never be justly laid to the charge of any one of us! If you have acted cruelly, even though it be to the meanest thing in creation, despise yourself, for you are of a lower order than the creature that you tortured; and if these men could have judged themselves aright, they would have despised themselves. They seem to me to have been the very meanest of mankind who, having such a gentle sufferer in their power, instead of showing any humanity to him, seemed as if they could not sufficiently abuse him, and indulged their vile nature to the utmost in mocking and persecuting him.

I. I hope that some spiritual profit may come to us while we are considering this terrible part of the suffering of our Lord; and, first, I want you, in imagination, to gaze upon MAJESTY IN MISERY.

There stands Jesus of Nazareth. I will not attempt to picture him. There has never yet been a painter who could portray the lineaments of that wondrous face. The highest art has never yet been able to satisfy itself upon that point even though it has borrowed its outline and its colours from the Scriptures themselves. The most skilful hand grows unsteady in the presence of One so glorious in his griefs. I will not, therefore, attempt to draw a portrait of my Lord and Master, but will simply ask you, by faith, to behold him, clothed with the garment that was without seam, bound, delivered over to the officers, and surrounded by them while they mocked and scoffed at him. Letting your eye rest upon him in a loving look, regarding him as the great centre of your heart's affection, what do you see – you who believe in his Deity, and who can say that he is 'very God of very God' to you?

If your eyes are opened by the Spirit of God, you will here see *Omnipotence held captive*. 'The men that held Jesus' did not really know who he was; he appeared to them to be a poor Galilean peasant, speaking the country brogue, they saw that he was a humble, lowly, emaciated man; and, as he had been committed to their charge, they held him as their prisoner. But they did not recognize that he was the Almighty God, the very Deity that created the heavens and the earth, for 'all things were made by him; and without him was not anything made that was made.' He was, at that very moment, 'upholding all things by the word of his power'; and, amid all his weakness, and in all his sufferings, he was still 'over all, God blessed for ever', whom all the holy angels continued to adore. Is it not a great mystery that omnipotence should thus be held captive? What a marvellous thing it is that he, who can create or who can destroy, according to the good pleasure of his own will, should take upon himself our nature, and in that nature should sink so low as to become subject even to the very coarsest and most cruel of mankind! What a wondrous stoop of condescension is here! Omnipotence allows itself to be bound, and never proves itself more truly omnipotent than when it restrains itself, and permits itself to be held as a prisoner by sinful men.

Look again at this Majesty in misery, and you will see *glory mocked*, for 'the men that held Jesus mocked him.' To them, he seemed to be a fit subject for ridicule and derision in professing to be a king, when he had neither an armed host nor multitudes of followers who could hope to stand for a single second against the mighty Caesar who held Israel in bondage. Ay, but there was a glory in Christ, which he had deigned to veil and to conceal for a while, but which angels still beheld and adored; yet these men were mocking him! There are some themes which seem to strike a speaker dumb, and this subject has something like this effect upon me. It appears to me amazing that the God, who had reigned in glory over myriads of holy angels, should be mocked by miscreants who could not even have lived an instant longer in his presence if he had not permitted them to do so; yet I see, in my text, that he, who made the heavens and the earth, stood there to be despised and rejected of men, and to be treated with the utmost contumely and scorn. I can make that statement, but you cannot realize what it means. This is one of those great mysteries of the faith that seem to stagger you. You believe it without the slightest hesitation; yet, the more you try really to grasp and comprehend it, the more it seems to elude you, and to tower above you. Thus, we see omnipotence, held captive, and glory mocked.

Next, we see *goodness smitten*, perfect, infinite, unutterable goodness stricken, bruised, assailed, assaulted: 'The men that held Jesus mocked him, and smote him.' To smite wickedness, is an act of justice; and even to lift the sword against oppression, may not always be a thing to be condemned; but to smite him who never did any man a wrong, but who has done all men some measure of good, and who has given to some men all conceivable good – ah, this is brutish indeed! The blessed Son of God, who stood there, had within his soul that mercy which endureth for ever, yet they smote him – there burned in his heart a love which many waters could not quench, and which the floods could not drown, yet they smote him! He had come here upon no errand of vengeance, but to bring peace and goodwill to men, and to set up a kingdom of joy and love; yet they bound him! Ah, me! it is wonderful that goodness should be so good as to submit to this shameful indignity; none but divine goodness would have submitted to it.

See what these mockers and smiters did next to our Lord. They produced a handkerchief, or a cloth of some kind, and they put it over his eyes. *Omniscience must seem to be blinded;* which, in truth, it cannot be; yet, in the Christ, there was the omniscience of the Godhead, and, to the utmost of their power, these men blinded him, in the hope that he might not see what they were doing. I know some who are trying to act thus at this present time. The only god that they have is a blind god. They believe in what they call 'the forces of nature', and then they condescendingly talk as though God was only the aggregate of the forces of nature working according to certain mechanical laws that can never be altered. The god in whom they profess to believe is a god that does not see.

They tell us that it is idle to pray, or to think that God takes any interest in such insignificant individuals as we are. Ah! I remember reading about those gods of the philosophers: 'They have mouths, but they speak not: eyes have they, but they see not: they have ears, but they hear not: noses have they, but they smell not: they have hands, but they handle not: feet have they, but they walk not: neither speak they through their throat. They that make them are like unto them; so is every one that trusteth in them.' 'But our God is in the heavens', seeing all that happens, and doing as he pleases among the hosts above and among men below. He is not now to be blindfolded, as he was once when he condescended to wear our nature, and to bear our sin. Yet it is wonderful that he should ever have permitted this indignity to be put upon him. The spouse in the Canticles truly sings, 'His eyes are as the eyes of doves by the rivers of waters, washed with milk, and fitly set' – exceeding the very stars of heaven for brightness – yet they covered them over! His eyes flamed with love, and in them there did gleam bright diamonds of pity for all the sorrows of mankind; yet those cruel men did hide those precious eyes of his, blindfolding the Christ of God!

Now, surely, they had made him suffer enough, far too much; yet again the infinite beauties of his blessed countenance were to be marred, for 'they struck him on the face.' 'Oh, but, had we been there', we say, 'our indignation would have burned against them for striking that dear face!' Yet we had need lay aside our indignation, and bring forward penitence instead, for we also have sometimes smitten that dear face of Jesus, which is as the sun of heaven, far brighter than the sun which lights up the world. All other beauties put together cannot equal the marvellous charms of that countenance which was marred more than any man's. There is nothing under heaven, or in heaven itself, that can rival the face of the Well-beloved; yet these men struck it! I think an angel might well shiver with horror if, for the first time, he heard that men had struck the face of his Lord. It was but his human face, it is true; but therein they struck at all of Deity that they could reach. It was man smiting God in the face. A slap in the face of Deity was what it really meant. Ah, me! that my Master should ever have had to endure such insult and pain – that he should ever have been willing to suffer such indignity as this – was there ever love like unto his?

Then the mockers said, 'Prophesy, who is it that smote thee?' That was *justice defied*. They seemed to say to our Lord, as they smote him, 'Tell us what our name is; say who struck that blow. Thou canst not resist it; thou canst not avenge thyself; but, at least, see if thou canst tell the name of him that smote thee. We defy thee so to do.' Ah! he had written down their names, and they will find out, one day, that he knows them all, for there are none who smite the Saviour who will not have their blows come back upon themselves unless they repent of their sin. There was justice defied, as 'they struck him on the face, and asked him, saying, Prophesy, who is it that smote thee?'

I say again that I am not able worthily to speak on such a theme as this, and I think I never shall be however long I may live. It is not within the compass of lips of clay, with words of air, to describe the condescending sufferings of him who, though he was rightly called 'Wonderful, Counsellor, The mighty God, The everlasting Father, The Prince of Peace' nevertheless stooped so low as to be mocked, smitten, blindfolded, and smitten again for your sakes and mine.

> Vexed, I try and try again,
> Still my efforts all are vain:
> Living tongues are dumb at best,
> We must die to speak of Christ.

The wonder of this Majesty in misery can be described in four words. The first wonder is that, under all this torture, our Lord was so *patient*. Not a flush of anger appeared on his cheek, not a flash of wrath from his eyes. He bore it all, bore it in his very soul, with divine patience, the very patience of 'the God of patience'.

The next wonder is, that he was *silent* under all this cruelty; not a word did he utter either in complaint or in condemnation of his assailants. This proved his true greatness. Eloquence is easy as compared with silence, and perhaps it would not have been true of Christ that 'never man spake like this Man', if it had not also been true of him that never man was silent like this Man. He fulfilled to the letter the ancient prophecy, 'He is brought as a lamb to the slaughter, and as a sheep before her shearers is dumb, so he openeth not his mouth.' Lord, teach us how to imitate thy patience and thy silence!

Notice, in the third place, how *eloquent* he was by that very silence. He said more for us, and more to us, by holding his tongue than if he had delivered himself of many burning sentences. It is matchless eloquence that is seen in the calm serenity of Christ in the presence of these cruel persecutors, in the forgiving character of Christ under the most exasperating circumstances, and in the patience of Christ under unparalleled sufferings.

And yet again, I see something so triumphant in our Saviour's griefs that, while I call him patient, silent, and eloquent, I must also call him *victorious*. His persecutors could not make him give way to anger. They could not destroy his mercy; they could not slay his love; they could not cause him to think of himself; they could not make him declare that he would go no further with his work of saving sinners now that men began to scoff at him, and smite him, and despitefully use him. No; the strong-souled Christ still perseveres in his merciful work, even as a mighty hunter pursues his game upon the mountain, leaping from crag to crag, and cliff to cliff, defying danger and death that he may secure the creature on whose track he has gone. So, O thou mighty Christ, thou didst accomplish thy glorious purpose of love and mercy! Thou didst lead captivity captive by suffering, to the bitter end, all that was inflicted upon thee, even unto the death of the cross.

Thus have I tried to picture Majesty in misery; but I have not been able to describe either Christ's Majesty or his misery as they deserve to be described. Muse on them, and pray the Spirit of God to give you such a sight of them as human nature by itself can never afford you.

II. Now I pass on to notice, secondly, that my test seems to me to show us SIN AT ITS SPORT.

All this sad scene represents what sin did when it had the opportunity – when all restraining bands were loosed, and it could act according to its own evil will. It also represents what sin is still doing, as far as it can, and what would always be the action of sin if it were not hindered by the almighty power of God.

What, then, does sin do in the hour of its liberty? I invite you to notice, first – and to pay particular attention to any part that may come home to yourself – *the levity of sin*. These men are grossly insulting the Christ of God; but, to them, it is a sport, a game. They play at blindfolding him; it is simply mirth and amusement to them. Sad indeed is it that sin should ever be what men call sport, yet I need scarcely remind you how often it is so, even now, to many. They run after it with the utmost eagerness, and they call it pleasure – they call that which is provoking God pleasure – they call that which crucified Christ pleasure! They say that 'they must see life', and they call that 'life' which forced from Jesus a bloody sweat, and which afterwards dragged him to a cruel death. And, alas! they say of many a sin, 'What a delight it is to us! Would you make our life miserable by taking away our enjoyments?' So it becomes a matter of enjoyment to them to smite Christ on the face, and to mock him! Perhaps I am addressing some who have even made the Bible into a jest-book; their puns and mirth have been pointed with passages of Holy Writ. Possibly, others have made rare fun out of some venerable Christian, some faithful servant of the living and true God. Well, sirs, if you have done so, I would have you know how heinous is your sin in thus making sport of the godly; such 'sport' as that, unless you repent of it, will damn you for ever; as surely as you live, it will shut you out from the great Father's love, and close the door of mercy against you, world without end. Yet that is how sin acts when it has its liberty; ay, and it sports even with the wounds of a crucified God! Alas, that it should ever do so!

Notice, next, *the utter wantonness of sin.* If these men really wanted to get amusement out of Christ, they were able to get it; but what need was there for them also to smite him? What need was there of all that superfluity of cruelty by which they put him to such shame and pain? If Christ must die, at least let him die in peace; why that spitting in his face, that terrible scourging, that awful aggravation of his griefs? It was because men will sin out of sheer wantonness. I have known some persons sin in such strange ways that I have wondered why they did it. It was not for pleasure; at least, I could not see any pleasure in it. It caused the man's own family to be utterly miserable, and brought them and himself, too, down to poverty; what mirth or merriment could there be in that? There are some who seem as if they could never be happy unless they were engaged in making themselves unhappy for ever and ever. They are not content without committing some extravagance in sin, and making their whole lives an outrageous series of rebellions against God. If any of you have ever been guilty of such wantonness in sin, may the Holy Spirit cause a gracious influence to steal over you, so that you will no longer grieve the Christ of God, but will yourself grieve that you should ever have sinned so shamefully against him!

Then note, next, *the cruelty of sin.* I have already asked, and I repeat the question – What need was there for these men to strike the Saviour? What pleasure could they derive from all the pain they caused to him? By the mouth of his ancient prophets, the Lord said, 'Oh, do not this abominable thing that I hate!' It was in their own interests that he thus pleaded with men, for he would not have them injure themselves; and sin is ever self-injury; it is a sort of suicide. Whenever a man does wrong, mischief must certainly come of it; and God knows this, so he beseeches men not to act so foolishly. And, oh! when a man mocks at true religion, rejects Christ, and postpones the day of repentance, he is piercing again that dear heart that bled for the unworthy, and grieving that blessed Spirit who still strives with the sons of men, though he is often vexed and grievously provoked by them. Why are you so unkind to your God? Surely, there can be no necessity for committing such a sin as this.

Then, observe *the desperate unbelief that there often is in sin.* These men would not have blindfolded Christ if they had really believed him to be the Son of God; but they acted as they did because they had no faith whatsoever in him. This is the great evil that lies at the root of most men's sins – they believe not in Jesus Christ, whom God hath sent. It is this of which the Spirit of God convinces men, as our Saviour foretold concerning him: 'He will convince the world of sin . . . because they believe not on me.' Yet there is nothing more reasonable, nothing more worthy to be believed, than the revelation of God as given to us in the Holy Scriptures; and a man has only to test and try for himself whether it be true, or not, and he shall soon have the proof of its verity in his own bosom. Let him really believe it, and then see whether it does not make him both holy and happy, and that shall be to him the test of its truth.

Notice, again, *how often there is in sin a kind of defiance of God.* If a boy were to come to his father, and were to say to him, 'I will do all manner of rude and unkind things to you, yet you will not chastise me', it would not be long before that father would make his son smart if he were himself worthy to be a father; but sinners act towards God in that kind of way. They often do to God what these persecutors did to Christ; so far as they can, they mock him, and smite him, and defy him. Am I addressing anyone who has ever called down upon his own person the curse of God? Beware lest that blasphemous prayer of yours be answered the next time you utter it, for it is God's way to answer prayer, and, mayhap, he will answer yours, and then where will you be? Some have even dared to defy God thus: 'Well, even if it be as you say, I am willing to take my chance; but I will not submit to God.' Ah, sir! Pharaoh tried that plan, and he repented of it, I think, when it was too late.

In the midst of the Red Sea, when the waters began to overwhelm him and all his mighty host, then he learned what were the consequences of saying, 'Who is the Lord, that I should obey his voice?' Every sin has in it a measure of defiance of God, it is like these men striking Christ upon the face, and saying to him, 'Prophesy, who is it that smote thee?'

I will not linger longer upon this part of my theme except just to say that there is one more thing about sin that is peculiarly lamentable, namely, *the multiplicity of sin*. Read the 65th verse: 'And many other things blasphemously spake they against him.' One thing, two things, twenty things, will not content them; they must say 'many other things' against him. When a man once gives himself up to sin, it is like getting into a current which bears him onward where, at first, he had no thought of going. If you wade into the waters of sin, it will not be long that you will be able to retain a foothold; and, by-and-by, unless the Lord shall in his grace prevent such a calamity, the rapid current will bear you away to your everlasting destruction. It is no use for you to say, 'Thus far will I go in sin, but no farther.' You cannot stop when you please; if you once commit yourself to the influence of sin, you know not whither it will carry you. Alas! alas! some men seem as if they never could sin enough to satisfy themselves. They multiply their transgressions beyond all count. Every iron of iniquity that they have is thrust into the fire. Both their hands are diligently engaged in doing mischief. Sometimes, they rise up early; but, more often, they sit up late – possibly, all the night through, that they may waste the more precious hours in their wickedness. So God is aggrieved, and Christ is wounded afresh by the sin of man. It is a sad, sad picture; I cast a veil over it, and turn to something brighter and better.

III. We have seen Majesty in misery, and sin at its sport; now, thirdly, let us see LOVE AT ITS LABOUR.

All that shame and suffering was endured by our Saviour for love of each of us who can truly say, 'He loved me, and gave himself for me.' All this blindfolding, and mocking, and smiting was borne by Christ for your sake, beloved, and mine. I will not try to describe it further, but I will ask you just to spend a minute or two in trying to realize that sad scene. For you – as much as if there were no other person in the whole universe – for you, the King of glory became the King of scorn, and bore all this despising and rejection of men. For you, John; for you, Mary; for you, old friend; for you, in your youth. If thou, whoever thou art, believest in him, he was thy Substitute. Thy faith gives thee the assurance that he was enduring all this for thee – for thee, I say, as much as if he had no other redeemed one, but had paid the ransom price all for thee. Less than this would not have sufficed for thee, though it is, indeed, sufficient for all the innumerable host redeemed by the precious blood of Jesus.

Let us, then, see love at its labour. I mean, our love to our Lord; though I might also speak of our Lord's love to us, and what it did for us. What shall our love do to show how grateful we are to Jesus for all that he endured for us? Well, first, *let it set penitence to confess*. Come, my heart, here is room for the display of thy grief. Why was Christ mocked in Jerusalem? Surely it was because thou hast mocked God with prayers that were no prayers, with hymns carelessly sung, with Scriptures read as if they were merely the writings of men, with professions of religion that were hollow and empty. Brothers and sisters, have not you some of these things to repent of? If you have mocked him thus, the mocking that he endured in the hall of the high priest was on your account.

And as he was blindfolded, let us weep because our unbelief has often blindfolded him. We imagined that he did not know about us, or that he had forgotten us. We thought that he could not see the end from the beginning, and that he would not be able to bring good out of evil. Let me ask you, dear friends, Have you not often made Christ to be a blindfolded Christ so far as your apprehension of him was concerned? If so, because you have thus blindfolded God by your unbelief, you are, by your sin, imitating the guilt of these men who literally blindfolded Christ.

And as we behold him smitten, let us again grieve as we remember how it was written of him, 'He was bruised for our iniquities: the chastisement of our peace was upon him; and with his stripes we are healed.' Every sin that we have ever committed made a gory furrow upon his precious back. Those black and blue bruises, that alternate upon his sacred shoulders, were caused by the cruel scourging to which each of us contributed our share by our trans-gressions. O beloved, weep as you see him bearing what you ought to have borne!

And when you read that they asked him taunting questions while his eyes were blindfolded, ask thyself, O child of God, whether thou hast not often done the same? Have you never asked for a sign, instead of walking by faith? I confess that I have sometimes wished that I could have some token or indication of what my Lord thought. Ah, that is what these cruel men sought from Christ; they tried to get him to convince them that he knew them when his eyes were blinded. O brothers and sisters, let us never seek a sign, as that wicked and adulterous generation did; but let us walk by faith, and not by sight, and implicitly trust our Lord. Because we have not trusted him as we should have done, but have demanded of him signs and tokens, we have been too much like these men who asked him, saying, 'Prophesy, who is it that smote thee?'

I said that we would see love at its labour, so I want you, next, to let your love *urge faith to confide in Christ*. Come, dear friends, in all this suffering of our Saviour, let us see fresh reasons for trusting ourselves more entirely in the hands of Christ. Those men held Jesus in order that neither death nor hell might ever be able to hold us. He was held in our stead, so he says concerning us, as he said concerning his disciples in the garden, 'If therefore ye seek me, let these go their way.' The great Substitute is held as a prisoner so that all, for whom he stood as Surety, might be set at liberty for ever.

He also was mocked; and to what end was that? We deserve eternal shame and contempt because of our sin, but he took all that shame upon himself, and made this wonderful exchange. As he put on the rags of our shame, he said to us, 'Take my glittering vesture, and wear it!' and now, the glory which he had with the Father from eternity, he has put upon his people, that they may be like him, and may be with him where he is for ever and ever. What a wonderful exchange is this! As Thomas read the Deity of Christ in his wounds, so do I read the eternal glory of his people in the mockery which he endured on their behalf.

When you see your Lord smitten, why is that but that there may be no smitings and no woundings for you now or for ever? You shall go free, for Jesus has borne all that you deserved to bear; he bore blow after blow that not one might ever fall upon you.

Why, too, was Jesus blindfolded but that we might be able to see? Our sin had blinded us to all that was worth seeing, but his death has taken away the scales, and we can now see because he was caused not to see. Because he suffered these miserable miscreants to bind his eyes, therefore are our eyes unbound today, and they shall be yet more unbound in that day when we shall behold him face to face, and be no more parted from him.

And why was Jesus blasphemed by the 'many other things' which they falsely laid to his charge? He was blasphemed that we might be justified. He was unrighteously accused and slandered in order that we might be able boldly to say, 'Who shall lay any thing to the charge of God's elect? It is God that justifieth. Who is he that condemneth? It is Christ that died.' Therefore, be ye glad, beloved. While ye sorrow over your Lord's griefs, rejoice over what those griefs have brought to you, and what they will continue to bring to you throughout eternity.

Now, lastly, let our love at its labour *arouse our zeal to consecration to our Lord*. Was he held captive? Then come, my most burning zeal, and inflame me with devotion to his cause. Was he held thus for me? Then he shall hold me fast, and never let me go. My Lord, I do surrender myself, my life, my all, to thee, to be thy willing captive for ever! Take these eyes, these lips, these hands, these feet, this heart, and as thou wast and art altogether mine, so let me be altogether thine. Is not this a fair requital? Does any child of God demur to that?

Then, next, as they did despise him, come, my soul, what sayest thou to this? Why, that I will despise the world that did despise my Lord and Saviour. O world, world, world, thou art a blind, blear-eyed, black-hearted thing to have treated my Master so! Shall I conform to thy customs? Shall I flatter thee? Shall I ask for thine applause? Nay, thou art crucified to me. As a felon nailed up to the cross, so, O world, art thou to me because thou hast crucified the Christ, the infinitely lovely Son of God! Henceforth, the world is crucified unto us, and we unto the world.

And as they blindfolded Jesus, what then? Why, I will be blindfolded, too; I will henceforth see no charm, no attraction, anywhere but in my Lord. Mine eyes shall behold him, and not another, in the glory that is yet to be revealed; and, today, I can say, with the psalmist, 'Whom have I in heaven but thee? and there is none upon earth that I desire beside thee.' Go through the world, beloved, blindfolded to all but Christ, and you shall do well.

And, as they struck Jesus on the face, what will you and I do to show how much we love that face which was so shamefully ill-treated? My heart brings up before me a vision of that 'sacred head, once wounded', encircled by the crown of thorns, that dear face, so bruised and battered, yet even then more beautiful than all the other loveliness of heaven beside. Jesus, Son of God, and Son of man, we do adore thee; and we haste to kiss those blessed feet of thine, in loving adoration, and we do it all the more because wicked men did smite thee upon the cheek! Reverence and love we gladly give to him who once was clouted by abjects, and who afterwards was nailed to the accursed tree.

And, inasmuch as these men said 'many other things blasphemously against Him', come, my brothers, let us say many things in his praise; and sisters, join us in the holy exercise. No one shall close our lips, faulty as they are, from speaking in honour of our dear Lord. Sometimes, with the prophet, we are ready to confess that we are men of unclean lips, and that we dwell in the midst of people of unclean lips; but, such as we are, we will render to him the calves of our lips, and give glory to his holy name. Never be ashamed to speak up for your Lord, beloved. Never blush to own that you belong to him. Nay, if you do blush at all, blush with shame that you do not love him more, and serve him better. By the memory of that dear face, blindfolded and smitten, while cruel men all around slander him with their blasphemous accusations, I charge you to –

> Stand up, stand up for Jesus,
> Ye soldiers of the cross!

God help you so to do!

Oh, that some here, who have never believed in Jesus Christ, would now begin to trust him! I do not invite you, just now, so much to believe in him in his glory as to believe in him in his shame. Was he really the Son of God, and did he suffer for guilty men all that we have been thinking of, and far more than that? Then, I must believe in him. To me, Jesus Christ seems to be a character that men could never have invented. He must be historical, for he is so original. Unaided human minds could never have thought out such a character. There are strange things in Buddhism, and other false religions, and men with wild imaginations have conceived curious notions concerning their gods; but I challenge anyone to show me, in any book except God's Book, anything that can parallel the story of the Eternal God himself becoming man in order to make atonement for the sins of his creatures, that is, the sins committed by them against himself. Yes, brothers and sisters, I must believe in him. What is more, I must believe that he died for me –

> That on the gross he shed his blood
> From sin to set me free.

Having so believed – I speak as God's witness to all who can hear me – I feel an inward peace that nothing can break, a holy joy that nothing can disturb, and a sacred calm which death itself shall not be able to destroy. I have been at the deathbeds of many of our brethren and sisters who have been accustomed to worship here, and who have been members of this church; and – note this testimony, I pray you – I have never seen one of them afraid to die. I have not met with one coward among them all; but I have heard some of them singing triumphantly in their last hours, as merrily as though it were their marriage day, while others have been as calm and quiet as if to die were but to go to bed, and sleep a while, and wake again in the morning. Believe ye in the Lord Jesus Christ, in this very Lord who stooped from the heights of glory to the depths of shame and suffering; and you also shall find that your confidence in him shall be rewarded even in this life; while, as for the world to come – ah! then, when there shall be no blindfolded eyes for him – no mockery and scorn and smiting for him – but all shall be glory for ever and ever, then you and I, if we are believers in him, shall eternally share his glory. God grant it, for Jesus Christ's sake! Amen.

4

OUR LORD'S TRIAL BEFORE THE SANHEDRIN[1]

And they all condemned him to be guilty of death.
MARK 14:64

THIS ONE SENTENCE is selected because custom demands a text; but in reality we shall follow the entire narrative of our Lord's trial before the high priests. We shall see how the Sanhedrin arrived at their unrighteous sentence, and what they did afterwards, and so, in a sense, we shall be keeping to our text. We have just been reading three passages – John 18:12– 24; Mark 14:53–65; and Luke 22:66–71. Please carry these in your minds while I rehearse the mournful story.

The narrative of our Lord's grief, if it be carefully studied, is harrowing in the extreme. One cannot long think of it without tears; in fact, I have personally known what it is to be compelled to leave my meditations upon it from excess of emotion. It is enough to make one's heart break fully to realize the sufferings of such an One, so lovely in himself and so loving toward us. Yet this harrowing of the feelings is exceedingly useful: the after result of it is truly admirable. After mourning for Jesus we are raised above our own mourning. There is no consolation under heaven at all like it; for the sorrows of Christ seem to take the sting out of our own sorrows, till they become harmless and endurable. A sympathetic contemplation of our Lord's grief so dwarfs our griefs that they are reckoned to be but light afflictions, too petty, too

---

[1] Sermon No. 1,643. Preached at the Metropolitan Tabernacle on Sunday morning, 5 February 1882.

insignificant, to be mentioned in the same day. We dare not write ourselves down in the list of the sorrowful at all when we have just seen the sharp pains of the Man of Sorrows. The wounds of Jesus distil a balm which heals all mortal ills.

Nor is this all, though that were much in a world of woe like this; but there is a matchless stimulus about the passion of the Lord. Though you have been almost crushed by the sight of your Lord's agonies, you have risen therefrom strong, resolute, fervent, consecrated. Nothing stirs our hearts' depths like his heart's anguish. Nothing is too hard for us to attempt or to endure for One who sacrificed himself for us. To be reviled for his dear sake who suffered such shame for us becomes no great affliction; even reproach itself when borne for him becomes greater riches than all the treasures of Egypt. To suffer in body and in mind, even unto death, for him were rather a privilege than an exaction: such love so swells our hearts that we vehemently pant for some way of expressing our indebtedness. We are grieved to think that our best will be so little; but we are solemnly resolved to give nothing less than our best to him who loved us and gave himself for us.

I believe also that full often careless hearts have been greatly affected by the sufferings of Jesus: they have been disturbed in their indifference, convinced of their ingratitude, weaned from their love of sin, and attracted to Christ by hearing what he bore on their behalf. No loadstone can draw human hearts like the cross of Christ. His wounds cause even hearts of stone to bleed. His shame makes obstinacy itself ashamed. Men never so plentifully fall before the great bow of God as when its arrows are dipped in the blood of Jesus. Those darts which are armed with his agonies cause wounds such as never can be healed except by his own pierced hands. These are the weapons which slay the sin and save the sinner; killing at one stroke both his self-confidence and his despair, and leaving him a captive to that conqueror whose glory it is to make men free.

This morning I would not only preach the doctrines that come out of the cross, but the cross itself. I suppose that was one of the great differences between the first preaching of all and the preaching after the Reformation. After the Reformation we had clearly ringing out from all pulpits the doctrine of justification by faith and other glorious truths, which I hope will be made more and more prominent; but the first fathers of the church set forth the same truths in a less theological fashion. If they dwell little upon justification by faith they were wonderfully full upon the blood and its cleansing power, the wounds and their healing efficacy, the death of Jesus and our eternal life. We will go back to their style for awhile, and preach the facts about our Lord Jesus Christ rather than the doctrinal inferences therefrom. Oh, that the Holy Spirit would so bring the sorrows of our Lord near to each heart that every one of us may know the fellowship of his sufferings, and possess faith in his salvation and reverent love for his person.

I. We will begin our narrative this morning by first asking you to think of THE PRELIMINARY EXAMINATION OF OUR BLESSED LORD AND MASTER BY THE HIGH PRIEST. They brought in our Lord from the garden bound; but they also kept fast hold upon him, for we read of 'the men that held him'. They were evidently afraid of their prisoner, even when they had him entirely in their power. He was all gentleness and submission; but conscience made cowards of them all, and they all therefore took a coward's care to hold him in their grasp. As the court had not yet gathered in sufficient numbers for a general examination, the high priest resolved that he would fill up the time by personally interrogating his prisoner.

He commenced his malicious exercise. The high priest asked Jesus *concerning his disciples.* We cannot tell what were the questions, but I suppose they were something like these: 'How is it that thou hast gathered about thee a band of men? What did they with thee? What was thine ultimate intention to do by their means? Who were they? Were they not a set of fanatics, or men discontented and ready for sedition?' I do not know how the crafty Caiaphas put his questions; but the Saviour gave no reply to this particular enquiry. What could he have said if he had attempted to answer? Ah, brothers, what good could he have said of his disciples? We may be sure he would say no ill. He might have said, 'Concerning my disciples, one of them has betrayed me; he has still the blood-money in his hand which you gave him as my price.

Another of them, down in the hall there, before the cock crows will deny that he ever knew me, and add oaths and cursing to his denial: and as for the rest, they have all forsaken me and fled.' Therefore our Lord said nothing concerning his disciples, for he will not turn the accuser of his own, whom he came, not to condemn, but to justify.

The high priest also asked him concerning *his doctrine*. I suppose he said to him, 'What new teaching is this of thine? Are *we* not sufficient to teach the people – the Scribes so learned in the law, the Pharisees so attentive to ritual, the Sadducees so philosophical and speculative? Why needest thou intrude into this domain? I suppose thee to be little more than a peasant's son: what is this strange teaching of thine?'

To this enquiry our Lord did answer, and what a *triumphant reply* it was! Oh that we could always speak, when it is right to speak, as meekly and as wisely as he! He said, 'I spake openly to the world; I ever taught in the synagogue and in the temple, whither the Jews always resort, and in secret I have said nothing. Why askest thou me? Ask them which heard me what I have said unto them: behold, they know what I have said.' Oh, brethren, no reply to slander can be compared with a blameless life. Jesus had lived in the full blaze of day where all could see, and yet he was able to challenge accusation and say, 'Ask them which heard me.' Happy is the man who has no need to defend himself because his works and words are solid testimonials to his uprightness and goodness. Our Saviour answered his questioner very gently, but yet most effectually, by his appeal to facts. He stands before us at once the mirror of meekness and the paragon of perfection, with slander like a wounded snake writhing at his feet. What a delight to have this triumphant pleader for our advocate, to urge his own righteousness in our defence! None can impugn his absolute perfection, and that perfection covers all his saints this day. Who shall accuse us now that Jesus has undertaken to plead for us?

This overwhelming answer, however, brought the Saviour *a blow from one of the officers of the court* who stood by. Was not this a most shocking deed? Here was the first of a new order of assaults. Hitherto we have not heard of strokes and blows; but now it is fulfilled, 'They shall smite the Judge of Israel with a rod upon his cheek.' This was the first of a long series of assaults. I wonder who the man was that struck the Master so. I could wish that the Master's reply to him may have influenced his heart to repentance; but if not, it is certain that he led the van in personal assaults upon our Lord's person: his impious hand first struck him. Surely if he died in impenitence the memory of that blow must remain as a never-dying worm within him. Today he cries, 'I was the first to smite him: I struck him on the mouth with the palm of my hand.' The old writers upon the Passion give us various details of the injuries inflicted upon the Saviour by that blow; but we attach no importance to such traditions, and therefore will not repeat them, but simply say that there was general belief in the church that this blow was a very grievous one, and caused the Saviour much pain. Yet while he felt that blow, and was perhaps half staggered by it, the Master did not lose his composure, or exhibit the least resentment. His reply was everything it ought to be. There is not a word too much. He does not say, 'God shall smite thee, thou whited wall', as did the Apostle Paul. We will not censure the servant, but we will far more commend the Master. He meekly said, 'If I have spoken evil, bear witness of the evil: but if well, why smitest thou me?' Enough, surely, if there remained any tenderness in the heart of the aggressor, to have made him turn his hand upon his own breast in penitential grief. One would not have wondered had he cried out, 'Forgive me, O thou divinely meek and gentle One, and let me henceforth be thy disciple.'

Thus have we seen the first part of our Lord's sufferings in the house of the high priest, and the lesson from it is just this – Let us be meek and lowly in heart as the Saviour was, for herein lay his strength and dignity. You tell me I have said that before. Yes, brethren, and I shall have to say it several more times before you and I have learned the lesson well. It is hard to be meek when falsely accused, meek when roughly interrogated, meek when a cunning adversary is on the catch, meek when smarting under a cruel blow which was a disgrace to a court of justice. You have heard of the patience of Job, but it pales before the patience of Jesus. Admire his forbearance, but do not stop at admiration; copy his example, write under this head-line and follow every stroke. O Spirit of God, even with Christ for an example, we shall not learn meekness unless thou dost, teach us; and even with thee for a teacher we shall not learn it unless we take his yoke upon us and learn of him; for it is only at his feet, and under thy divine anointing that we shall ever become meek and lowly of heart, and so find rest unto our souls.

The preliminary examination is therefore over, and it has ended in no success whatever for the high priest. He has questioned Jesus and he has smitten him, but the ordeal brings nothing to content the adversary. The prisoner is supremely victorious, the assailant is baffled.

II. Now comes a second scene, THE SEARCH FOR WITNESSES AGAINST HIM. 'The chief priests and all the council sought for witness against Jesus to put him to death; and found none.' A strange court that meets with the design to find the prisoner guilty, resolved in some way or other to compass his death. They must proceed according to the forms of justice, and so they summon witnesses, though all the while they violate the spirit of justice, for they ransack Jerusalem to find witnesses who will perjure themselves to accuse the Lord. Every man of the council is writing down somebody's name who may be fetched in from the outside, for the people have come from all parts of the land to keep the Passover, and surely some may be hunted up who, in one place or another, have heard him use an actionable mode of speech. They fetch in, therefore, everyone that they can find of that degraded class who will venture upon perjuring themselves if the bribe be forthcoming. They scour Jerusalem to bring forth witnesses against Jesus; but they had great difficulty in accomplishing their design, because they were bound to examine the witnesses apart, and they could not make them agree. Lies cannot be easily made to pair with each other, whereas truths are cut to the same pattern.

Moreover, many sorts of witnesses that they could readily find they did not dare to bring forward. Witnesses were forthcoming who could testify that Jesus had spoken against the tradition of the elders; but in that some who were in the council, namely, the Sadducees, were agreed with him to a large extent. It would never do to bring forward a charge about which they would not be unanimous. His denunciations of the Pharisees could not be the charge, for these pleased the Sadducees; neither could they allege his outcry against the Sadducees, for in this the Pharisees were agreed with him. You recollect how Paul, when brought before this Sanhedrin, took advantage of their division of opinion and cried, 'I am a Pharisee, the son of a Pharisee; of the hope and resurrection of the dead I am called in question'; and in this manner created a dissension among the conclave, which for a time wrought in his favour. Our Lord took higher and nobler ground, and did not stoop to turn their folly to his own benefit; yet, they being conscious of their internal feuds, cautiously avoided those points upon which they were not in harmony.

They might have brought forward their old grievance that the Lord Jesus did not observe the Sabbath after their fashion; but then it would have come out more publicly that he had healed the sick on the Sabbath. It would not do to publish that fact, for who would think of putting a person to death for having opened the eyes of one born blind, or having restored a withered arm on the Sabbath-day? That kind of witness was therefore set aside. But might they not have found some witnesses to swear that he had talked about a kingdom that he was setting up? Might not this readily have been made to mean sedition and rebellion? Yes, but then that was rather a charge to allege against him before Pilate's civil court, whereas theirs was an ecclesiastical tribunal. Moreover, there were Herodians in the council who were very restive under the Roman yoke, and could not have had the face to condemn anyone for being a patriot; and beside, the people outside would have sympathized with Jesus all the more if they had supposed that he would lead them on rebelling against Caesar. Therefore they could not urge that point. They must have been greatly puzzled to know what to do; especially when even on those points which they decided to bring forward the witnesses no sooner opened their mouths than they contradicted each other.

At last they had it. There came two whose evidence was somewhat agreed; and they asserted that on a certain occasion Jesus Christ had said, 'I will destroy this temple that is made with hands, and within three days I will build another made without hands.' Here was blasphemy against the holy and beautiful house of the Lord, and this would serve their turn. Now, the Saviour had said something which was a little like the testimony of these false witnesses, and a misunderstanding had made it more like it; but still their statement was a lie, and none the less a lie because a shadow of truth had fallen upon it, for the worst kind of lie is that which is manufactured out of a truth: it does more mischief a great deal than if it were a falsehood from stem to stern. The Saviour had not said, 'I will destroy this temple': he said, 'Destroy this temple', that is to say, 'Ye will destroy it, and ye may destroy it.' He had not referred to the Jerusalem temple at all; this spake he concerning the temple of his body which would be destroyed. Christ has never said, 'Destroy this temple which is made with hands, and I will build another without hands': in his language there is no allusion to hands at all. These refinements were of their own inventing, and his language gave no colour for them. He had not said, 'I will build another'; he had said, 'I will raise it up', which is quite a different thing. He meant that his body, after being destroyed, would be raised up again on the third day. They had altered a word here and a word there, the mood of one verb and the form of another, and so they made out our Lord to say what he never thought of. Yet even on that charge they did not agree. One said one thing upon it, and another said another, so that even this paltry accusation could not be brought against the Saviour. Their patched-up falsehood was made of such rotten stuff that the pieces would not hold together. They were ready to swear to anything that came into their perjured imaginations, but they could not be got to swear any two of them to the selfsame thing.

Meanwhile the Lord himself *stands silent;* like the sheep before her shearers, he is dumb, and openeth not his mouth; and I suppose the reason was partly that he might fulfil the prophecy, partly because the grandeur of his soul could not stoop to contend with liars, and most of all because his innocence needed no defence. He that is in some measure guilty is eager to apologize and to extenuate: his excuses usually suggest to men of experience the belief that there may be some ground for the accusation. He that is perfectly innocent is in no haste to answer his slanderers, for they soon answer one another. Our Lord did not desire to get into a vain jangle with them, and so to lead them on to utter still more falsehoods. If speech can do no good then indeed silence is wise:

when the only result would have been to provoke his enemies to add to their iniquities, it was magnanimous compassion which led the slandered Saviour to hold his speech.

We must not refrain from noticing *the comfort* which in some degree had been ministered to our Lord by the accusation which came most to the front. He stands there, and he knows they are about to put him to death, but they themselves remind him that their power over him has no longer lease than three days, and at the end of that short time he will be raised up again, no more to be at their disposal. His enemies witnessed the resurrection to him. I say not that his memory was weak, or that he would possibly have forgotten it amid his sorrows, but yet our Lord was human, and modes of comfort which are valuable to us were also useful to him. When the mind is tortured with malicious falsehood, and the whole man is tossed about by pains and griefs, it is good for us to be reminded of the consolations of God. We read of some who were 'tortured, not accepting deliverance', and it was the hope of resurrection which sustained them. Our Lord knew that his soul would not be left in the abodes of the dead, neither should his flesh see corruption, and the false witnesses brought this vividly before his mind. Now, indeed, could our Redeemer say, 'Destroy this temple, and in three days I will raise it up.' These ravens have brought the Saviour bread and meat. In these dead lions our glorious Samson has found honey. Sustained by the joy that was set before him he despises the shame. Strange that out of the mouths of those who sought his blood there should come the memorial of one of his greatest glories.

Now, brethren, here again we learn the same lesson as before, namely, let us gain meekness, and prove it by our power to hold our tongues. Eloquence is difficult to acquire, but silence is far more hard to practice. A man may much sooner learn to speak well than learn not to speak at all. We are in such a hurry to vindicate our own cause that we damage it by rash speech: if we were calm, gentle, quiet, forbearing as the Saviour was, our pathway to victory would be much more easy.

Observe, again, *the armour with which Christ was clad:* see the invulnerable shield of his holiness. His life was such that slander could not frame an accusation against him which would last long enough to be repeated. So frail were the charges that, like bubbles, they vanished as soon as they saw the light. Our Lord's enemies were utterly baffled. They hurled their darts against him, but, as if they fell upon a shield of blazing diamond, every arrow was broken and consumed.

Learn also this other lesson that we must expect to be mis-represented: we may reckon that our words will have other meanings to ungracious ears than those which we intended; we may expect that when we teach one thing which is true they will make us out to have stated another which is false; but let us not be overwhelmed by this fiery trial as though it were some strange thing. Our Lord and Master has endured it, and the servants must not escape. Wherefore endure hardness as good soldiers of Jesus Christ, and be not afraid.

Amid the din of these lies and perjuries, I hear the still small voice of a truth most precious, for like as Jesus stood for us at the bar, and they could not cause an accusation to abide upon him, so when we shall stand in him at the last great day, washed in his blood and covered with his righteousness, we too shall be clear. 'Who shall lay anything to the charge of God's elect?' If Satan should appear as the accuser of the brethren, he will be met by the voice, 'The Lord rebuke thee, O Satan, even the Lord that hath chosen Jerusalem rebuke thee: is not this a brand plucked out of the burning?' Yes, beloved, we too shall be cleared of slander. Then shall the righteous shine forth as the sun in the kingdom of their Father. The glorious righteousness of him who was falsely accused shall deliver the saints and all iniquity shall stop her mouth.

III. But I must not dwell too long even on such themes as these, and therefore I pass on to THE PERSONAL INTERROGATION which followed upon the failure to bring forward witnesses. The high priest, too indignant to sit still, rises and stands over the prisoner like a lion roaring over his prey, and begins to question him again. It was an unrighteous thing to do. Should the judge who sits to administer law set himself to prove the prisoner guilty, or, what is worse, shall he try to extort confession from the accused which may he used against him? It was a tacit confession that Christ had been proved innocent up till then. The high priest would not have needed to draw something out of the accused one if there had been sufficient material against him elsewhere. The trial had been a dead failure up to that point, and he knew it, and was red with rage. Now he attempts to bully the prisoner, that he may extract some declaration from him which may save all further trouble of witnesses and end the matter. The question was forced home by a solemn adjuration, and it effected its purpose, for the Lord Jesus did speak, though he knew that he was thereby furnishing a weapon against himself. He felt under bond to answer the high priest of his people when he used such adjuration, bad man as that high priest was; and he could not draw back from a charge so solemn lest he should seem by his silence to deny the truth upon which the salvation of the world is made to hinge.

So when the high priest said to him, 'Art thou the Christ, the Son of the Blessed?' how distinctly and outspoken was the Master's reply. Though he knew that his death would thus be compassed, he witnessed a good confession. He plainly said, 'I am', and then he added to that declaration, 'Ye shall see the Son of man' – so he brings out his humanity as well as his deity, 'sitting on the right hand of power, and coming in the clouds of heaven.' What a majestic faith! It is wonderful to think that he should be so calm as to confront his mockers, and assert his glory while he was in the depths of shame.

He did as good as say, 'You sit as my judges, but I shall soon sit as your judge; I seem to you to be an insignificant peasant, but I am the Son of the Blessed; you think that you will crush me, but you never will; for I shall speedily sit at the right hand of the power of God, and come in the clouds of heaven.' He speaks boldly, as well became him. I admire the meekness that could be silent, I admire the meekness that could speak gently, but I still more wonder at the meekness that could speak courageously, and still be meek. Somehow or other, when we rouse ourselves to courage, we let in harshness at the same door, or if we shut out our anger, we are very apt to forget our firmness. Jesus never slays one virtue to make room for another. His character is complete, full-orbed, perfect, whichever way we look at it.

And surely, brethren, this must have brought another sweet consolation to our divine Master's heart. While smarting under that cruel blow, while writhing under those filthy accusations, while enduring such contradiction of sinners against himself, he must have felt satisfied from within in the consciousness of his Sonship and his power, and in the prospect of his glory and triumph. A well of water springs up within his soul as he foresees that he shall sit at the right hand of God, and that he shall judge the quick and the dead, and vindicate his redeemed. It is a wise thing to have these consolations always ready to hand. The enemy may not see their consolatory power, but we see it. To us from beneath the altar there issues forth a stream whose gentle flow supplies our spirits with a quiet gladness such as all earth's waters can never rival. Even now we also hear the Father say, 'I am thy shield and thy exceeding great reward.'

Notice, ere we pass away from this point, that, practically, the trial and the interrogation ended in our Lord's being *condemned because of his avowal of his deity*. They said, 'Ye have heard the blasphemy: what think ye? And they all condemned him to be guilty of death.' I cannot make out at all those people who call themselves Unitarians, and deny our Lord's deity. Unitarians we also are, for we believe in one God, and one God only; but they tell us that this blessed Christ our Master is not God, and yet they own that he was the most excellent of men, the most perfect of human beings. I cannot see it myself. He seems to me to be a blasphemer, and nothing else, if he be not God; and the Jews evidently held that opinion, and treated him accordingly. If he had not said that God was his Father, they would not have been so enraged against him. They put him to death because of the assertion of his deity, and the declaration that he would sit at the right hand of power and judge the world. Today multitudes are willing to take Christ as a teacher, but they will not have him as the Son of God. I do not doubt that the Christian religion might be received in many places if it were shorn of its strength; if, in fact, its very soul and bowels were torn out of it, by setting forth Jesus as one of the prophets and nothing more. Hear how our wise men talk of him as one of a line of great reformers, such as Moses, Samuel, Elijah, and they often add Confucius and Muhammad. Do we give place to this? No, not for an instant. He is verily the Son of the Blessed. He is divine, or false. The accusation of blasphemy must lie against him if he be not the Son of the Highest.

IV. We must now pass on and linger for a second or two over THE CONDEMNATION. They condemned him out of his own mouth: but this, while it wore the semblance of justice, was really unjust. The prisoner at the bar has affirmed that he is the Son of God. What next? May he not speak the truth? If it be the truth he must not be condemned, but adored. Justice requires that an enquiry be made as to whether he be the Christ, the Son of the Blessed, or not. He has claimed to be the Messiah. Very well, all those in the court are expecting the Messiah; some of them expect him to appear very speedily. May not this be the sent one of the Lord? Let an enquiry be made into his claims. What is his lineage? Where was he born? Have any prophets attested him? Has he wrought miracles? Some such enquiries are due to any man whose life is at stake. You cannot justly condemn a man to die without examining into the truth of his defence, for it may turn out that his statements are correct. But, no, they will not hear the man they hate, the mere claim condemns him; it is blasphemy, and he must die.

He says he is the Son of God. Come, then, Caiaphas and council, call for witnesses for the defence. Enquire whether blind eyes have been opened and the dead raised up. Ask whether he has wrought miracles such as no man ever wrought in the midst of Israel through-out all time. Why not do this? O no, he must be taken from prison and from judgment, and none shall declare his generation. The less enquiry the more easy to condemn him unjustly. He has said he is the Christ and the Son of God, he is therefore guilty of death. Alas, how many there are who condemn Christ's doctrine without making due enquiries into it – condemn it on the most trivial grounds. They come to hear a sermon, and perhaps find fault with the mannerism of the preacher, as if that were sufficient reason for denying the truth which he preaches; or else they say, 'This is so strange – we cannot believe it.' Why not? Are not strange things sometimes true, and is not many a truth wondrously strange until you get familiar with it? These men will not condescend to hear Christ's proof of claim: they will make no enquiry. In this, like the Jewish priests, they practically cry, 'Away with him! Away with him!'

He is condemned to die, and the high priest rends his clothes. I do not know whether he wore at that time the robes in which he ministered, but doubtless he wore some garb peculiar to his sacerdotal office, and this he rent. Oh, how significant! The house of Aaron and the tribe of Levi had their garments rent, and the temple, within a few hours, rent its veil from the top to the bottom: for priests and temple were alike abolished. They little knew it, but in all they did there was a singular significance: those rent garments were an index of the fact that now the Aaronic priesthood was for ever rent, and the great Melchizedek's priesthood had come in, for the true Melchizedek there and then stood before them in all the majesty of his patience.

Observe that *they were all agreed;* there were no dissentients; they had taken care, I have no doubt, not to let Nicodemus and Joseph of Arimathaea know anything about this meeting of theirs. They held it in the night, and they only rehearsed it in the early morning, for the sake of keeping their old Rabbinical law that they must try prisoners by daylight. They hurried up the trial, and any that might have spoken against their bloodthirsty sentence were kept out of the way. The assembly was unanimous. Alas for the unanimity of ungodly hearts against Christ! It is wonderful that there should be such quarrels among Christ's friends, and such unity among his foes, when the point is to put him to death. I never heard of quarrels among devils, nor did I ever read of sects in hell: they are all one in their hatred of the Christ and of God. But here are we split up into sections and parties, and often at war with one another. O Lord of love, forgive us: King of concord, come and reign over us, and bring us into a perfect unity around thyself.

The sentence was 'death'. I say nothing of it but this. Death was the sentence due to me, the sentence due to you, and they laid it upon our Substitute. 'Worthy of death' – they said – all of them. All hands were held up; all voices said 'Yea, yea' to the verdict. Yet there was no fault in him. Say rather, there was every excellence in him. As I hear Jesus condemned to die my soul falls at his feet and cries, 'Blessed Lord, now hast thou taken my condemnation; there is, therefore, none for me. Now hast thou taken my cup of death to drink, and henceforth it is dry to me. Glory be to thy blessed name, henceforth and for ever.'

V. I am almost glad that my time is so far advanced, for I must needs set before you the fifth and most painful scene. No sooner have these evil men of the Sanhedrin pronounced him guilty of death, than the servants, the guards, and those that kept the high priests' hall, eager to please their masters, and all touched with the same brute-like spirit which was in them, straightway began to *abuse* the infinite majesty of our Lord. Consider THE ABUSE. Let me read the words: 'Some began to spit on him.' 'Began to spit on him!' Thus was contempt expressed more effectively than by words. Be astonished, O heavens, and be horribly afraid. His face is the light of the universe, his person is the glory of heaven, and they 'began to spit on him.' Alas, my God, that man should be so base! Some went further, and they 'covered his face'. It is an Eastern custom to cover the face of the condemned, as if they were not fit to see the light, nor fit to behold their fellow men. I know not whether for this reason, or in pure mockery, they covered his face, so that they could not see it, and he could not see them. How could they thus put out the sun and shut up bliss. Then when all was dark to him we read that they began to say, 'Prophesy, Who is he that smote thee?' Then another did the like, and many were the cruel cuffs they laid about his blessed face.

The mediaeval writers delighted to talk about the teeth that were broken, the bruises on the checks, the blood which flowed, the flesh that was bruised and blackened; but we dare not thus imagine. Scripture has cast a veil, and there let it abide. Yet it must have been an awful sight to see the Lord of glory with his face bestained by their accursed phlegm and bruised with their cruel fists. Here insult and cruelty were combined: ridicule of his prophetic claims and dishonour to his divine person. Nothing was thought bad enough. They invented all they could of shame and scorn, and he stood patient there though a single flash of his eye would have consumed them in a moment.

Brothers, sisters, this is what our sin deserved. A shameful thing art thou, O sin! Thou dost deserve to be spit upon! This is what sin is constantly doing to Christ. Whenever you and I sin we do, as it were, spit in his face: we also hide his eyes by trying to forget that he sees us; and we also smite him whenever we transgress and grieve his Spirit. Talk not of cruel Jews: let us think of ourselves, and let us be humbled by the thought. This is what the ungodly world is ever doing to our blessed Master. They also would hide his eyes which are the light of the world: they also despise his gospel, and spit upon it as an utterly worn out and worthless thing: they also do despite to the members of his body through his poor afflicted saints who have to bear slander and abuse for his dear sake.

And yet over all this I seem to see a light most blessed. Christ must be spit upon, for he has taken our sin: Christ must be tortured, for he is standing in our stead. Who is to be the executioner of all this grief? Who shall take upon himself the office of putting Christ to shame? Our redemption was being wrought out this way – who shall be the drudge to perform this miserable work? Fling in the clusters richer than the grapes of Eshcol; fling them in, but who shall tread them out and laboriously extract the wine, the generous wine which cheereth God and man? The feet shall be the willing feet of Christ's own adversaries: they shall extort from him that which shall redeem us and destroy all evil. I rejoice to see Satan outwitted, and his malice made to be the means of his own overthrow. He thinks to destroy Christ, and by that deed he destroys himself. He pulls down evil upon his own head and falls into the pit which he has digged. Thus shall all evil ever work for the good of the Lord's people; yea, their greatest good shall ofttimes come out of that which threatened their ruin, and wrought in them the utmost anguish. Three days must the Christ suffer and die and lie in the grave; but after that he must bruise the serpent's head and lead captivity captive, and that by the means of the very suffering and shame which he is now enduring; in like manner shall it happen to his mystical body, and Satan shall be bruised under our feet shortly.

I leave this subject, hoping that you will pursue it in your meditations, Here are three observations.

First, *how ready should we be to bear slander and ridicule for Jesus' sake*. Do not get into a huff, and think it a hard thing that people should mock at you. Who are you, dear sir? Who are you? What can you be if compared with Christ? If they spat upon him, why should they not spit upon you? If they buffeted him, why should they not buffet you? Shall your Master have all the rough of it? Shall he have all the bitter, and you all the sweet? A pretty soldier you, to demand better fare than your Captain!

How earnestly, next, ought we to honour our dear Lord. If men were so eager to put him to shame, let us be ten times more earnest to bring him glory. Is there anything we can do today by which he may be honoured? Let us set about it. Can we make any sacrifice? can we perform any difficult task which would glorify him? Let us not deliberate, but at once do it with our might. Let us be inventive in modes of glorifying him, even as his adversaries were ingenious in the methods of his shame.

Lastly, *how surely and how sweetly may all who believe in him come and rest their souls in his hands.* Surely I know that he who suffered this, since he was verily the Son of the Blessed, must have ability to save us. Such griefs must be a full atonement for our transgressions. Glory be to God, that spittle on his countenance means a clear, bright face for me. Those false accusations on his character mean no condemnation for me. That putting him to death proves the certainty of our text last Sabbath morning, 'Verily, verily, I say unto you, he that believeth on me hath everlasting life.' Let us sweetly rest in Jesus, and if ever our faith is agitated, let us get away to the hall of Caiaphas, and see the Just standing for the unjust, the Faultless One bearing condemnation for sinners. Let us in the high priest's hall judge and condemn every sin and every doubt, and come forth glorying that the Christ has conquered for us, and that we now wait for his appearing with delight. God bless you, brothers, for Christ's sake. Amen.

5

NEVERTHELESS, HEREAFTER[1]

Jesus saith unto him, Thou hast said [or said so],
nevertheless, I say unto you, Hereafter shall ye see
the Son of man sitting on the right hand of power,
and coming in the clouds of heaven.
MATTHEW 26:64

OUR LORD, BEFORE HIS ENEMIES, was silent in his own
defence, but he faithfully warned and boldly avowed the truth. His
was the silence of patience, not of indifference; of courage, not of
cowardice. It is written that 'before Pontius Pilate he witnessed a
good confession', and that statement may also be well applied to
his utterances before Caiaphas, for there he was not silent when it
came to confession of necessary truth. If you will read the chapter
now open before us, you will notice that the high priest adjured
him, saying, 'Art thou the Christ, the Son of God?', to which he
replied at once, 'Thou hast said it.' He did not disown his
Messiahship; he claimed to be the promised one, the messenger
from heaven, Christ the anointed of the Most High. Neither did
he for a moment disavow his personal deity; he acknowledged and
confessed that he was the Son of God. How could he be silent
when such a vital point as to his person was in question? He did
not hold them in suspense, but openly declared his Godhead by
saying, 'I am'; for so are his words reported by one of the evangelists. He then proceeded to reveal the solemn fact that he would
soon sit at the right hand of God, even the Father. In the words of

---

[1] Sermon No. 1,364. Preached at the Metropolitan Tabernacle, date not known.

our text he declared that those who were condemning him would see him glorified, and in due time would stand at his bar when he would come upon the clouds of heaven to judge the quick and dead according to our gospel. See, then, dear brethren, in a few words, the great truths of our holy religion clearly set forth by our Lord Jesus; he claimed to be the Christ of God, and the Son of God, and his brief statement by implication speaks of Jesus dead, buried, and risen, and now enthroned at the right hand of God in the power of the Father, and Jesus soon to come in his glorious second advent to judge the world in righteousness. Our Lord's confession was very full, and happy is he who heartily embraces it.

I intend to dwell upon three catch-words around which there gathers a world of encouraging and solemn thought. The first is *'nevertheless'*, and the second is *'hereafter'*; what the third is you shall know hereafter, but not just now.

I. 'NEVERTHELESS', said Christ, 'hereafter shall ye see the Son of man sitting at the right hand of power, and coming in the clouds of heaven.' This, then, is the string from which we must draw forth music. *'Nevertheless'*, which being interpreted by being pulled in pieces, signifies that truth is never-the-less sure because of opposition. 'Nevertheless', not one atom the less is the truth certain to prevail, for all that you say or do against it. Jesus will surely sit at the right hand of power, and come in due season upon the clouds of heaven. Let us dwell for a little time upon this important fact, that truth is none the less certain because of the opposition of men and devils.

Observe, first, that *the Saviour's condition when he made use of that 'nevertheless' was no proof that he would not rise to power.* There he stood, a poor, defenceless, emaciated man, newly led from the night-watch in the garden and its bloody sweat. He was a spectacle of meek and lowly suffering led by his captors like a lamb to the slaughter, with none to speak a word on his behalf. He was surrounded by those who hated him, and he was forsaken by his friends. Scribes, Pharisees, priests, were all thirsting for his heart's blood. A lamb in the midst of wolves is but a faint picture of Christ standing there before the Sanhedrin in patient silence. And yet, though his present condition seemed to contradict it, he who was the faithful and true witness spake truly when he testified, 'Nevertheless, hereafter ye shall see the Son of man coming in the clouds of heaven. Despite my present shame and suffering, so it shall be.'

He gives himself that lowly, humble title of Son of man, as best indicating himself in his condition at that time. 'Hereafter ye shall see the Son of man sitting at the right hand of power, and coming in the clouds of heaven.' The humiliation of Christ did not in the least endanger his after glory. His sufferings, his shame, his death, did not render it any the less certain that he would climb to his throne. Nor did the cavillings of his opposers keep him for one instant from his place of honour. I wish you to remember this, for there is a great principle in it. There are many poor weak-minded people who cannot take sides with a persecuted truth, nor accept anything but the most popular and fashionable form of religion. They dare not be with truth when men spit in its face, and buffet it, and pour contempt upon it; but it will be victorious none the less, although cowards desert it and false-hearted men oppose it. If it stand alone at the bar of the world, a culprit to be condemned – if it receive nothing but a universal hiss of human execration – yet, if it be the truth, it may be condemned, but it will be justified; it may be buried, but it will rise; it may be rejected, but it will be glorified, even as it has happened to the Christ of God. Who would be ashamed of truth at any time when he knows the preciousness of it? Who will tremble because of present opposition when he foresees what will yet come of it? What a sublime spectacle – the Man of Sorrows standing before his cruel judges in all manner of weakness and poverty and contempt, at the same time heir of all things, and appointed, nevertheless, to sit at the right hand of power and to come in the clouds of heaven.

Nor may we think only of his condition as a despised and rejected man; for he was, on his trial, charged with grievous wrong, and about to be *condemned by the ecclesiastical authorities.* The scribes, learned in the law, declared that he blasphemed; and the priests, familiar with the ordinances of God, exclaimed, 'Away with him; it is not meet that he should live.' The high priest himself gave judgment that it was expedient for him to be put to death. It is a very serious thing, is it not, when all the ecclesiastical authorities are against you – when they are unanimous in your condemnation? Yes, verily, and it may cause great searching of heart; for no peaceable man desires to be opposed to constituted authority, but would sooner have the good word of those who sit in Moses' seat. But this was not the last time in which the established ecclesiastical authorities were wrong, grievously wrong. They were condemning the innocent, and blaspheming the Lord from heaven. Nor, I say, was this the last time in which the mitre and the gown have been upon the side of cruel wrong; yet this did not un-Christ our Saviour or rob him of his deity or his throne. On the same principle human history brings before us abundance of instances in which, nevertheless, though scribes, priests, bishops, pontiffs, and popes condemned the truth, it was just as sure, and became as triumphant, as it had a right to do. There stands the one lone man, and there are all the great ones around him – men of authority and reputation, sanctity and pomp – and they unanimously deny that he can ever sit at the right hand of God; 'But, nevertheless', saith he, 'hereafter ye shall see the Son of man at the right hand of power.' He spoke the truth; his declaration has been most gloriously fulfilled hitherto. Even thus over the neck of clergy, priests, pontiffs, popes, his triumphant chariot of salvation shall still roll, and the truth – the simple truth of his glorious gospel – shall, despite them all, win the day, and reign over the sons of men.

Nor is this all. Our Lord at that time was *surrounded by those who were in possession of earthly power*. The priests had the ear of Pilate, and Pilate had the Roman legions at his back. Who could resist such a combination of force? Craft and authority form a dreadful league. One disciple drew a sword, but just at the time when our Lord stood before the Sanhedrin that one chivalrous warrior had denied him; so that all the physical force was on the other side. As a man he was helpless when he stood bound before the council. I am not speaking now of that almighty power which faith knows to have dwelt in him; but as to human power, he was weakness at its weakest. His cause seemed at the lowest ebb. He had none to stand up in his defence – nay, none to speak a word on his behalf; for, 'Who shall declare his generation?' And yet, for all that, and even because of it, he did rise to sit at the right hand of power, and he shall come in the clouds of heaven. So if it ever comes to pass, my brother, that thou shouldst be the lone advocate of a forgotten truth – if thy Master should ever put thee in all thy weakness and infirmity in the midst of the mighty and the strong, do not thou fear or tremble; for the possession of power is but a trifle compared with the possession of truth, and he that has the right may safely defy the might of the world. He shall win and conquer, let the princes and powers that be take to themselves what force and craft they choose. Jesus, nevertheless, wins, though the power is all against him, and so shall the truth which he represents, for it wears about it a hidden power which baffles all opponents.

Nor was it merely all the power, there was *a great deal of furious rage against him*. That Caiaphas, how he spoke to him! 'I adjure thee', saith he, 'by God.' And after he has spoken he rends his garments in indignation, his anger burns like fire; but the Christ is very quiet, the Lamb of God is still, and looking his adversary in the face, he says, 'Nevertheless, hereafter thou shalt see the Son of man sitting at the right hand of power, and coming in the clouds of heaven.' He was strong, and therefore calm; confident, and therefore peaceful; fully assured, and therefore patient. He could wait, for he believed; and his prophecy was true, notwithstanding the high priest's rage. So if we meet with any man at any time who gnashes his teeth upon us, who foams in passion, who dips his pen into the bitterest gall to write down our holy faith, who is indefatigable in his violent efforts against the Christ of God – what mattereth it? 'Nevertheless, ye shall see the Son of man sitting at the right hand of power.' 'Yet have I set my king upon my holy hill of Zion', said Jehovah; and he declared the decree though the heathen raged and the people imagined a vain thing. Well may he smile at rage who is so sure of victory.

Yes, but it was not one person that raged merely. The people of Jerusalem, and the multitudes that had come up to the Passover, bribed and egged on by the priests and the Pharisees, were all hot after our Saviour's death, clamouring, 'Crucify him, crucify him'; and yet there he stood, and as he heard their tumult, and anticipated its growing demand for his blood, he lost not his confidence, but he calmly said, 'Nevertheless, hereafter, shall ye see the Son of man sitting at the right hand of power.' Behold his perfect inward peace, and see how he manifests it by a bold confession in the very teeth of all his adversaries. 'Ye may be as many as the waves of the sea; and ye may foam and rage like the ocean in a storm, but the purpose and the decree of God will, nevertheless, be fulfilled; ye cannot let or hinder it one whit. Ye, to your everlasting confusion, shall see the Son of man sitting at the right hand of power.'

Beloved, you know that after he had said this our Lord was taken before Herod and Pilate, and at last was put to death; and he knew all this, foreseeing it most clearly, and yet it did not make him hesitate. He knew that he would be crucified, and that his enemies would boast that there was an end of him and of his kingdom. He knew that his disciples would hide themselves in holes and corners, and that nobody would dare to say a word concerning the man of Nazareth; he foreknew that the name of the Nazarene would be bandied about amid general opprobrium, and Jerusalem would say, 'That cause is crushed out; that egg of mischief has been broken'; but he, foreseeing all, that, and more, declared, 'Nevertheless, hereafter ye shall see the Son of man sitting at the right hand of power, and coming in the clouds of heaven.' I cannot help harping upon the text – I hope I shall not weary you with it, for to me it is music. I do not like running over the word *'nevertheless'* too quickly. I like to draw it out and repeat it as 'never-the-less'. No, not one jot the less will his victory come. Not in the least degree was his royal power endangered or his sure triumph imperilled. Not even by his death and the consequent scattering of his disciples was the least hazard occasioned; but, indeed, all these things wrought together for the accomplishment of the divine purpose concerning him, and the lower he stooped the more sure he was to rise ultimately to his glory.

And now, beloved, it is even so. The man Christ Jesus was despised and rejected of men, but at this moment he sits at the right hand of power; all power is given to him in heaven and in earth, and therefore does he bid us proclaim his gospel. There is not an angel but does his bidding; providence is arranged by his will, for 'the government shall be upon his shoulder, and his name shall be called Wonderful, Counsellor, the mighty God, the everlasting Father, the Prince of Peace.' Atoning work is done, and, therefore, he sits. His work is well done, and, therefore, he sits on the right hand of God, in the place of honour and dignity. Before long he will come. We cannot tell when; he may come tonight, or he may tarry many a weary year; but he will surely come in person, for did not the angels say to the men of Galilee, as they stood gazing into heaven, 'This same Jesus shall so come in like manner as ye have seen him go into heaven'? He shall come with blast of trumpet and with thousands of angelic beings, all doing him honour. He shall come with flaming fire to visit the trembling earth. He shall come with all his Father's glories on, and kings and princes shall stand before him, and he shall reign amongst his ancients gloriously. The tumults of the people, and the plotting of their rulers, shall be remembered in that day, but it shall be to their own eternal shame; his throne shall be none the less resplendent.

I beg you to learn the spiritual lesson which comes out of this. I have already indicated it, and it is this – never be afraid to stand by a losing cause. Never hesitate to stand alone when the truth is to be confessed. Never be overawed by sacerdotalism, or daunted by rage, or swayed by multitudes. Unpopular truth is, nevertheless, eternal, and that doctrine which is scouted and cast out as evil today shall bring immortal honour to the man who dares to stand by its side and share its humiliation. Oh, for the love of the Christ who thus threw a *'nevertheless'* at the feet of his foes, follow him whithersoever he goeth. Through flood or flame, in loneliness, in shame, in obloquy, in reproach, follow him! If it be without the camp, follow him! If every step shall cost you abuse and scorn, follow still; yea, to prison and to death still follow him, for as surely as he sitteth at the right hand of power so shall those who love him and have been faithful to his truth sit down upon his throne with him. His overcoming and enthronement are the pledges of the victory both of the truth and of those who courageously espouse it.

Thus have we sounded our first great bell – 'NEVERTHELESS'. Let its music ring through the place and charm each opened ear.

II. The second bell is 'HEREAFTER'. 'Nevertheless, hereafter'. I like the sound of those two bells together; let us ring them again. 'Nevertheless, *hereafter*'. The hereafter seems in brief to say to me

71

that *the main glory of Christ lies in the future*. Not today, perhaps, nor tomorrow will the issue be seen! Have patience! Wait a while. 'Your strength is to sit still.' God has great leisure, for he is the Eternal. Let us partake in his restfulness while we sing, '*Nevertheless, hereafter*'. O for the Holy Spirit's power at this moment; for it is written, 'he will show you things to come.'

It is one great reason why the unregenerate sons of men cannot see any glory in the kingdom of Christ because to them it is such a future thing. Its hopes look into eternity; its great rewards are beyond this present time and state, and the most of mortal eyes cannot see so far. Unregenerate men are like Passion in John Bunyan's parable: they will have all their good things now, and so they have their toys and break them, and they are gone, and then their hereafter is a dreary outlook of regret and woe. Men of faith know better; and like Patience in the same parable, they choose to have their best things last, for that which comes last, lasts on for ever. He whose turn comes last has none to follow him, and his good things shall never be taken away from him. The poor, purblind world cannot see beyond its own nose, and so it must have its joys and riches at once. To them speedy victory is the main thing, and the truth is nothing. Is the cause triumphant today? Off with your caps, and throw them up, and cry 'Hurrah!' no matter that it is the cause of a lie. Do the multitudes incline that way? Then, sir, if you be worldly-wise, run with them. Pull off the palm branches, strew the roads, and shout 'Hosanna to the hero of the hour!' though he be a despot or a deceiver. But not so – not so with those who are taught of God. They take eternity into their estimate, and they are contented to go with the despised and rejected of men for the present, because they recollect the hereafter. They can swim against the flood, for they know whither the course of this world is tending. O blind world, if thou wert wise, thou wouldst amend thy line of action, and begin to think of the hereafter too; for, brethren, the hereafter will soon be *here*.

What a short time it is since Adam walked in the garden of Eden; compared with the ages of the rocks, compared with the history of the stars, compared with the life of God, it is as the winking of an eye, or as a flash of lightning. One has but to grow a little older, and years become shorter, and time appears to travel at a much faster rate than before, so that a year rushes by you like a meteor across the midnight heavens. When we are older still, and look down from the serene abodes above, I suppose that centuries and ages will be as moments to us; for to the Lord they are as nothing. Suppose the coming of the Lord should be put off for ten thousand years – it is but supposition – but if it were, ten thousand years will soon be gone, and when the august spectacle of Christ coming on the clouds of heaven shall really be seen, the delay will be as though but an hour had intervened. The space between now and then, or rather the space between what is 'now' at this time, and what will be 'now' at the last – how short a span it is! Men will look back from the eternal world and say, 'How could we have thought so much of the fleeting life we have lived on earth, when it was to be followed by eternity? What fools we were to make such count of momentary, transient pleasures, when now the things which are not seen, and are eternal, have come upon us, and we are unprepared for them!' Christ will soon come, and at the longest, when he cometh, the interval between today and then will seem to be just nothing at all; so that 'hereafter' is not as the sound of far-off cannon, nor as the boom of distant thunder, but it is the rolling of rushing wheels hastening to overtake us.

'Hereafter'! 'Hereafter'! Oh, when that hereafter comes, how overwhelming it will be to Jesus' foes! Now where is Caiaphas? Will he now adjure the Lord to speak? Now, ye priests, lift up your haughty heads! Utter a sentence against him now! There sits, your victim upon the clouds of heaven. Say now that he blasphemes, and hold up your rent rags, and condemn him again. But where is Caiaphas? He hides his guilty head; he is utterly confounded, and begs the mountains to fall upon him. And, oh, ye men of the Sanhedrin, who sat at midnight and glared on your innocent victim, with your cold, cruel eyes, and afterwards gloated over the death of your martyred Prince, where are ye now – now that he has come with all his Father's power to judge you? They are asking the hills to open their caverns and conceal them; the rocks deny them shelter. And where, on that day, will you be; you who deny his deity, who profane his Sabbath, who slander his people, and denounce his gospel – oh, where will you be in that tremendous day, which as surely comes as comes tomorrow's rising sun? Oh, sirs, consider this word – 'Hereafter'! I would fain whisper it in the ear of the sinner, fascinated by his pleasures. Come near and let me do so – *hereafter!* I would make it the alarm for the sleeping transgressor, who is dreaming of peace and safety, while he is slumbering himself into hell. Hereafter! Hereafter! Oh, yes, ye may suck the sweet, and eat the fat, and drink as ye will; but hereafter! hereafter! What will ye do hereafter when that which is sweet in the mouth shall be as gall in the belly, and when the pleasures of today shall be a mixture of misery for eternity? Hereafter! Oh, hereafter! Now, O Spirit divine, be pleased to open careless ears, that they may listen to this prophetic sound.

To the Lord's own people there is no sound more sweet than that of 'hereafter'. 'Hereafter ye shall see the Son of man coming in the clouds of heaven.' Welcome, welcome, welcome, welcome, Redeemer, Saviour! Welcome in every character in which thou comest. What acclamations and congratulations will go up from the countless myriads of his redeemed, when first the ensigns of the Son of man shall be seen in the heavens! On some one of earth's mornings, when the children of men shall be 'marrying and giving in marriage', while saints shall be looking for his appearing, they shall first of all perceive that he is actually coming. Long desired, and come at last. Then the trumpet shall be heard, waxing exceeding loud and long, ringing out a sweeter note to the true Israel than ever trumpet heard on the morn of Jubilee. What delight! What lifting up of gladsome eyes! What floods of bliss! Oppression is over, the idols are broken, the reign of sin is ended, darkness shall no more cover the nations. He cometh, he cometh; glory be to his name!

> Bring forth the royal diadem,
> And crown him Lord of all.

O blessed day of acclamations! how shall heaven's vault be rent with them when his saints shall see for themselves what was reserved for him and for them in the 'hereafter'. 'Ye shall see the Son of man at the right hand of power, and coming in the clouds of heaven.'

That word 'hereafter', my brothers and sisters, is, at this moment, our grandest solace, and I wish to bring it before you in that light. Have you been misunderstood, misrepresented, slandered because of fidelity to the right and to the true? Do not trouble yourself. Vindicate not your own cause. Refer it to the King's Bench above, and say, 'Hereafter, hereafter'. Have you been accused of being mad, fanatical, and I know not what besides, because to you party is nothing, and ecclesiastical pride nothing, and the stamp of popular opinion nothing; because you are determined to follow the steps of your Master, and believe the true and do the right? Then be in no hurry; the sure hereafter will settle the debate. Or are you very poor, and very sick, and very sad? But are you Christ's own? Do you trust him? Do you live in fellowship with him? Then the hope of the hereafter may well take the sting out of the present. It is not for long that you shall suffer; the glory will soon be revealed in you and around you. There are streets of gold symbolic of your future wealth, and there are harps celestial emblematical of your eternal joy. You shall have a white robe soon, and the dusty garments of toil shall be laid aside for ever. You shall have a far more exceeding and an eternal weight of glory; and therefore the light affliction which is but for a moment may well be endured with patience. Have you laboured in vain? Have you tried to bring souls to Christ, and had no recompense? Fret not, but remember the hereafter. Many a labourer, unsuccessful to the eye of man, will receive a 'Well done, good and faithful servant' from his Master in that day. Set little store by anything you have, and wish but lightly for anything that you have not. Let the present be to you, as it really is, a dream, an empty show, and project your soul into the hereafter, which is solid and enduring; for, oh! what music there is in it! – what delight to a true child of God! 'Nevertheless, hereafter'.

I feel half inclined to have done, and to send you out of the place, singing all the way, 'Nevertheless, hereafter'. The people outside might not understand you, but it would be a perfectly justifiable enthusiasm of delight.

III. Now, thirdly. Where am I to look for my third bell? Where is the third word I spoke of? In truth, I cannot find it in the version which we commonly use, and there is no third word in the original, and yet the word I am thinking of is there. The truth is that the second word, which has been rendered by 'hereafter', bears another meaning; I will give you what the Greek critics say, as nearly as can be, the meaning of the word is, 'HENCEFORWARD'. 'Henceforward ye shall see the Son of man sitting at the right hand of power, and coming in the clouds of heaven.' *'Henceforward'.* That is another word, and the teaching gathered out of it is this; *even in the present there are tokens of the victory of Christ.* 'But', says one, 'did Christ say to those priests that henceforward they should see him sitting at the right hand of power?' Yes, yes, that is what he meant. He meant, 'You look at me and scorn me; but, sirs, you shall not be able to do this any longer, for henceforward you shall see for yourselves that I am not what I appear to be, but that I sit at the right hand of power. Henceforward, and as long as you live, you shall know that galling truth.' And did that come true? Yes, it came true that night; for when the Saviour died there came a messenger unto the members of the Sanhedrin and others, and told them that the veil of the temple was rent in twain. In that moment, when the man of Nazareth died, that splendid piece of tapestry seemed to tear itself asunder from end to end as if in horror at the death of its Lord. The members of that council, when they met each other in the street and spoke of the news, must have been dumb in sheer astonishment; but while they looked upon each other, the earth they stood upon reeled and reeled again, and they could scarcely keep their feet. This was not the first wonder which had that day startled them, for the sun had been beclouded in unnatural darkness. At midday the sun had ceased to shine, and now the earth ceases to be stable. Lo, also, in the darkness of the evening, certain members of this council saw the sheeted dead, newly arisen from their sepulchres, walking through the streets; for the rocks rent, the earth shook, and the graves opened, and the dead came forth and appeared unto many. Thus early they began to know that the man of Nazareth was at the right hand of power.

Early on the third morning, when they were met together, there came a messenger in hot haste, who said, 'The stone is rolled away from the door of the sepulchre. Remember that ye placed a watch, and that ye set your seal upon the stone. But early this morning the soldiers say that he came forth. He rose, that dreaded One whom we put to death, and at the sight of him the keepers did quake and became as dead men.' Now, these men – these members of the Sanhedrin – believed that fact; and we have clear evidence that they did so, for they bribed the soldiers, and said, 'Say ye, his disciples came and stole away his body while we slept.' Then did the word also continue to be fulfilled, and they plainly saw that Jesus whom they had condemned was at the right hand of power. A few weeks passed over their heads, and, lo, there was a noise in the city, and an extraordinary excitement. Peter had been preaching and three thousand persons in one day had been baptized into the name which they dreaded so much; and they were told, and they heard it on the best of evidence, that there had been a wonderful manifestation of the Holy Spirit, such as was spoken of in the book of the prophet Joel. Then they must have looked one another in the face, and stroked their beards, and bitten their lips, and said one to another, 'Did he not say that we should see him at the right hand of power?' They had often to remember that word, and again and again to see its truth, for when Peter and John were brought before them, it was proven that they had restored a lame man, and these two unlearned and ignorant men told them that it was through the name of Jesus that the lame were made to leap and walk. Day after day they were continuously obliged, against their will, to see, in the spread of the religion of the man whom they had put to death, that his name had power about it such as they could not possibly gainsay or resist. Lo, one of their number, Paul, had been converted, and was preaching the faith which he had endeavoured to destroy. They must have been much amazed and chagrined, as in this also they discerned that the Son of man was at the right hand of power.

'Yes', say you, 'but did they see him coming in the clouds of heaven?' I answer, yes. Henceforth they saw that also, for they began to have upon their minds forebodings, and dark thoughts. The Jewish nation was in an ill state, the people were getting disquieted, impostors were rising, and the leading men of the nation trembled as to what the Romans would do. At last there came an outbreak, and the imperial power was defied, and then such of them as still survived began to realize the words of Christ. When they saw the comet in the sky, and the drawn sword hanging over Jerusalem, when they saw the city compassed about with armies, when they marked the legions dig the trenches, and throw up the earthworks and surround the devoted city, while all around was fire and famine; when from every tower upon the walls they could see one of their own countrymen nailed to a cross, for the Romans put the Jews to death by crucifixion by hundreds, and even by thousands – then must they have begun to see the coming of the Son of man. And when, at last, the city was destroyed and a firebrand was hurled even into the holy place, and the Jews were banished and sold for slaves till they would not fetch the price of a pair of shoes, so many were they and so greatly despised – then they saw the Son of man coming in the clouds of heaven to take vengeance on his adversaries.

Read the text as meaning, 'Henceforward, ye shall see the Son of man at the right hand of power, and coming in the clouds of heaven.' It is not the full meaning of the passage, but it is a part of that meaning, beyond all question.

Beloved, even at the present time we may see the tokens of the power of Christ among us. Only tokens, mark you; I do not want to take you off from the hereafter, but henceforward and even now there are tokens of the power of our Lord Jesus. Look at revivals. When they break out in the church, how they stagger all the adversaries of Christ. They said – yes, they dared to say – that the gospel had lost all its power – that, since the days of Whitefield and Wesley, there was no hope of the masses being stirred, yet when they see, even in this house, from Sabbath to Sabbath, vast crowds listening to the word, and when some few months ago no house could be built that was large enough to accommodate the thronging masses who sought to hear our American brethren, then were they smitten in the mouth, so that they could speak no more, for it was manifested that the Lord Christ still lives, and that, if his gospel be fully and simply preached, it will still draw all men to him, and souls will be saved, and that not a few.

And look ye, in the brave world outside, apart from religion, what influences there are abroad which are due to the power of the Christ of God. Would you have believed it twenty years ago that in America there should be no more a slave; that united Italy should be free of her despots? Could you have believed that the Pope would be whining about his being a prisoner in the Vatican, and that the power of antichrist would be shorn away? No, the wonders of history, even within the last few years, are enough to show us that Christ is at the right hand of power. Come what will in the future, mark ye this, my brethren, it will never be possible to uphold tyranny and oppression long, for the Lord Christ is to the front for the poor and needy of the earth. O despots, you may do what you will, and use your craft and policy, if you please, but all over this world the Lord Jesus Christ has lifted up a plummet and set up a righteous standard, and he will draw a straight line, and it will pass through everything that offends, that it may be cut off; and it will also pass over all that is good and lovely, and right, and just, and true, and these shall be established in his reign among men. I believe in the reign of Christ. Kings, sultans, czars – these are puppets all of them, and your parliaments and congresses are but vanity of vanity. God is great, and none but he. Jesus is the King in all the earth. He is the man, the King of men, the Lord of all. Glory be to his name. As the years progress we shall see it more and more, for he has had long patience, but he is beginning now to cut the work short in righteousness. He is baring his right arm for war and that which denies manhood's just claims, that which treads upon the neck of the humanity which Christ has taken, that which stands against his throne and dominion, must be broken in pieces like a potter's vessel, for the sceptre in his hand is a rod of iron, and he will use it mightily. The Christ, then, gives tokens still of his power. They are only tokens, but they are sure ones, even as the dawn does not deceive us, though it be not the noontide.

And oh, let me say, there be some of you present who are enemies of Christ, but you also must have perceived some tokens of his power. I have seen him shake the infidel by the gospel till he has said, 'Almost thou persuadest me to be a Christian.' He has taken him in the silence of the night and probed his conscience; in his gentleness and love, and pity he has led the man to think, and though he has not altogether yielded, yet he has felt that there is a solemn power about the Christ of God. Some of the worst of men have been forced to own that Christ has conquered them. Remember how Julian, as he died, said, 'The Nazarene has overcome me; the Nazarene has overcome me.' May you not have to say that in the article of death, but oh that you may say it now. May his love overpower you, may his compassion win you, and you will see in your own salvation tokens of his power.

But I must have done, for my time has fled, but I desire to add that it will be a blessed thing if everyone here, becoming a believer in Jesus, shall henceforward see him at the right hand of power and coming in the clouds of heaven. Would to God we could live with that vision full in view, believing Jesus to be at the right hand of power, trusting him and resting in him. Because we know him to be the Lord, strong and mighty, the Lord mighty in battle, we ought never to have a doubt when we are doing what is right. We ought never to have a doubt when we are following Jesus, for he is more than a conqueror, and so shall his followers be. Let us go on courageously, trusting in him as a child trusts in his father, for he is mighty upon whom we repose our confidence.

Let us also keep before our mind's eye the fact that he is coming. Be ye not as the virgins that fell asleep. Even now my ear seems to hear the midnight cry, 'Behold, the bridegroom cometh!' Arise, ye virgins, sleep no longer, for the bridegroom is near. As for you, ye foolish virgins, God grant that there may yet be time enough left to awake even you, that you may yet have oil for your lamps before he comes. He comes we know not when, but he comes quickly. Be ye ready, for in such an hour as ye think not the Son of man cometh. Be ye as men that watch for their Lord, and as servants that are ready to give in their account, because the master of the house is near.

In that spirit let us come to the Lord's table, as often as we gather there, for he has said to us, 'Do this until I come.' Outward ordinances will cease when he comes, for we shall need no memorial when the Lord himself will be among us. Let us here pledge him in the cup. That he is coming we do verily believe; that he is coming we do joyfully proclaim. Is it a subject of joy to you? If not –

> Ye sinners seek his face,
> Whose wrath ye cannot bear;
> Bow to the sceptre of his grace,
> And find salvation there.

God bless you, for Christ's sake.

6

AN AWFUL CONTRAST[1]

Then did they spit in his face.
MATTHEW 26:67

And I saw a great white throne, and him that sat on it,
from whose face the earth and the heaven fled away.
REVELATION 20:11

GUIDED BY OUR TEXT in Matthew's Gospel, let us first go in thought to the palace of Caiaphas the high priest, and there let us, in deepest sorrow, realize the meaning of these terrible words: 'Then did they spit in his face.' There is more of deep and awful thunder in them than in the bolt that bursts overhead, there is more of vivid terror in them than in the sharpest lightning flash: 'Then did they spit in his face.'

Observe that these men, the priests, and scribes, and elders, and their servitors, did this shameful deed after they had heard our Lord say, 'Hereafter shall ye see the Son of man sitting on the right hand of power, and coming in the clouds of heaven.' It was in contempt of this claim, in derision of this honour which he foretold for himself, that 'then did they spit in his face', as if they could bear it no longer, that he, who stood to be judged of them, should claim to be their Judge; that he, whom they had brought at dead of night from the garden of Gethsemane as their captive, should talk of coming in the clouds of heaven: 'Then did they spit in his face.'

[1] Sermon No. 2,473. Preached at the Metropolitan Tabernacle on Sunday evening, 11 July 1886.

Nor may I fail to add that they thus assaulted our Lord after the high priest had rent his clothes. My brethren, do not forget that the high priest was supposed to be the representative of everything that was good and venerable among the Jews. The high priest was the earthly head of their religion; he it was who, alone of mortal men, might enter within the mysterious veil; yet he it was who condemned the Lord of glory, as he rent his clothes, and said, 'He hath spoken blasphemy; what further need have we of witnesses? behold, now ye have heard his blasphemy.' It makes me tremble as I think of how eminent we may be in the service of God, and yet how awfully we may be enemies of the Christ of God. Let none of us think that, though we even clamber up to the highest places in the church, we are therefore saved. We may be high priests, and wear the Urim and the Thummim, and put on the breastplate with all its wondrous mystic stones, and bind around us the curious girdle of the ephod, and yet, for all that, we may be ringleaders in expressing contempt of God and of his Christ. It was when Caiaphas, the high priest, had pronounced the word of condemnation against Christ, that 'then did they spit in his face.' God grant that we may never take upon ourselves any office in the church of God, and then, girt about with the authority and influence which such an office might lend to us, be the first to pour derision and contempt upon the Christ of God! Yet I do not hesitate to say that when men look to the earthly priesthood instead of looking to Christ, the great High Priest, when men are taught to trust in the mass instead of trusting in Christ's one sacrifice for sin upon the cross, it is then that the very priests do lead the way in spitting in his face. Antichrist never more surely dwells anywhere than in the place where Christ is thus dishonoured, and none do him such dire disgrace as those who ought to bow at his feet, and lift him high among the sons of men, yet who reject him, and refuse his rightful claims.

'Then did they spit in his face', after he had proclaimed his Godhead as King and Judge of all, and after the man who ought to have been his principal earthly servant had turned arch-traitor, and led the way in contempt of him by accusing him of blaspheming. 'Then did they spit in his face.'

There are two or three thoughts that come to my mind when I think that these wicked men did actually spit in Christ's face – in that face which is the light of heaven, the joy of angels, the bliss of saints, and the very brightness of the Father's glory. This spitting shows us, first, *how far sin will go*. If we want proof of the depravity of the heart of man, I will not point you to the stews of Sodom and Gomorrah, nor will I take you to the places where blood is shed in streams by wretches like to Herod and men of that sort. No, the clearest proof that man is utterly fallen, and that the natural heart is enmity against God, is seen in the fact that they did spit in Christ's face, did falsely accuse him, and condemn him, and lead him out as a malefactor, and hang him up as a felon that he might die upon the cross. Why, what evil had he done? What was there in his whole life that should give them occasion to spit in his face? Even at that moment, did his face flash with indignation against them? Did he look with contempt upon them? Not he; for he was all gentleness and tenderness even towards these his enemies, and their hearts must have been hard and brutal indeed that 'then did they spit in his face.' He had healed their sick, he had fed their hungry, he had been among them a very fountain of blessing up and down Judaea and Samaria; and yet, 'then did they spit in his face.' I say again, relate not to me the crimes of ancient nations, nor the horrible evils committed by uncivilized men, nor the more elaborate iniquities of our great cities; tell me not of the abominations of Greece or Rome – this – this, in the sight of the angels of God, and in the eyes of the God of the angels, is the masterpiece of all iniquity: 'Then did they spit in his face.' To enter into the King's own palace, and draw near to his only-begotten Son, and to spit in his face – this is the crime of crimes which reveals the infamous wickedness of men. Humanity stands condemned of the blackest iniquity now that it has gone as far as to spit in Christ's face.

My meditation also turns towards the Well-beloved into whose face they spat; and my thought concerning him is this, *how deep was the humiliation he had to endure!* When he was made sin for us, though he himself knew no sin; when our Lord Jesus Christ took upon himself the iniquities of his people, and was burdened with the tremendous weight of their guilt, it became incumbent upon the justice of God to treat him as if he were actually a sinner. He was no sinner, and he could be none; he was perfect man and perfect God, yet he stood in the place of sinners, and the Lord caused to meet upon him the iniquity of all his people. Therefore, in the time of humiliation, he must not be treated as the Son of God, neither must he be held in honour as a righteous man; he must first be given up to shame and to contempt, and then to suffering and to death; and, consequently, he was not spared this last and most brutal of insults: 'Then did they spit in his face.' O my Lord, to what terrible degradation art thou brought! Into what depths art thou dragged through my sin, and the sin of all the multitudes whose iniquities were made to meet upon thee! O my brothers, let us hate sin; O my sisters, let us loathe sin, not only because it pierced those blessed hands and feet of our dear Redeemer, but because it dared even to spit in his face! No one can ever know all the shame the Lord of glory suffered when they did spit in his face. These words glide over my tongue all too smoothly; perhaps even I do not feel them as they ought to be felt, though I would do so if I could. But could I feel as I ought to feel in sympathy with the terrible shame of Christ, and then could I interpret those feelings by any language known to mortal man, surely you would bow your heads and blush, and you would feel rising within your spirits a burning indignation against the sin that dared to put the Christ of God to such shame as this. I want to kiss his feet when I think that they did spit in his face.

Then, once more, my thoughts run to him again in this way, I think of *the tender omnipotence of his love*. How could he bear this spitting when, with one glance of his eye, had he been but angry, the flame might have slain them, and withered them all up? Yet he stood still even when they did spit in his face; and they were not the only ones who thus insulted him, for, afterwards, when he was taken by the soldiers into Pilate's hall, they also spat upon him in cruel contempt and scorn.

> See how the patient Jesus stands,
> Insulted in his lowest case!
> Sinners have bound the Almighty hands!
> And spit in their Creator's face.

How could he bear it? Friends, he could not have borne it if he had not been omnipotent. That very omnipotence, which would have enabled him to destroy them, was omnipotence of love as well as omnipotence of force. It was this that made him – if I may so say – 'restrain himself', for there is no omnipotence like that which doth restrain omnipotence. Yet so it was that he could endure this spitting from men; but can you think of this marvellous condescension without feeling your hearts all on fire with love to him, so that you long to do some special act of homage to him, by which you may show that you would fain recompense him for this shame if you could?

I will not say more about that point, for the shameful fact stands indelibly recorded in the Scripture: 'Then did they spit in his face'; but I want to bring the truth home, brethren, and to show you how we may have done to Christ what these wicked men did. 'Oh!' says one, 'I was not there; I did not spit in his face.' Listen; perhaps you have spat in his face, perhaps even *you* have spat in his face. You remember that touching hymn that we sometimes sing –

> My Jesus! say what wretch has dared
>   Thy sacred hands to bind?
> And who has dared to buffet so
>   Thy face so meek and kind?
>
> My Jesus! whose the hands that wove
>   That cruel thorny crown?
> Who made that hard and heavy cross
>   That weighs thy shoulders down?
>
> My Jesus! who with spittle vile
>   Profaned thy sacred brow?
> Or whose unpitying scourge has made
>   Thy precious blood to flow?
>
> 'Tis I have thus ungrateful been,
>   Yet, Jesus, pity take!
> Oh, spare and pardon me, my Lord,
>   For thy sweet mercy's sake!

There are still some who spit in Christ's face by *denying his Godhead*. They say, 'He is a mere man; a good man, it is true, but only a man'; though how they dare say that, I cannot make out, for he would be no good man who claimed to be God if he was not God. Jesus of Nazareth was the basest of impostors who ever lived if he permitted his disciples to worship him, and if he left behind him a life which compels us to worship him, if he was not really and truly God; therefore, of all those who declare that he is not God – and there is a very great company of them even amongst the nominally religious people of the present day – we must sorrowfully, but truthfully say, 'Then did they spit in his face.'

They also do the same who *rail at his gospel*. There are many, in these days, who seem as if they cannot be happy unless they are tearing the gospel to pieces. Especially is that divine mystery of the substitutionary sacrifice of Christ the mark for the arrows of the wise men, I mean those who are wise according to the wisdom of this world. We delight to know that our Lord Jesus Christ suffered in the room and place and stead of his people.

> He bore that we might never bear
> His Father's righteous ire.

Yet I have read some horrible things which have been written against that blessed doctrine, and as I read them I could only say to myself, 'Then did they spit in his face.' If there is anything that is beyond all else the glory of Christ, it is his atoning sacrifice; and if ever you thrust your finger into the very apple of his eye, and touch his honour in the tenderest possible point, it is when you have aught to say against his offering of himself a sacrifice unto God, without blemish and without spot, that he might put away the iniquities of his people. Wherefore judge yourselves in this matter, and if ye have ever denied Christ's deity, or if ye have ever assailed his atoning sacrifice, it might truly have been said of you, 'Then did they spit in his face.'

Further, this evil is also done *when men prefer their own righteousness to the righteousness of Christ*. There are some who say, 'We do not need pardon, we do not want to be justified by faith in Christ, we are good enough already', or, 'We are working out our own salvation; we mean to save ourselves.' O sirs, if you can save yourselves, why did Jesus bleed upon the cross? It was a superfluity indeed that the Son of God should die in human form if there be a possibility of salvation by your own merits; and if you prefer your merits to his, it must be said of you also, 'Then did they spit in his face.' Your righteousnesses are only filthy rags; and if you prefer these to the fair white linen which is the righteousness of saints, if you think to wash yourselves in your tears, and so you despise that precious blood apart from which there is no purging of our sin, still to you does our text apply, 'then did they spit in his face', when they preferred their own righteousness to Christ's.

I have often spoken to you about the parable of the prodigal son; but, possibly, your case is more like that of the elder brother in the parable; you have your portion of goods, it is all your own, and you are keeping it. You are rich, and increased in goods, and have need of nothing. You are self-righteous, you think that you can do very well without God and without Christ, and you half suspect that God can hardly do without you. You are doing so very well in the observance of rites and ceremonies, and the performance of charity and devotions that, if *you* go into the far country, you will cut a very respectable figure; you will be one of those excellent citizens of that country who will, in due time, send some poor prodigal into *your* fields to feed your swine. I am inclined to believe that your case is even more sad and hopeless than that of the prodigal himself. You, too, have gone far away from God, you are living without him. He is not in all your thoughts, you could almost wish that there were no God, for then there would be no dark cloud hovering in the distance to spoil your summer's day, no fear of storms to come to mar the joy of the hour. Just as truly as of the avowed infidel who openly rejects Christ, it must be said of you, 'Then did they spit in his face.'

The same thing is, oh! so sadly true *when anyone forsakes the profession of being a follower of Christ*. There are some, alas! who, for a time, have appeared to stand well in the Church of God – I will not judge them – but there have been some who, after making a profession of religion, have deliberately gone back to the world. After seeming for a while to be very zealous, they have become worldly, careless, and perhaps even lascivious and vile. They break the Sabbath, they neglect the Word of God, they forsake the mercy-seat; and their last end is worse than their first. When a man forsakes Christ for a harlot, when he gives up heaven for gold, when he resigns the joys he professed to have had in Christ in order that he may find mirth in the company of the ungodly, it is another instance of the truth of these words, 'Then did they spit in his face.' To prefer any of these things to Christ, is infamous; and the mere act of spitting from the mouth seems little compared with this sin of spitting with the very heart and soul, and pouring contempt upon Christ by choosing some sin in preference to him. Yet, alas! how many are thus still spitting in Christ's face. Perhaps some now present are doing it.

If, dear friends, our conscience in any measure accuses us of this sin, *let us at once confess it;* let us humble ourselves before the Lord; and with the very mouth that spat upon him, let us kiss the Son lest he be angry, and we perish from the way, when his wrath is kindled but a little.

And when we have confessed the sin, *let us believe that he is able and willing to forgive us.* I know that it requires a great act of faith, when sin is consciously felt, to believe in the splendour of divine mercy; but, dear friends, do believe it. Do the Lord Jesus the great honour of saying to him, 'Gracious Lord, wash me in thy precious blood; though I did spit in thy face, wash me in that cleansing fountain, and I shall be whiter than snow'; and according to your faith, so shall it be done unto you. You shall have the forgiveness even of this great sin if you confess it, and believe that Christ is both able and willing to forgive it.

And when you have done that, then *let your whole life be spent in trying to magnify and glorify him* whom you and others have defamed and dishonoured. Oh, I think that, if I had ever denied Christ's Deity, I should want to stand in this pulpit night and day to revoke what I had said, and to declare him to be the Son of God with power! I think that, if I had ever set up anything in opposition to him, I should want day and night to be setting him up above everything else, as indeed, I long to do. Come, Christian brethren and sisters, let us do something unusual in Christ's honour; let us find out something or invent something fresh, either in the company of others or all by ourselves, by which we may further glorify his blessed name.

Yet once more, if ever anybody should despise us for Christ's sake, let us not count it hard, but *let us be willing to bear scorn and contempt for him*. Let us say to ourselves, '"Then did they spit in his face." What, then, if they also spit in mine? If they do, I will "hail reproach, and welcome shame", since it comes upon me for his dear sake.' See, that wretch is about to spit in Christ's face! Put your cheek forward, that you may catch that spittle upon your face, that it fall not upon him again, for as he was put to such terrible shame, every one who has been redeemed with his precious blood ought to count it an honour to be a partaker of the shame, if by any means we may screen him from being further despised and rejected of men.

There, dear friends, I have not preached, I have just talked very, very feebly, and not at all as I wished and hoped I might be able to do, about this wonderful text: 'Then did they spit in his face.'

Now try to follow me, just for a few minutes, while I let you see that same face in a very different light. Our second text is in the 20th chapter of the Revelation, at the 11th verse – 'And I saw a great white throne, and him that sat on it, *from whose face the earth and heaven fled away;* and there was found no place for them.'

This passage needs no words of mine to explain it. Notice how the apostle begins: *'I saw'*. Oh, I wish I had the power to make you also see this great sight! Sometimes, vividly to realize a truth even once, is far better than to have merely heard it stated ten thousand times. I remember the story of a soldier who was employed in connection with one of the surveys of Palestine. He was with some others of the company in the valley of Jehoshaphat, and without thinking seriously of his words, he said to his comrades, 'Some people say that, when Christ shall come a second time to judge the world, the judgment will take place in the valley of Jehoshaphat, in this very place where we now are.' Then he added, 'When the great white throne shall be set, I wonder whereabouts I shall be.' It is said that he carelessly exclaimed, 'I shall sit here upon this big stone', and he sat down; but in an instant he was struck with horror, and he fainted, because in the act of sitting down he had begun to realize somewhat of the grandeur and the terror of that tremendous scene. I wish I knew how to do or say anything by which I could make you realize this scene that John saw in vision. The Lord Jesus Christ went up to heaven from the top of Olivet in his own proper body, and he shall so come in like manner as he was taken up into heaven; but he shall come, not the lowly Man of sorrows, but as Judge of all seated upon a great white throne; and John says, 'I saw it.' As we sang, a few minutes ago –

> The Lord shall come! but not the same
> As once in lowliness he came;
> A silent lamb before his foes,
> A weary man, and full of woes.
>
> The Lord shall come! a dreadful form,
> With rainbow wreath and robes of storm;
> On cherub wings, and wings of wind,
> Appointed Judge of all mankind.

I wish, dear friends, that even in your dreams you might see this sight, for, though I have no trust in dreams by themselves, yet any realization of this great truth will be better than the mere hearing of it.

'I saw', said John, 'a great white throne.' He saw *a throne,* for Christ now reigns, he is King of kings, and Lord of lords; and when he comes again, he will come in the power of universal sovereignty as the appointed Judge of all mankind. He will come upon a throne.

That throne is said to be *white.* What other throne can be so described? The thrones of mere mortals are often stained with injustice, or bespattered with the blood of cruel wars; but Christ's throne is white, for he doeth justice and righteousness, and his name is truth.

It will also be a *great* white throne – a throne so great that all the thrones of former kings and princes shall be as nothing in comparison with it. The thrones of Assyria, and Babylon, and Persia, and Greece, and Rome, shall all seem only like tiny drops of dew to be exhaled in a moment; but this great white throne shall be the recognized seat of the King of kings, the Sovereignty over all sovereignties: 'I saw a great white throne.'

John not only saw the great white throne, but also *'HIM that sat upon it.'* What a wondrous sight was that! John saw him, whose eyes are 'as a flame of fire, and his feet like unto fine brass, as if they burned in a furnace.' John saw him whose divine majesty shall shine resplendent even through the nail-prints which he shall still wear when seated on the great white throne. What a sight it was to John, who had leaned his head upon Christ's bosom, to behold that same Master, whom he had seen die upon the cross, now sitting upon the throne of universal judgment: 'I saw a great white throne, and him that sat upon it.'

Now notice what happened: *'from whose face the earth and the heaven fled away.'* As soon as ever this great white throne appeared, heaven and earth began to roll away like a wave receding from the shore. What must HE be before whose face heaven and earth shall retreat as in dismay?

Observe, first, *Christ's power.* He does not drive away the heaven and the earth; he does not even speak to them; the sight of his face is all that is needed, and the old heaven, and the old sin-stained earth, shall begin to flee away, 'the elements shall melt with fervent heat, the earth also and the works that are therein shall be burned up'; and all that by the mere showing of Christ's face. He does not have to lift his arm, he has not to seize a javelin, and to hurl it at the condemned earth; at the sight of his face, heaven and earth shall flee away.

Behold the terror of *Christ's majesty.* And what will you do in that day – you who did spit in his face, you who did despise him? What will you do in that day? Suppose the great judgment day had already come, suppose that the great white throne was just over yonder, and that when this service was over, you must appear with all the risen dead before your Judge. One would have to say, 'I have refused him; how shall I dare to look in his face?' Another would cry, 'He drew me once, I felt the tugging of his love, the drawings of his Spirit; but I resisted, and would not yield. How can I meet him now? How can I look him in the face?' Another will have to say, 'I had to strive hard to escape from the grasp of his hand of mercy; I stifled conscience, and I went back into the world.' You will all have to look into that face, and that face will look at all of you. One will have to say, 'I gave up Christ for the world.' 'I gave him up for the theatre', another must say. 'I gave him up for the dancing saloon', another will say. 'I gave him up for the love of women', another will say. 'I gave him up that I might carry on my business as I could not carry it on if I was a true Christian; I gave up Christ for what I could get.' You will have to say all this, and that very soon. As surely as you see me upon this platform now, you shall see the King upon the great white throne then, that King who was once despised and rejected of men.

O sirs, I would that ye would think of all this! It is not one hundredth part so much my concern as it is yours; I am not afraid to see Christ's face, for he hath looked on me in love, and blotted out all my sin, and I love him, and long to be with him for ever and ever. But if you have never had that look of love, if you have never been reconciled to him, I ask you; by the love you bear yourselves, to begin to think about this matter. Begin to prepare to meet this King of men, this Lord of love, who, as surely as he is the Lord of love, will be the King of wrath, for there is no anger like the anger of love. There is no indignation like 'the wrath of the Lamb', of which we read a few minutes ago. Divine love, when it has become righteous indignation, burns like coals of juniper, and is quenchless as hell. Wherefore –

> Ye sinners, seek his grace,
> Whose wrath ye cannot bear;
> Fly to the shelter of his cross,
> And find salvation there;

and ere heaven and earth begin to flee away from the face of him who sits upon the throne, and ere ye yourselves begin to cry to the rocks to cover you and the mountains to hide you from that face – seek ye his face with humble penitence and faith, that you may be prepared to meet him with joy in that last tremendous day.

If what I have been saying be all a dream, dismiss it, and go your ways to your sins; but if these things be the very truth of God – and verily they are – do act as sane men should, think them over, and prepare to meet your Judge. God help you to do so, for Christ's sake! Amen.

7

SECOND-HAND[1]

Sayest thou this thing of thyself,
or did others tell it thee of me?
JOHN 18:34

I EXPLAINED, this morning, why our Saviour put that question to Pilate. The Roman governor had asked him 'Art thou the King of the Jews?' And Jesus as good as said to him, 'Have you, of your own knowledge, seen anything in me that looks like setting up to be a king in opposition to Caesar? You intend, by asking me that question, to enquire whether I have led a rebellion against your government, or the imperial authority which you represent. Now, has there been anything which you have observed which would have led you to make this enquiry, or do you only ask it because of what the Jews have been saying in their enmity against me?' You will see, dear friends, that our Lord asked this question in order that he might get from Pilate's own lips the acknowledgment that he had not seen any sign of sedition or rebellion in him, and that it might be proved that the charge had been brought to Pilate by those outside, and had not come from the Roman governor himself.

We will, now, forget Pilate for a while, for I want to use this question in two ways with reference to ourselves. First, I shall utilize it as *a warning against second-hand cavils at Christ and his gospel*. Some people have a large stock of them, and we might say to, each one of these cavillers, 'Sayest thou this thing of thyself, or did others tell it thee?' Then, in the second place, I shall use the

---

[1] Sermon No. 2,624. Preached at the Metropolitan Tabernacle on Sunday evening, 12 February 1882.

text as *a warning against all second-hand religion,* pressing this question home upon each one who speaks up for Christ, 'Sayest thou this thing of thyself, or did others tell it thee?'

I. We will begin with the opponents of the Lord Jesus, and consider our text, first, as A WARNING AGAINST SECOND-HAND CAVILS AT CHRIST AND HIS GOSPEL.

There are a great many people in the world who really do not know why they oppose religion; and if you ask them the reason, they repeat some old bit of scandal, some stale slander upon Jesus and his cross, and they give that as their answer. I firmly believe that there are thousands, who are ranked among the opposers of the gospel, who have not anything to say against Christ of their own knowledge; but others have told them something or other, and they go on repeating and reiterating the old exploded obsolete objections that have been demolished thousands of times, and I suppose they and others of their kind will keep on doing the same thing right to the end of time.

As soon as ever Jesus Christ's gospel was launched upon the world's sea, it had to encounter opposing winds, and storms, and tempests. Like a scarred veteran, the gospel has had battle after battle to fight. In our Lord's own day, it was opposed most vigorously. His apostles found that, wherever they went, their feet were dogged by those who railed at Jesus and his Word; and when the apostles had all fallen asleep, the early churches found that they had need of an order of men who became the apologists for the gospel, and who bravely stood up to defend it against the attacks of divers heathen philosophers, and sceptics, and heretics who arose wherever the truth was preached. Everywhere, there was opposition to the gospel of our Lord Jesus Christ, and his servants girded up their loins to do battle for him and for his truth.

That great campaign has continued even down to this day, and there is this very remarkable fact about it, that, at the present moment, most of the objections that are brought against the gospel are those that were answered and silenced some hundreds of years ago; and, even when they appeared, all those centuries back, they were then only reproductions of some older objections which had been answered, and, as the defenders of the faith thought, had been trampled out, like sparks of fire trodden under foot. But, somehow, an ill wind has begun to blow again, and the fire, which some hoped was finally extinguished, has burned up once more. Originality in scepticism has almost ceased to be; we scarcely ever hear anything fresh in the way of heresy nowadays. We are troubled with the very errors which our forefathers answered a hundred years ago; yet the adversaries of the truth go on cleaning and sharpening again their blunted shafts, that they may once more shoot them at the great shield of faith, which is impervious to their puny assaults, for it can quench even the most fiery darts of the devil himself. The modern arrows of scepticism will be broken against that glorious shield, yet they will probably be gathered up by another generation that will follow the present one, and the heretics and objectors in the future will do just as their fathers did before them. I want, at this time, to put to any caviller whom I may be addressing, the question of our Lord to Pilate, 'Sayest thou this thing of thyself, or did others tell it thee?'

And, first, I ask you to observe that there are many unreasonable prejudices. *Some persons have great prejudices against the Bible.* I will not repeat what they say; but I should like to ask every person who thinks ill of this blessed Book, 'Have you read the Bible through, and read it thoroughly? Have you studied it? Are your objections your own? Come, now; did you make them yourself?' It is almost always found that objections are like the axe the young prophet was using, they are borrowed; and often, they are objections against a Book which has not been read at all, and which has not been allowed to exercise its own influence upon the heart and the judgment of the person who is prejudiced against it to his own hurt. Other people have told men such-and-such things, so they shut the Book, and refuse to look into it for themselves.

There are other people who are *prejudiced against public worship.* You see, I am starting at the very beginning, those matters with regard to religion which are elementary. Of course, we are told that we shut ourselves up on a Sunday in these dreary buildings of ours, and here we sit, in a horrible state of misery, listening to the most awful twaddle that ever was taught, our singing being nothing better than droning, and the whole of our worship being something very terrible! If I were to read to you the descriptions of an English Sabbath which I have sometimes seen in newspapers, they might make you almost weep tears of blood to think that we poor souls should suffer so much as we do; only you know that we are altogether unconscious of any such suffering. We really have been under the notion that we very much enjoyed ourselves while worshipping the Lord in his house. Many of us have the idea that the Sabbath is the happiest day in all the week to us, and that, when we hear the gospel preached, it is sweeter than music to us, and makes our hearts leap within us for very joy. Of course, we are very much obliged to our friends for telling us how dull and how unhappy we are, and for wishing us to be in a better condition. We can only say that, not being enabled to perceive any of these sorrows, we would advise them to retain their pity, and exercise it upon themselves, for they certainly need it far more than we do. To any of you who make remarks of the kind I have indicated, I say, Do your difficulties concerning public worship really arise out of your attending the house of God – out of your hearing the gospel preached – out of your joining in the songs and praises of God's people? Oh, no! it is those people who never come to our services who believe the Sabbath to be dull, the house of God to be dreary, and the preaching of the gospel to be a monotonous sound from which every sensible man would escape. I put the question of my text to every person who is prejudiced against the Bible, and prejudiced against our public worship in God's house, 'Sayest thou this thing of thyself, or did others tell it thee?'

Sometimes, *the prejudice concerns the preacher*. I will not say that it is so about myself; though I have had in my time more than my fair share of it. 'Hear him?' says one; 'I would not go across the road to listen to such a fellow.' Many have said that, and the preacher, whoever he may be, is condemned without a hearing. If the objector were asked to give a reason for his prejudice, he might answer by quoting the old lines –

> I do not like you, Dr Fell,
> The reason why, I cannot tell;
> But this I know, and know full well,
> I do not like you, Dr Fell.

I should like to say to everybody who is prejudiced against any servant of Christ, 'Sayest thou this of thyself?' Those absurd stories about the preacher – did you really hear them yourself, or did somebody tell you them? Would you like to be judged by the mere idle tittle-tattle of the street or of the newspapers? And if you would not, then be an honest, reasonable man, and at least give the servant of God a hearing before you condemn him or his message; and, take my word for it, the most-abused preacher is very likely to be the very man whom God will bless the most. Not the one who is most praised, but the one who is most censured by the world, is probably the man who has been most faithful to his Master and to the gospel committed to his charge. At any rate, be honest enough to reply to the question which our Lord put to Pilate, 'Sayest thou this thing of thyself, or did others tell it thee?'

There is a remark sometimes made, and I fear it is a very common one, 'Oh, I would not be a Christian, I would not be religious, for *it makes men so dreadfully miserable!*' Now, friend, sayest thou this of thyself, or did somebody else tell it thee? Come, now, you say that religion is such a miserable thing; have you tried it for yourself? Have you experienced the misery that comes out of prayer – out of faith – out of repentance – out of love to God – out of being pardoned – out of having a good hope of heaven? Have you ever proved what that dreadful misery is? I think, if you had ever really tested these things for yourself, your verdict would be the very reverse, and you would join with us in singing the lines that express what many of us most firmly believe about this matter –

> 'Tis religion that can give
> Sweetest pleasures while we live;
> 'Tis religion must supply
> Solid comfort when we die.

Yet you go on repeating that slander upon religion though you cannot prove it to be true, and might easily learn its falseness. Do let me appeal to you. Had you a godly mother? 'Yes,' you say, 'and it was her life that prevents my being altogether an unbeliever.' I thought so; but, if I remember her aright, she was a quiet good soul who, in her home, tried to make everybody happy; and though she had not much pleasure in her son, for he was wayward and wilful, yet there was no unkindness on her lip, the law of love always ruled the house. She was a weak and feeble creature, who derived but slender gratification from any of the outward enjoyments of life; but she had a deep, secret spring of peace and joy which kept her calm, and quiet, and happy; and now that she has gone to be with God, she has left a gleam of sunlight still behind in her sweet memory. You did not get from your mother, nor from other godly friends, your belief that religion makes men miserable; and I venture to say that, so far as you have had any actual personal observation of it, you have been inclined to come to quite the opposite verdict, and to confess that, though you do not know how it is, yet, somehow or other, godliness does give, to the people who possess it, peace of mind, and happiness of heart, and usefulness of life.

There is another slander that is spread abroad very widely, and that is, *that the doctrine of the grace of God* – the doctrine which we try to preach from this pulpit,– has no sanctifying effect – that, on the contrary, it *is likely to lead people into sin* – that if we preach, 'He that believeth on the Son hath everlasting life,' and do not preach up good works as the way of salvation, it is clear that such teaching will lead people into sin. Clear, is it? It is not so to me; but, my friend, will you answer this question, 'Sayest thou this thing of thyself, or did others tell it thee?' Is it not a matter of history that there never have been stricter living men than the Puritans? What is the great quarrel against John Calvin himself but that, when he ruled in Geneva, he was too stern and too exacting in his requirements? It is an odd thing – is it not? – that these doctrines of grace should, on the one hand, make men too strict as a matter of fact, and yet that the wiseacres who object to them should say that these doctrines are likely to lead into sin those who accept them? It is not found to be so by those who believe them. Let me again appeal to any candid objector. My dear sir, did you ever prove what it is to believe in the great love of God to you – that, for the sake of his dear Son, out of pure, unmerited grace, he has chosen you, and saved you, and appointed you to eternal life? Did you ever believe that, and then feel, as a natural consequence, that you would go and live in sin? I know that you never did, but that it was quite the reverse. 'Here,' said some boys to a companion, 'we are going to rob an orchard; come along with us, Jack.' 'No,' said he, 'my father would not approve of such a thing.' 'But your father is very fond of you, and never beats you as our fathers do.' 'Yes,' said the boy, 'my father loves me very much, and I love him very much, and that is the reason why I am not going to rob the orchard, and so to grieve him.' Now, you believe in the beating of the boys by the rod of the law, do you not? And we, on the other hand, feel that; because God loves us, and will in his infinite mercy continue to love us, therefore we must keep out of sin as much as we possibly can. We cannot do that horrible thing which would grieve his blessed Spirit. So I ask you, as truthful men, not to repeat that old slander concerning the doctrines of grace leading to sin, until you have really had some reason to assert it because of what you yourselves have witnessed in the lives of Christian people. Do not say it again until you can truly say it from your own experience or observation; do not repeat it simply because others tell it to you.

Yes, and there are some who say that *there is no power in prayer,* – that we may pray, if we like, but that we cannot change the purposes of God – that the laws of nature are fixed and immutable, and, therefore, to pray is a piece of absurdity. 'Sayest thou this thing of thyself, or did others tell it thee?' I will speak personally to you. Did you ever try to pray? Did you ever put this matter to the test – whether God will hear prayer or no? I do not think you can have put it to a fair test, and I would like you to see whether God will or will not hear even your prayer if you cry to him. If any say to me, 'God does not hear prayer,' I have scarcely the patience to give them an answer. I live from day to day crying to God for this or that favour which I receive as certainly and as constantly as ever my sons had their meals when they sat at my table. I knew how to give good gifts to my children, and I know that my heavenly Father gives good gifts to me. My evidence, of course, is only that of one man, and it may not suffice to convince others, though many of you here could add your testimony to mine; but I should like all objectors just to give prayer a fair trial before they are quite so sure about the inefficacy of it. Let them see whether real prayer, offered in the name of Jesus, will not be heard even in their case. Certain I am that there is not anywhere on the face of the globe a praying man who does not bear this testimony – that God hears him. And if any say, 'We do not pray, and do not believe that God hears prayer,' what evidence have you to bring? You are out of court altogether, for you know nothing about the matter; but the man who does pray, and then says, 'God hears me,' is the man to be a witness, and the one who has a right to be heard. I have told you, more than once, what the Irishman said when there were five witnesses to prove that he had committed murder. He said to the judge, 'You must not condemn me on their evidence; there are only five people here who saw me do it, but I can bring fifty people who did not see me do it;' but that was no evidence at all; and, in like manner, there are many who say, 'You bring a certain number of people, who pray, to prove that God hears them; but we can bring ten times as many, who do not pray, and who do not get heard.' What has that to do with the matter? Where is the evidence? You say it not of yourself but merely repeat, second-hand, what has been said by others, so often, and so foolishly, that it sickens one to hear it.

It is beginning to be questioned, in many quarters, nowadays, whether there is any real effect produced by prayer, except that of exciting certain pious emotions in the breasts of those who pray. This is a very pretty statement! We ought to be extremely obliged to those superior persons who allow that even so much may be done! I wonder they do not assert that prayer is ridiculous, or hypocritical, or immoral. Their moderation puts us under obligations. And yet I do not know: when I look again at their admission, I thank them for nothing, for they as good as call us fools. Do they think that we perform a useless exercise merely for the sake of exciting pious emotions? We must be grievous idiots if we can receive benefit from a senseless function. We are not willing to whistle to the wind for the sake of the exercise. We should not be content to go on praying to a God who could be proved to be both deaf and dumb. We have still some little common sense left, despite what our judicious friends consider to be our fanaticism. We are sure that we obtain answers to prayer. Of this fact I am certain, and I solemnly declare that I have received of the Lord that which I have asked at his hands. I am not alone in such testimony, for I am associated with multitudes of men and women who bear witness to the same fact, and declare that they sought the Lord, and he heard them. Take care, brethren and sisters, to record all instances of answered prayer, so as to leave this unbelieving generation without excuse. Accumulate the facts, and demonstrate the grand truth. Multiply the testimonies, till even the philosophers are obliged to admit both the phenomena and the deduction rightly drawn from them.

There is one other gross slander to which I would reply, and that is, a saying that goes round among troubled consciences – *that Christ will not receive sinners* – that the very guilty cannot be saved – that Christ can forgive and deliver up to a certain point; but if you get beyond that, he is no longer willing to pardon. Dear hearer, has that foolish and wicked notion entered thy head? Then, I ask thee, 'Sayest thou this thing of thyself?' Didst thou ever prove it to be true? Hast thou ever sought his face? Hast thou cried to him for mercy? 'Yes,' you say, 'I have.' And then, further, have you thrown yourself at his feet, trusting him to save you, and have you been refused? I know you have not; there was never a sinner yet, who fell down before him, and determined to lie there and perish if he did not speak a word of mercy, to whom the Lord has not, sooner or later, spoken the grace-word which has sent that poor sinner on his way rejoicing. I would at least like you to go and see whether Christ will receive you or not, before you say that he will not do so. Say not that the door of his mercy is shut, but go in while it is still open. If he casts you out, then he will have broken his word, for he has said, 'Him that cometh to me, I will in no wise cast out.' Do not give him the lie, and say that he will cast you out till you have yourself proved that it is so; and that, I know, will never be the case. I am afraid that there is another being who has been whispering that vile insinuation into your ear, and he is your arch-enemy, who is seeking your destruction, and therefore he has come, and told you this falsehood against the infinitely-loving and gracious Saviour. Believe him not; but come even now, and put your trust in Jesus, and you shall find that he will give to you eternal life.

I have thus examined the question of my text with reference to the opponents of the gospel, and I shall now leave that part of the subject, praying the Holy Spirit to bless it to all whom it may concern.

II. Now, in the second place, I am going to speak briefly, but with much earnestness, to the many here present who are friends of the gospel, but who have only a SECOND-HAND RELIGION, if they have any at all. I want to have a word with you, dear friends, about this matter. You and I have been talking a great deal about Christ. Now, have we been simply quoting what others have said? Have we been making extracts from other people's experience; or is what we have said something that we can say of ourselves, and not what others have told us?

For, brethren, first, *a second-hand testimony for Christ is a powerless thing.* Take a man – as I am afraid is often done – with no grace in his heart, and send him to Oxford or Cambridge, with the view of making him a parson; teach him the sciences, and languages, and mathematics, and give him a degree. His friends want to get a living for him, and the bishop's chaplain proceeds to examine him. The first question ought to be, Is this young man a Christian? Is he truly converted? Does he know the Lord? Does he understand in his own soul the things he is going to preach to others? For, if he does not, what good can he do in the Christian ministry? Perhaps he is sent to a school of theology, to learn the various systems of doctrine. He must read the judicious Hooker, he must study Jeremy Taylor, he must take lessons in elocution and rhetoric. Then, possibly, his friends buy him some litho-graphed sermons that he may read, and they get him some books, that he may make extracts from them to put into the sermons he preaches. Suppose that man is all the while unconverted, suppose that he does not know anything about the working of the grace of God in his own soul, what is the good of him as a teacher of others? No good at all; at any rate, at the best, he may be only as good as one of those newly-invented phonographs which can repeat what is spoken into them. This man can read out what he has selected from other books; but that is all. We will suppose that he is a very decent sort of fellow – an amiable gentleman, well-instructed, well-behaved, and so on; but all that he has to say is what other people have told him.

But now put into that man's pulpit, only for one Lord's-day, a preacher who has known what it is to feel the burden of sin, and to have it removed by faith in Jesus. Let him begin to speak to the people, in downright earnest, about the pangs and sorrows of true repentance; let him tell them about their need of the new birth, and about his experience of obtaining that great blessing; and how, by sovereign grace, he was brought out of the darkness into the light, and even from death to life. Let that man be moved to speak of the peace of pardon through the precious blood, and of the joys of heaven laid up for all believers, and then the people will wake up, I will warrant you. This is something very different from the preaching to which they have been accustomed, and they will soon feel the power of it.

Yet the Lord sometimes uses even a preacher who does not himself understand the truth he proclaims. I know a man, who went and heard a certain minister preach, or rather, read a sermon, and it was such a good one that the hearer's conscience was smitten by it. The discourse was about the new birth; and, the next morning, the man went off to the clergyman, and said, 'Sir, I want you to explain this matter further to me, for I am dreadfully distressed by what you preached last night.' What, think you, did this preacher say? He said, 'Well, Jonathan, I am sure I never meant to cause anybody any uneasiness; what was it that gave you such trouble?' 'Why,' replied he, 'it was that part of the sermon where you said that we must be born again.' So the preacher said, 'Well, here is the discourse. You see, by the dates upon it, that I have used it thirteen times before, so I could not have made it with any special view to your case. I am very sorry, indeed, that it caused you any discomfort, and I will never preach it again if it brings people into trouble in this style.'

That was all the help the poor man could get from the parson, so he went out, and found a true servant of God, who knew the truth himself, and was not a second-hand retailer of it, and, through conversation with him, and prayer, and the reading of the Scriptures, he was brought into peace and liberty. I need hardly tell you that he does not go to hear that second-hand preacher now; he listens to a far humbler minister, who, nevertheless, preaches what he has tasted and handled of the good Word of life. Now, if any of you are going to be Sunday-school teachers, or street-preachers, do not begin to talk about what somebody else has told you. Go and say what you yourself know, of a heart first broken by the power of the Holy Spirit, and then bound up by the application of the atonement of the Lord Jesus Christ. Tell out your message, in a living way from the heart to the heart, or else your hearers will feel that there is no power about it, however nicely you put the truth, and however sweetly you describe it. There is all the difference between personal testimony to the truth and a parrot-like repetition of it, that there is between the living and the dead. Let us only bear witness to what we do really know, and then no one will need to ask us what our Lord asked Pilate, 'Sayest thou this thing of thyself, or did others tell it thee?'

Now, further, the same thing is true *with regard to professors*. We have many friends who come, at different times, to join the church, and their stories greatly vary. Some who come to see me cannot say much, and they think that I shall be very dissatisfied with them because they make a great muddle of their narrative, and there is not much that comes out after all. But the people with whom I am least satisfied are those who reel off their yarn by the yard; they have it all ready to repeat, and everything is arranged as prettily as possible. Yes; and as I listen to it, I know that someone has told them what to say, and they have learned it all for me to hear. But I like far better the testimony that I have to pick out in little bits, but which I know comes fresh from the heart of the trembling convert.

Sometimes, it costs the poor soul a tear or a real good cry, and I have to go round about in all manner of ways to get hold of the story at all; but that shows that it is true, and that the man never borrowed it. I like to hear the experience of a believer, when he comes straight out of the world and out of the ways of sin, to confess his faith in Christ. He does not know anything about the terms that Christian people use. He has not learned our phrases; and it is a great delight to hear it all fresh and new. Yet it is always the same story in all the essential parts of it. However strangely he may narrate it, it tallies with that of others in the main points. Take the experience of a Christian man who has been brought up in the sanctuary from his childhood, and extract the pith and marrow of it. Now take the experience of a man who has been a horse-racer, a drunkard, a swearer, but who has been truly converted, and extract the pith of that. Talk to a peer of the realm who has become an heir of the kingdom of heaven, and take the pith of his experience. Now get a chimney-sweep who has been brought to the Lord, and get the pith of his experience; put them all side by side, and you will not know one from the other. There are always the same essential marks – death, birth, life, food – Christ in the death, the life, the birth, the food – repentance, faith, joy, the work of the Spirit of God. But it is very sweet to hear the story told in the many different ways in which the converts tell it. The true child of grace is ever the same in heart, although the outward appearance may continually vary.

But, dear friends, whenever you begin to make a profession of religion, take care that you never profess more than you really possess. Go just as far as you can go yourself, by the grace of God, and do not repeat what others tell you. To borrow another man's experience is dishonest. If it is not mine, how dare I say that it is? It is also very apt to be self-deceptive, for a man may repeat another person's experience until he really thinks he did pass through it himself, just as a man may repeat a lie until it almost ceases to be a lie because he himself gets to believe what at first he knew was not true. That borrowing of the experience of others is usually unavailing with those who have had much to do with men, for we who do know the Lord, and are familiar with his people, very readily trip up those who only repeat what they have learned.

Freemasons recognize one another by various grips and signs. A man may, perhaps, find out one of the grips, but he does not learn them all, and at last he gets caught, and people say to him, 'You are pretending to be what you really are not.' Take, again, a man's handwriting; someone may imitate my writing for a long while, but, at last, he does not copy some peculiar dash, or stroke, or mark, which is characteristic of my style, and those who know say, 'That is not Mr Spurgeon's writing; it is a forgery.' So there is a something – a sort of freemasonry – about Christianity. People may learn some of our grips, and signs, and passwords; but, by-and-by, they make a blunder, and we say, 'Ah! you are an impostor.' They may try to write after the fashion of a child of God, and they may make the pot-hooks, and hangers, and straight strokes; but, as they get on further, there is a something or other that comes out in the long run, which proves that they are only copyists after all. Therefore, I say to you, dear friends – Do not attempt to repeat what others have told you about experimental godliness, but let your testimony only consist of what you can truly say out of your own heart and soul.

Let this be the case also *with regard to every man, whether he makes a profession of religion or not.* May God grant that all that we think we know, we may really know in our own souls, and not have because we have borrowed it from others! In religion, proxies and sponsors are altogether out of place. I pray you never to be guilty of that horrible blasphemy – for I think that it is nothing less than that – of standing up before God, and promising that a child shall keep his commandments, and walk in the same all the days of its life. Remember that, in religion, there are certain things that must be personal. For instance, every man must be himself born; another person cannot be born for you. In like manner, 'Ye must be born again' – personally, for yourself. There is no possibility of another person experiencing that new birth for you. If a man lives, he must eat for himself. You cannot take my meals for me; it is I myself who must eat them. And we must eat the flesh and drink the blood of Christ by faith, each one for himself or herself; nobody can do it for another.

In daily life, each man must be clothed for himself. You may wear silk and satin, you may be dressed in the best broadcloth; but you cannot be clothed on my behalf, I must be myself dressed, or else go naked. So must each man put on the robe of Christ's righteousness, or be naked to his shame before God. Every man must repent of his own sin – make confession of his own sin – believe in the Lord Jesus Christ for himself – love God for himself – obey the Lord for himself; and there is no possibility of any other person, by any means, doing this for you. There must be personal godliness, or else there is no godliness at all. So, whenever you feel inclined to say for yourself, 'I believe that I am a Christian; I believe this and I believe that;' let this question come home to you, 'Sayest thou this thing of thyself, or did others tell it thee?'

And, lastly, brethren and sisters in Christ, let me utter a word specially for your ears. *Never get, in your prayers, or in your talk, an inch beyond your actual experience.* Our calling is a very high one; and one of the most serious difficulties in the way of ever attaining its greatest height is the impression that we have reached it when we have not. My own impression is, that some brethren might have been well-nigh perfect if they had not thought that they were so already, but they missed the blessing through that very thought. Many a man might have become wise, but he imagined that he had learned wisdom, so he never really was wise. You know that, if you see a man who thinks that he is wise, you say to yourself, 'How very foolish he is!' And you speak truly, too. The doorstep of wisdom is a consciousness of ignorance, and the gateway of perfection is a deep sense of imperfection. Paul was never so nearly perfect as when he cried, 'O wretched man that I am! who shall deliver me from the body of this death?'

But if he had sat down, and, said, 'I have attained, and am already perfect,' then would he have been in a fair way of missing the blessing of God. No, dear brothers or sisters, say no more than you can justify. There are many who do that in business; mind that you do not so act in spiritual matters. Look at that shop window: what a wonderful display! Now go inside the shop; why, there is nothing there! No, for the man has all his goods in the window. You would at once say to yourself, if he wanted to deal with you, 'I shall not trust him very deeply.' Ah! and do we not know some who, spiritually, have all their goods in the window? It is a grand thing to have a great stock in reserve. Never mind if it is in the cellar, where you cannot yourself see it; it is none the worse for being out of sight.

The great thing for all Christians is to have a good background, something behind that is real; so that, if you pray, or if you speak to another, you will be prepared to back it up. I remember trying to be a blessing to a very shrewd boy in a Sunday school class when first I knew the Lord. I told him the gospel: 'He that believeth and is baptized shall be saved.' Then he asked me a straight question, 'Teacher, have you believed?' I replied, 'Yes, I hope so.' He said, 'Don't you know, teacher? You ought to.' 'Yes,' I answered, 'yes, I do know; I have believed in Jesus.' 'Well, teacher,' he enquired next, 'have you been baptized?' I replied, 'Yes, I have.' 'Then,' said he, 'teacher, you are saved.' I said, 'I hope so.' 'But,' he insisted, 'you *are*.' Just so, and I found that I must say so, too, and that I must not use even Christ's words unless I meant to back them up by my own consistent character; otherwise I was throwing suspicion on my Master's veracity. May the Lord bring us up to this point of Christian honesty – that, when we cannot truthfully say a thing from our own experience, we will be honest enough to resolve, 'I shall not say it till I *can* truly say it.'

When you think of a verse of a hymn, and it is a little in advance of your own position, wait till you come up to that point. There are numbers of hymns that I laid by, in that fashion, years ago. I wished that I could sing them, yet they seemed to stick in my throat, and I could not. But my throat has been cleared a good deal lately, and I have been obliged at last to feel that I must have those very hymns, for they have become true to my soul, and have made my experience a very happy one. Do not be in too much of a hurry in spiritual things any more than in temporal affairs. If you cannot eat meat, stick to your milk. Milk is for babes, so keep to milk till you outgrow it. You will choke with that tough bit of meat; you had better leave it for somebody else. Do not find fault with it; it is good for strong men, they do not want to be always drinking milk. Do not deny the strong man his meat, but let him have as much as he likes of it; as for yourself, if you are a babe in grace, keep to your milk diet. 'As newborn babes, desire the unadulterated milk of the Word, that ye may grow thereby: if so be ye have tasted that the Lord is gracious.' But, in all your testimony, do not go beyond what is actually true to yourself, and often let my text lay its hand upon your shoulder, and repeat this searching enquiry, 'Sayest thou this thing of thyself, or did others tell it thee?'

May God grant a rich blessing to you all, dear friends, for our Lord Jesus Christ's sake! Amen.

8

THE KING IN PILATE'S HALL[1]

Pilate therefore said unto him, Art thou a king then? Jesus
answered, Thou sayest that I am a king. To this end was I
born, and for this cause came I into the world, that I should
bear witness unto the truth. Every one that is of the truth
heareth my voice.

JOHN 18:37

OUR LORD was being cross-questioned by an unscrupulous,
vacillating, contemptuous Roman official. So, as our blessed Lord
and Master did not escape the ordeal of malicious questioning,
let no disciple of his imagine that he will escape. 'The disciple is
not above his master, nor the servant above his lord. It is enough
for the disciple that he be as his master, and the servant as his
lord.' Sooner or later the day will come when the profession that
you have made shall be questioned and tested. To some of Christ's
followers, this time of trial comes very soon after their conversion;
others are assailed at a later period. The cool, calm, calculating
doubter suggests a question about this or that, and everything that
can be moved is shaken. Just as Pilate said to Christ, 'Art thou a
king then?' so will men say to you, 'Are you a Christian? Are you
really believing in Jesus? Have you been born again? Are you a
new creature in Christ Jesus? Are you fully sanctified?' And they
will make these enquiries in such a tone of contemptuous ridicule
that you will need all your strength, and all your patience, and an
increase in your faith, and in all your graces, if you are to witness

[1] Sermon No. 2,826. Preached at the Metropolitan Tabernacle on Sunday evening,
4 May 1884.

a good confession, as your Master did before Pontius Pilate. When such a time comes to you, I cannot suggest to you a better model for your answer than that which your Lord gave to the Roman governor. At first, he did not answer Pilate: 'Jesus gave him no answer.' And a large portion of the inquisitive questioning to which we have to submit is not worth answering; nor is it worth while for you and me to go up and down the world fishing for questions, or inviting the objections and cavillings of sceptics, because we think ourselves so exceedingly clever that we are easily able to answer them. Believe me, you will have quite enough to do if you catch on your shield all the fiery darts that come without your invitation. You will have no need to ask to be led into temptation, or to seek permission to rush into it. Our Saviour invited no questions from Pilate; he did not even condescend to answer all that Pilate had to say to him; and the best thing for a Christian to do, in many of his times of trial, is to say, with David, 'I was dumb with silence. I held my peace, even from good; and my sorrow was stirred.'

When the Master did reply, he set us an example that we may safely follow. Observe how he replied – without any tartness, without even the appearance of anger. He was very courteous towards Pilate; he put what he had to say in a fashion which would commend itself to him. He knew that Pilate's chief jealousy was about his being a king, and he tried to remove it by explaining that his kingdom was not of this world, else would his servants fight for him so that he should not be delivered to the Jews. I cannot conceive of replies, to such a man as Pilate, more suitable, more calculated to have done him good if there had been any soil in Pilate's heart upon which the good seed could have fallen with the hope of growth. I pray that you and I, when we are assailed and questioned, may be wise as serpents, and harmless as doves, giving a reason for the hope that is in us with meekness and fear, answering, not with the object of displaying our own skill or learning, but always with the motive of seeking the good of the questioner, if, peradventure, God may grant unto him repentance that he may come to the knowledge of the truth. I admire, and hold up as an example to you, the exceeding sweetness of our Saviour's replies to his carping critic.

Note, however, how bold he was, as well as wise and gentle: 'Thou sayest that I am a king.' He does not flinch from admitting the truth, however distasteful it may be to his hearer. If this truth troubles Pilate after our Saviour's explanation that his kingdom is not of this world, he cannot deny the fact that he really is a king, for he must speak the truth come what may of it. I fear that, sometimes, in our endeavours to be sweet in disposition, we have not been strong in principle. 'Charity' is a word that is greatly cried up nowadays; but, often, it means that, in trying to be courteous, we have also been traitorous. Our speech has been soft and smooth, but it has not been sincere and true. Did you never catch yourself wishing to trim off the corners of a truth – or, at least, seeking if you could not omit something that might prejudice your hearer? If so, let me tell you plainly that he who wishes to alter any truth has already begun to lie. Though he may not actually do it, yet the very wish to change the truth in any degree is a proof of perversity of heart which needs to be repented of and forgiven. We have already turned aside from the right path when we do not dare to say what God has taught us. Our Saviour never acted like that; he was always true, transparent, clear, faithful. There was never in him any holding back even in the least degree; as he said to Pilate, 'Thou sayest that I am a king. To this end was I born, and for this cause came I into the world, that I should bear witness unto the truth.' Oh, that we might learn from our Saviour the sacred art of blending Christlike gentleness with holy courage, and Christlike courage with gentleness such as his!

Observe, too – for it is worthy of notice – how modestly and unobtrusively our Saviour answered Pilate's questioning. It is an unhappy circumstance that some men seem as if they cannot speak boldly without having somewhat of pride mixed with their courage. Full often, our very virtues lie quite near to the borders of vice. We aim at what is right; but, alas! we go beyond it, or we fall short of it, or hit the target where our shots do not count. Ah, Lord, what imperfect creatures we are! But our Saviour was perfect in every respect. He only answered the questions of Pilate when it was right for him to answer them, and even then he seemed to take the words wherewith to frame his answer out of Pilate's own mouth: 'Thou sayest that I am a king. It is even as thou hast said.'

Our gracious Master is very straightforward, yet how modest he is! He seems to hide himself even behind Pilate's words. He does not hide the truth; yet, in a perfectly sinless way, he somewhat conceals himself. I wish we could imitate him in that respect. Even when we are, like Bayard, 'without fear, and without reproach,' we are very apt, at the same time, to be without any desire for the conflict against evil, or any wish to obtrude ourselves, in the least degree, upon the attention of others, even if a protest would be right from us. We never see any of this false shame in our Saviour; so, if we have at all given way to it in the past, let us never repeat that sin.

The words of Paul, in his first Epistle to Timothy, are very properly rendered in the Revised Version, 'Christ Jesus, who before Pontius Pilate witnessed *the* good confession.' It was more than *a* good confession that our Lord Jesus witnessed before Pontius Pilate, so the definite article is rightly used, and '*the* good confession' stands out prominently as an example for all his followers. It is concerning that good confession that I am about to speak as the Holy Spirit shall graciously guide me.

I. First, let us ask, – WHAT WAS 'THE GOOD CONFESSION' THAT JESUS WITNESSED BEFORE PONTIUS PILATE?

I think the good confession of our Lord was, first, *his avowal of his kingship:* 'Thou sayest that I am a king.' Dear friends, do not forget that our Saviour was, at that time, a prisoner in bonds, on trial for his life. As far as the eye could see, he appeared to be absolutely in the power of Pilate – a man who was destitute of any kind of conscience, and who cared nothing what means he employed so long as he could attain his own evil ends. There stands Jesus, a bound prisoner, before one who can order him to be put to death; and the judge contemptuously says to him, 'Art thou a king then?', and he answers, with great gentleness, but most decidedly and undoubtedly, 'I am a king, even as thou sayest.' I think I see Pilate's lip curl; I can imagine the supreme contempt with which he looked upon the miserable victim before him, disowned by his own countrymen, who had brought him there because, in their hate, they wished to have him put to death; yet he talks about being a king! It may have been a merry jest for Pilate at the moment, but he did not dare to make it one afterwards. His wife would have stopped him had he sought to find amusement in Jesus of Nazareth. At the time, it must all have seemed very strange to him. It takes a great deal of courage for a man to avow that which seems to be improbable; and, indeed, impossible. He knows it is true, but the other man thinks it is a piece of fanaticism. 'Ridiculous nonsense,' says he; and he scorns the idea with a sardonic grin. It is not easy, then, for a humble-minded spirit just as determinedly to avow it. I believe that there is many a man, who could stand upon a public platform, and announce his convictions to an infuriated crowd, who would not dare to say the same things to a single individual. It took more courage for Christ to speak to Pilate alone as he did, than it has done for many a man to stand and burn at the stake; yet the Saviour did it. Calmly, and deliberately, he avowed the truth, blessed be his holy name! 'I am a king,' said he, and so he is. In our hearts, we own his sovereignty over us as individuals, and his supremacy over the entire church. Nay, more, his Father hath given him power over all flesh, that he should give eternal life to as many as he has given him. He hath said it, 'Yet have I set my King upon my holy hill of Zion,' 'and he shall reign for ever and ever,' and all loyal hearts cry, 'Hallelujah!' It was a good confession for the Nazarene, clothed in the common smock-frock of a Galilean peasant, with gory sweat still upon his brow, with the ropes that bound him still about his wrists, with the howling savagery of his countrymen behind him, to say to Pilate, 'I am a king.'

Next, Christ's 'good confession' was *his announcement of a spiritual kingdom*. Pilate could not comprehend what he meant when he said, 'My kingdom is not of this world; if my kingdom were of this world, then would my servants fight, that I should not be delivered to the Jews.' A spiritual kingdom! Pilate would not have given the smallest Roman coin for such a kingdom as that. Our Saviour's own countrymen did not understand what he meant by a spiritual kingdom 'not of this world'. They were looking for a temporal prince, an earthly leader who would deliver them from the Roman yoke; but Jesus asserts that his kingdom, whatever it is, and wherever it is, is a spiritual thing. This is the testimony that we also are trying to bear today; and, sometimes, we have to bear it before the very temporal power that thinks the church is an instrument to be used for its own purposes – a sort of mental and moral police force to keep, people in order, the officers themselves to be kept in order, and dressed, governed, fed, and maintained by Act of Parliament, and not able to lift so much as a little finger should the State forbid them to do so. This is a doctrine which needs some courage to utter it even now; but it is to be spoken, and must be spoken, more and more loudly. Christ's kingdom is not of this world; it borrows no power from the secular arm, and would not accept it if it were offered. It is a rule of spirit over spirit, of mind over mind, of truth over the souls of men; and that man is a faithful witness for Christ who can unflinchingly bear this testimony even before the greatest and the proudest of the land. Our Saviour did so when he said to Pilate, 'My kingdom is not of this world.'

Another part of Christ's 'good confession' was *a declaration of his life purpose:* 'To this end was I born, and for this cause came I into the world, that I should bear witness unto the truth.' There is many a man who is pursuing a calling which he would scarcely like to own, and there are others who think that their calling can be best pursued by stealthy, crafty, Jesuitical plans; but it was not so with the Saviour. He boldly declared the purpose for which he had come into the world; why should he conceal it? He who seeks to bear witness to the truth should himself be true enough to avow what the object of his witness is; and the Saviour did so, before Pilate, and wherever he was. All his life long he was a witness to the truth, he was himself the truest man who ever lived. It is beautiful to notice the truth of the Lord Jesus Christ even in small particulars. There is no rhetoric about our Saviour's speech, because rhetoric is too often but a lie. He speaks as simply as a child; there is no attempt at any display of learning in our Saviour's teaching. Because it is all solid truth, and divine revelation, there is no need that he should use the jargon of the schools, or call himself a Rabbi, or doctor. He spake with authority, and you can see how simply, how plainly, how heartily, he did it. There was no particular garb to attract attention to the Saviour, no priestly robes with which to dignify a kind of babyish authority; but he was a man among men, speaking what he knew in the language of the people which they could understand. There was no pomp, or ceremony, or show about his life; and, especially, there was no sham or pretence. He was what he seemed to be, and he seemed to be just what he was. If you look upon any other man, you can see some attempt to hide his deficiencies, or to increase his influence by an appearance of greater strength than actually exists. In the Saviour, you see him altogether as he is. He wears his heart upon his sleeve. He speaks straight on, and never turns aside to crooked ways. He never blushes or stammers, why should he do so? What has he to conceal? His teaching is delivered as from a mountain-top and men may stand, and gaze; and, the longer they gaze, the better will they see what he wishes them to see. He has no curtain behind which there is something concealed; all is as open as the day. As a truthful man, he was a fit witness to bear testimony to the truth. And what a breaker of idols, what a smasher of all shams, he was! Pharisees, and Sadducees, and Herodians got but short shrift from him. Nothing false could stand before him. Even a scourge of small cords, when it was held in his hands, sufficed to sweep the buyers and sellers from the temple; but when he used the sledge-hammer of denunciation, who could resist him? His fan was in his hand, and he did thoroughly purge his floor. And this was his life purpose – that he might bear witness to the truth, and he avowed that purpose even before Pontius Pilate.

Our Saviour also witnessed 'the good confession' *by his avowal that there is such a thing as positive truth:* 'To this end was I born, and for this cause came I into the world, that I should bear witness unto the truth.' There is need of just such witness as that today. 'Now be very careful upon that point,' says one; 'do you mean to say that there really is such a thing as the truth?' By your leave, dear sir, or without it, I will venture to assert that there is. 'That reply is a very bigoted one; because, if there is a doctrine that is "the truth", then that which is contrary to it is a lie.' Precisely so; and by your leave, or without your leave, again I say that it is so, and it must be so in the natural order of things. If this doctrine be true, then that which contradicts it cannot be true. If God has spoken thus, that which is opposed to God, and his truth, is not from him, and cannot stand on the same footing with that which is divinely revealed. It takes a good deal of courage to say that nowadays. If you go into society, you will get three cheers if you declare that you are an Agnostic – that you do not know anything, you are not sure of anything. Others say that, whatever a man believes, or does not believe, it really does not matter provided he is perfectly sincere; that is to say, if a man sincerely takes prussic acid, it will not kill him; and if he sincerely goes without food, he will not starve; and if he sincerely refuses to breathe, he will do as well as those that do breathe, which is another lie. The statue of Christ was set up among the statues of Plato, and Socrates, and other notable men; and some thought it was an honour to Christ, but it was not. They would crown Christ, so they say, among the great ones of earth. Ah! but they cannot crown him unless they 'crown him Lord of all'. Our blessed Saviour is honestly intolerant. He says, 'He that believeth and is baptized shall be saved, but he that believeth not shall be damned.' Because he loves the souls of men, he will not bolster up the fiction of universal charity, and even before the Broad-church or No-church Pilate, he says that he has come to bear witness to the truth; so there is the truth, and that which is contrary to it is not truth.

One other point in our Lord's 'good confession' was *his separation of characters*, for he went on to say to Pilate – and I fear that most of us would have left out that sentence – 'Every one that is of the truth heareth my voice.' Do you hear that declaration, Pilate? You are the Roman procurator – a very great man, and this poor prisoner of yours, whose life is now at your mercy, tells you plainly that every one that is of the truth heareth his voice. Then, Pilate, if you are of the truth, you will have to sit at his feet, and listen to his words, and learn of him. I can well conceive what Pilate thought as he turned on his heel, and contemptuously asked, 'What is truth?' He had heard quite enough of such talk as that; he did not want any more of such close dealing. But therein lies the glory of the Master, that he is not content with merely teaching truth, but, in his good confession before Pontius Pilate, he presses it home even upon his judge, and divides and separates between the precious and the vile. So must you and I do, dear friends, if we are faithful followers of 'the faithful Witness'. I dare not preach to this congregation as if you were all Christians, for you are not. I dare not deliver even one discourse under the delusion that all my hearers are saved; for, alas! they are not. This is the fault with multitudes of sermons – that they seem to carry the whole congregation to heaven when, possibly, the major part of those present may be going down to hell. That will not do. Remember what the Lord said to the prophet Jeremiah, 'If thou take forth the precious from the vile, thou shalt be as my mouth.' But if there be no winnowing fan in our hand, to separate the chaff from the wheat, we are not like to Christ, nor has Christ sent us on his service. In this 'good confession' of his, we see how clearly and solemnly – gently, I admit, but still most decidedly – he made a division and separation of characters, and gave a test by which Pilate could judge himself if he had been willing to do so.

II. The time will not suffice for me to go fully into all the teaching of my text, but I want to ask, in the second place – To WHAT TRUTH DID OUR LORD WITNESS?

He said to Pilate that he was born; that proves his humanity. He also said that he came into the world; and that, I think, shows his divinity as well as his humanity. He came on purpose to bear witness to the truth, and I believe that the life of Christ witnessed, not only to all doctrinal truth, but also to everything that is true, especially to true-heartedness, simplicity, sincerity. His life was a testimony against all guile, craftiness, cunning, concealment; in that sense, it was as testimony to the truth.

But with regard to special truths to which he testified, did not his very coming here, and being born, bear witness to *the grand truth that God is love, and that God loves men?* The Infinite takes upon himself the nature and form of an infant. The Illimitable is encased within a human body. 'The Word was made flesh, and dwelt among us.' We never can have a clearer testimony to the thoughtful care of God to men than we find in the coming of the Son of God as the Son of man, except this – that, being found in fashion as a man, he proved the love of God to sinners by the tears which he wept over the guilty and perishing, and, best of all, by the blood which he shed for many for the remission of sins. As ye see Christ dying on the accursed tree, say, 'Behold, what manner of love the Father hath bestowed upon us.' He willeth not the death of any, but longs that they should turn unto him and live. The

Saviour's death for the guilty proves that 'God so loved the world, that he gave his only begotten Son, that whosoever believeth in him should not perish, but have everlasting life.' All his life long, the Saviour was bearing witness to this grand truth. Oh, that we may none of us dare to doubt it after he has backed it up by a life of self-abnegation, and a death of sublime self-sacrifice!

He also bore witness, all through his life, to *the spirituality of true religion*. He was always teaching truth like this: 'God is a Spirit: and they that worship him must worship him in spirit and in truth.' He wore no phylactery, he assumed no airs of an ascetic; even in his eating and drinking, he was like other men, insomuch that they said of him that he was 'a man gluttonous, and a wine bibber' – a vile charge, without an atom of truth in it. He taught that true religion consisted not in long prayers, but in entering into the closet, and sincerely seeking the Father's face; it was not fasting thrice in the week, but it was truly praying, 'God be merciful to me a sinner;' it was not giving alms in public, and sounding a trumpet before him, and in secret devouring widows houses; but it consisted in love to God and love to man. It was the work of the Holy Spirit upon the heart that Jesus preached, and he grandly witnessed against all the idolatrous and false forms of faith which, even down to this day, prostitute his blessed name.

In that sad hour, our Lord Jesus was also a wonderful witness to *the enmity of men to God*. He in whom there was no roughness or sternness, as there was in John the Baptist, came as the Messenger of love and mercy, for God sent him not into the world to condemn the world, but that the world through him might be saved. He was the great Householder's Son, who was, 'last of all' sent to receive the fruits of the vineyard, but the husbandmen said, 'This is the heir; come, let us kill him, and let us seize on his inheritance.' The men of this world were never so base – they never displayed so much of their utter malice against God as when they took his Son, and put him to a cruel and ignominious death. This was the culmination of human guilt. All the adulteries, and murders, and unnatural vices and accursed blasphemies, that had ever defiled the race of mankind have not so certainly proved it to be a desperately fallen thing as the murder of the Son of God, the Saviour and the Friend of men. This appalling crime of deicide stands out without a parallel in the history of the universe. There was no guilt in the Lord Jesus for which he deserved to die; yet, with wicked hands, they crucified and slew him.

Our Saviour was also ever a witness to *the great necessity of a new creation, a change of heart, a regeneration.* To Nicodemus he said, 'Ye must be born again;' and to his disciples, 'Except ye be converted, and become as little children, ye shall not enter into the kingdom of heaven.' He also preached the absolute necessity of faith in himself, and did not mince the matter in the least: 'He that believeth on the Son hath everlasting life: and he that believeth not the Son shall not see life, but the wrath of God abideth on him.' To all this, Jesus steadfastly witnessed in life and in death.

And to this truth also he bore witness, *that salvation was to be found only in himself.* 'As Moses lifted up the serpent in the wilderness, even so must the Son of man be lifted up; that whosoever believeth in him should not perish, but have eternal life.' 'If any man thirst, let him come unto me, and drink.' His teaching was always concerning himself: 'I am the way, the truth, and the life.' 'Come unto me, all ye that labour and are heavy laden, and I will give you rest.' He never hesitated to bear witness to the truth so it was but natural that part of his 'good confession' before Pilate should be this plain declaration, 'To this end was I born, and for this cause came I into the world, that I should bear witness unto the truth.'

III. Now I will try briefly to answer a third question, – WHAT HAD THIS 'GOOD CONFESSION' OF JESUS TO DO WITH PILATE?

I answer, first, that it gave Pilate *a reason for acting justly.* It ought to have helped to stir any little conscience that Pilate still had left, and also to allay the jealousy which he may have felt because of the Saviour's royal claims. Our Lord spoke thus out of kindness to Pilate.

I think, however, that the main reason for our Saviour's testimony was that *it gave Pilate an opportunity to learn the truth.* Had his soul been like the good soil, had he really ever been the subject of sovereign grace, he would have said to Jesus, 'I will gladly hear what this truth is if thou wilt tell it to me.' He would, at least, have spared time enough to hear from his strange prisoner what this truth was. There must have been an unusual force about our Saviour's few short sentences that ought to have convinced even Pontius Pilate of his evident sincerity. Those eyes, so gentle, yet so piercing, must have looked Pilate through and through. The tones of his voice must have been very different from anything to which Pilate had been accustomed in the courts of Nero. Jesus spoke as no other man had ever spoken in Pilate's hall before; and had there been anything hopeful about him, he would have said, 'Good Master, tell me what that truth is to which thou bearest witness.'

And I say to you, who are not converted, if you desire to be right with God, you will want to know what this truth is for which the Lord Jesus lived and died. And when you do know it, if there is the right principle in your heart, then you will believe it; and, believing it, you will be assuredly saved. There is such life-giving truth in the Saviour's teaching that you have but to hear it, and turn it over in your mind, and weigh it with the best judgment that you have, to be convinced that it is most certainly true. So I put it to you, if it be true, will you not believe it? Believing it, will you not yield to it, and let it reign over your whole being, for it is truth from the mouth of the King? It is the sceptre in the hand of King Jesus, with which he rules over the hearts of all his loyal subjects.

IV. Now, to finish, I have to ask, – WHAT HAS THIS TO DO WITH OURSELVES?

It has something to do with every one of us, whether we own Christ or not. First, it suggests to our hearts this question – *Are we of the truth?* For, if we are of the truth, we shall hear Christ's voice. It is the voice of the King eternal, immortal, invisible. He is the King of truth, and he rules over truthful minds. Coming to be the chief witness to all truth, he really occupies the throne of truth. Now, dear friends, are we of the truth? For, if we are not, we shall not accept Christ; but if we are, we shall be glad to have him as our King. I ask any man here, who has hitherto refused Christ, whether he is not conscious of something missing from his life. Are you not sometimes half inclined to believe in Jesus? Do you not have to do violence to your conscience by what you call reason, but by what I venture to say is a most unreasonable travesty of all good reasoning? If you would but let that reason of yours go its own way, and follow the track of truth, I believe that, ere long, by God's grace, you would be sitting at the Saviour's feet, and learning of him.

The next thing that this testimony of Christ has to do with us is this. If, on our behalf, he witnessed 'the good confession' for the truth before Pontius Pilate, then it behoves you and me, not only to believe, but *to bear witness to the truth*. Brothers and sisters in Jesus, this looks to me to be but a small thing for us to do. If the Son of God has come into this world on our behalf, and has not been ashamed to call us brethren, and to espouse our cause even at the cost of his life, I say that it looks to me to be but a small thing that he should ask of us that, if with our heart we believe in him, we should with our mouth make confession of him – that, if we believe in him, we should also, be baptized in his name, for it is his will that we should make an open confession before men if we really are his disciples.

There are new fashions in theology, and new gods lately come up, and new christs, and all manner of nonsense and novelty; but I am a follower of the old Christ, who is the same, yesterday, and today, and for ever; and I glory in being a fool for Christ's sake if it be a foolish thing to follow the Man of Nazareth, the Christ of Calvary, who died as the Substitute for all who believe in him; that, by the shedding of his precious blood, he might reconcile them unto God for ever.

I appeal to some, who I believe do really love my Lord and Master, but who are, like Saul of old, hiding away out of sight. Are, you never going forth to fight for your King? Will you still continue in the ways of the world, and yet profess to be a lover of the Lord? Cowards that you are, come out boldly for Jesus! If you are on Christ's side, avow it. There, never was a cause that better deserved to be openly confessed than his. If Christ be God, follow him; but if Satan be God, serve him. If the world be worth your love, give your love to the world, and say so, and do not come sneaking in among Christians as if you belonged to them. But if the Lord Jesus Christ be worthy of your love, give it to him, and say that you have done so. Come to the front, unite with his people, share the scorn that falls upon them; and whenever any man wishes to set Christ in the pillory, say to him, 'Put me there, too, for I am one with him, and have taken up his cause.' When he comes – and he soon will come in all the glory of his Father and of his holy angels, he who has denied him before men he will deny before the assembled universe; but he who has confessed him before men, him will he confess in the presence of his Father and of his holy angels

May that be my lot, and yours, dear friends, without a single exception, for his dear name's sake! Amen.

9

JESUS, THE KING OF TRUTH[1]

Pilate therefore said unto him, Art thou a king then? Jesus
answered, Thou sayest that I am a king. To this end was I
born, and for this cause came I into the world, that I should
bear witness unto the truth. Every one that is of the truth
hereth my voice.

JOHN 18:37

THE SEASON IS ALMOST ARRIVED when by the custom of
our fellow-citizens we are led to remember the birth of the holy
child Jesus, who was born 'king of the Jews'. I shall not, however,
conduct you to Bethlehem, but to the foot of Calvary; there we
shall learn, from the Lord's own lips, something concerning the
kingdom over which he rules, and thus we shall be led to prize
more highly the joyous event of his nativity.

We are told, by the Apostle Paul, that our Lord Jesus Christ
before Pontius Pilate witnessed a good confession. It was a good
confession as to the manner of it, for our Lord was truthful, gentle,
prudent, patient, meek, and yet, withal, uncompromising and
courageous. His spirit was not cowed by Pilate's power, nor ex-
asperated by his sneers. In his patience he possessed his soul, and
remained the model witness for the truth – both in his silence and
in his speech. He witnessed a good confession also, as to the matter
of it; for, though he said but little, that little was all that was
needful. He claimed his crown rights, and, at the same time,
declared that his kingdom was not of this world, nor to be

---

[1] Sermon No. 1,086. Preached at the Metropolitan Tabernacle on Thursday
evening, 19 December 1872.

sustained by force. He vindicated both the spirituality and the essential truthfulness of his sovereignty. If ever we should be placed in like circumstances, may we be able to witness a good confession too! We may never, like Paul, be made to plead before Nero; but, if we should, may the Lord stand by us, and help us to play the man before the lion! In our families, or among our business acquaintances, we may have to meet some little Nero, and answer to some petty Pilate; may we then also be true witnesses. O that we may have grace to be prudently silent or meekly outspoken, as the matter may require, in either case being faithful to our conscience and our God! May the sorrowful visage of Jesus, the faithful and true witness, the Prince of the kings of the earth, be often before our eye, to check the first sign of flinching, and to inspire us with dauntless courage!

We have before us, in the words of the text, a part of our Saviour's good confession touching his kingdom.

I. Note, first of all, that OUR LORD CLAIMED TO BE A KING. Pilate said, 'Art thou a king, then?' asking the question with a sneering surprise that so poor a being should put forth a claim to royalty. Do you wonder that he should have marvelled greatly to find kingly claims associated with such a sorrowful condition? The Saviour answered, in effect, 'It is even as thou sayest, I am a king.' The question was but half earnest; the answer was altogether solemn: 'I am a king.' Nothing was ever uttered by our Lord with greater certainty and earnestness.

Now, notice, that our Lord's claim to be a king *was made without the slightest ostentation or desire to be advantaged thereby.* There were other times when, if he had said 'I am a king,' he might have been carried upon the shoulders of the people, and crowned amid general acclamations. His fanatical fellow countrymen would gladly have made him their leader at one time; and we read that they would have 'taken him by force and made him a king.' At such times he said but little about his kingdom, and what he did say was uttered in parables, and explained only to his disciples when they were alone. Little enough did he say in his preaching concerning his birthright as the Son of David and a scion of the royal house of Judah; for he shrank from worldly honours, and disdained the vain glories of a temporal diadem. He who came in love to redeem men, had no ambition for the baubles of human sovereignty. But now, when he is betrayed by his disciple, accused by his countrymen, and in the hands of an unjust ruler; when no good can come of it to himself; when it will bring him derision rather than honour; he speaks out plainly and replies to his interrogator, 'Thou sayest that I am a king.'

Note well *the clearness of our Lord's avowal;* there was no mistaking his words: 'I am a king.' When the time has come for the truth to be spoken, our Lord is not backward in declaring it. Truth has her times most meet for speech, and her seasons for silence. We are not to cast our pearls before swine, but when the hour has come for speech we must not hesitate, but speak as with the voice of a trumpet, giving forth a certain sound, that no man may mistake us. So, though a prisoner given up to die, the Lord boldly declares his royalty, though Pilate would pour derision upon him in consequence thereof. O, for the Master's prudence to speak the truth at the right time, and for the Master's courage to speak it when the right time has come. Soldiers of the cross, learn of your Captain.

Our Lord's claim to royalty *must have sounded very singularly in Pilate's ear.* Jesus was, doubtless, very much careworn, sad, and emaciated in appearance. He had spent the first part of the night in the garden in an agony; in the midnight hours he had been dragged from Annas to Caiaphas, and from Caiaphas to Herod; neither at daybreak had he been permitted to rest, so that, from sheer weariness, he must have looked very unlike a king. If you had taken some poor ragged creature in the street, and said to him, 'Art thou a king, then?' the question could scarcely have been more sarcastic. Pilate, in his heart, despised the Jews as such, but here was poor Jew, persecuted by his own people, helpless and friendless; it sounded like mockery to talk of a kingdom in connection with him. Yet never earth saw truer king! None of the line of Pharaoh, the family of Nimrod, or the race of the Caesars, was so intrinsically imperial in himself as he, or so deservedly reckoned a king among men by virtue of his descent, his achievements, or his superior character. The carnal eye could not see this, but to the spiritual eye it is clear as noonday. To this day, pure Christianity, in its outward appearance, is an equally unattractive object, and wears upon its surface few royal tokens. It is without form or comeliness, and when men see it, there is no beauty that they should desire it. True, there is a nominal Christianity which is accepted and approved of men, but the pure gospel is still despised and rejected. The real Christ of today, among men, is unknown and unrecognised as much as he was among his own nation eighteen hundred years ago. Evangelical doctrine is at a discount, holy living is censured, and spiritual-mindedness is derided. 'What,' say they, 'This evangelical doctrine, call you it the royal truth? Who believes it nowadays? Science has exploded it. There is nothing great about it; it may afford comfort to old women, and to those who have not capacity enough for free thought, but its reign is over, never to return.' As to living in separation from the world, it is called Puritanism, or worse. Christ in doctrine, Christ in spirit, Christ in life – the world cannot endure as king. Christ chanted in cathedrals, Christ personified in lordly prelates, Christ surrounded by such as are in king's houses, he is well enough; but Christ honestly obeyed, followed, and worshipped in simplicity, without pomp or form, they will not allow to reign over them.

Few nowadays will side with the truth their fathers bled for. The day for covenanting to follow Jesus through evil report and shame appears to have gone by. Yet, though men turn round upon us, and say, 'Do you call your gospel divine? Are you so preposterous as to believe that your religion comes from God and is to subdue the world?' – we boldly answer; 'Yes!' Even as beneath the peasant's garb and the pale visage of the Son of Mary we can discern the Wonderful, the Counsellor, the Mighty God, the Everlasting Father, so beneath the simple form of a despised gospel we perceive the royal lineaments of truth divine. We care nothing about the outward apparel or the external housing of truth; we love it for its own sake. To us, the marble halls and the alabaster columns are nothing, we see more in the manger and the cross. We are satisfied that Christ is the king still where he was wont to be king, and that is not among the great ones of the earth, nor among the mighty and the learned, but amongst the base things of the world and the things which are not, which shall bring to nought the things that are, for these hath God from the beginning chosen to be his own.

Let us add, that our Lord's claim to be a king *shall be acknowledged one day by all mankind*. When Christ said to Pilate, according to our version, 'Thou sayest that I am a king,' he virtually prophesied the future confession of all men. Some, taught by his grace, shall in this life rejoice in him as their altogether lovely King. Blessed be God, the Lord Jesus might look into the eyes of many of us, and say, 'Thou sayest that I am a king,' and we would reply, 'We do say it joyfully.' But the day shall come when he shall sit upon his great white throne, and then, when the multitudes shall tremble in the presence of his awful majesty, even such as Pontius Pilate, and Herod, and the chief priests, shall own that he is a king! Then to each of his astounded and overwhelmingly convinced enemies he might say, 'Now, O despiser, thou sayest that I am a king,' for to him every knee shall bow, and every tongue shall confess that he is Lord!

Let us remember, here, that when our Lord said to Pilate, 'Thou sayest that I am king' *he was not referring to his divine dominion*. Pilate was not thinking of that at all, nor did our Lord, I think, refer to it: yet, forget not that, as divine, he is the King of kings and Lord of lords. We must never forget that, though he died in weakness as man, yet he ever lives and rules as God. Nor do I think he referred to *his mediatorial sovereignty*, which he possesses over the earth for his people's sake; for the Lord has all power committed unto him in heaven and in earth, and the Father has given him power over all flesh, that he may give eternal life to as many as are given him. Pilate was not alluding to that, nor our Lord either, in the first place; but he was speaking of *that rule which he personally exercises over the minds of the faithful, by means of the truth*. You remember Napoleon's saying, 'I have founded an empire by force, and it has melted away; Jesus Christ established his kingdom by love, and it stands to this day, and will stand.' That is the kingdom to which our Lord's word refers, the kingdom of spiritual truth in which Jesus reigns as Lord over those who are of the truth. He claimed to be a king and the truth which he revealed, and of which he was the personification, is, therefore, the sceptre of his empire. He rules by the force of truth over those hearts which feel the power of right and truth, and therefore willingly yield themselves to his guidance, believe his word, and are governed by his will. It is as a spiritual Lord that Christ claims sovereignty among men; he is king over minds that love him, trust him, and obey him, because they see in him the truth which their souls pine for. Other kings rule our bodies, but Christ our souls; they govern by force, but he by the attractions of righteousness; theirs is, to a great extent, a fictitious royalty, but his is true, and finds its force in truth.

So much, then, upon Christ's claims to be a king.

II. Now, observe, secondly, that OUR LORD DECLARED THIS KINGDOM TO BE HIS MAIN OBJECT IN LIFE. 'To this end was I born, and for this cause came I into the world.' To set up his kingdom was the reason why he was born of the virgin. To be king of men, it was necessary for him to be born. He was always the Lord of all; he needed not to be born to be a king in that sense, but to be king through the power of truth, it was essential that he should be born in our nature. Why so? I answer, first, because it seems unnatural that a ruler should be alien in nature to the people over whom he rules. An angelic king of men would be unsuitable; there could not exist the sympathy which is the cement of a spiritual empire. Jesus, that he might govern by force of love and truth alone, became of one nature with mankind; he was a man among men, a real man – but a right noble and kingly man, and so a King of men.

But, again, the Lord was born *that he might be able to save his people*. Subjects are essential to a kingdom; a king cannot be a king if there be none to govern. But all men must have perished through sin, had not Christ come into the world and been born to save. His birth was a necessary step to his redeeming death; his incarnation was necessary to the atonement.

Moreover, truth never exerts such power as when it is embodied. Truth spoken may be defeated, but truth acted out in the life of a man is omnipotent, through the Spirit of God. Now, Christ did not merely speak the truth, but he *was* truth. Had he been truth embodied in an angelic form, he had possessed small power over our hearts and lives; but perfect truth in a human form has royal power over renewed humanity. Truth embodied in flesh and blood has power over flesh and blood. Hence, for this purpose was he born. So when ye hear the bells ringing out at Christmas, think of the reason why Jesus was born; dream not that he came to load your tables and fill your cups; but in your mirth look higher than all earth-born things. When you hear that in certain churches there are pompous celebrations and ecclesiastical displays, think not for this purpose was Jesus born. No; but look within your hearts, and say, for this purpose was he born: that he might be a King, that he might rule through the truth in the souls of a people who are by grace made to love the truth of God.

And then he added, 'For this cause came I into the world;' that is, he came out of the bosom of the Father that he might set up his kingdom, *by unveiling the mysteries which were hid from the foundation of the world*. No man can reveal the counsel of God, but one who has been with God; and the Son who has come forth from the ivory palaces of gladness, announces to us tidings of great joy! For this cause also came he into the world, from the obscure retirement of Joseph's workshop, where, for many years he was hidden like a pearl in its shell. It was needful that he should be made known, and that the truth to which he witnessed should be sounded in the ears of the crowd.

Since he was to be a King, he must leave seclusion, and come forth to do battle for his throne; he must address the multitudes on the hillside; he must speak by the seashore; he must gather disciples, and send them forth by two and two to publish on the housetops the secrets of mighty truth! He came not forth because he loved to be seen of men, or courted popularity; but for this purpose – that, the truth being published, he might set up his kingdom. It was needful that he should come out into the world and teach, or truth would not be known, and consequently could not operate. The sun must come forth, like a bridegroom out of his chamber, or the kingdom of light will never be established; the breath must come forth from the hiding-place of the winds, or life will never reign in the valley of dry bones. During three years, our Lord lived conspicuously, and emphatically 'came into the world'. He was seen of men so closely as to be beheld, looked upon, touched, and handled. He was intended to be a pattern, and therefore, it was needful that he should he seen. The life of a man who lives in absolute retirement may be admirable for himself and acceptable with God, but it cannot be exemplary to men: for this cause the Lord came forth into the world, that all he did might influence mankind. His enemies were permitted to watch his every action, and to endeavour to entrap him in his speech, by way of test; his friends saw him in privacy and knew what he did in solitude; thus his whole life was reported – he was observed on the cold mountainside at midnight, as well as in the midst of the great congregation. This was permitted to make the truth known, for every action of his life was truth, and tended to set up the kingdom of truth in the world.

Let us pause here. Christ is a king, a king by force of truth in a spiritual kingdom; for this purpose was he born, for this cause came he into the world. My soul, ask thyself this question – Has this purpose of Christ's birth and life been answered in thee? If not, what avails Christmas to thee? The choristers will sing, 'Unto us a child is born; unto us a Son is given.' Is that true to thee? How can it be unless Jesus reigns in thee, and is thy Saviour and thy Lord? Those who can in truth rejoice in his birth are those who know him as their bosom's Lord, ruling their understanding by the truth of his doctrine; their admiration by the truth of his life; their affections by the truth of his person. To such he is not a personage to be portrayed with a crown of gold and a robe of purple, like the common theatrical kings of men; but one brighter and more heavenly, whose crown is real, whose dominion is unquestionable, who rules by truth and love! Do we know this King?

This question may well come home to us, for, beloved, there are many who say, 'Christ is my King,' who know not what they say, for they do not obey him. He is the servant of Christ who trusts in Christ, who walks according to Christ's mind, and loves the truth which Jesus has revealed: all others are mere pretenders.

III. But now I must pass on. Our Lord, in the third place, REVEALED THE NATURE OF HIS ROYAL POWER. I have already spoken on that, but I must do so again. We should have thought the text would have run thus: 'Thou sayest that I am a king; to this end was I born, and for this cause came I into the world, that I should establish my kingdom.' It is not so in words, but so it must mean, for Jesus was not incoherent in his speech. We conclude that the words employed have the same meaning as that which the context suggests, only it is differently expressed. If our Lord had said, 'That I might establish a kingdom', he might have misled Pilate; but when he availed himself of the spiritual explanation, and said that his kingdom was truth, and that the establishment of his kingdom was by bearing witness to the truth, then, though Pilate did not understand him – for it was far above his comprehension – yet, at any rate, he was not misled.

Our Lord, in effect, tells us that truth is the pre-eminent characteristic of his kingdom, and that his royal power over men's hearts is through the truth. Now, the witness of our Lord among men was emphatically upon real and vital matters. He dealt not with fiction, but with facts; not with trifles, but with infinite realities. He speaks not of opinions, views, or speculations, but of infallible verities. How many preachers waste time over what may be or may not be! Our Lord's testimony was pre-eminently practical and matter-of-fact, full of verities and certainties. I have sometimes, when hearing sermons, wished the preacher would come to the point, and would deal with something that really concerned our soul's welfare.

What concern have dying men with the thousand trivial questions which are flitting around us? We have heaven or hell before us, and death within a stone's throw; for God's sake do not trifle with us, but tell us the truth at once! Jesus is king in his people's souls, because his preaching has blessed us in the grandest and most real manner, and set us at rest upon points of boundless importance. He has not given us well-chiselled stones, but real bread. There are a thousand things which you may not know, and you shall be very little the worse for not knowing them; but O, if you do not know that which Jesus has taught, it shall go ill with you. If you are taught of the Lord Jesus, you shall have rest for your cares, balm for your sorrows, and satisfaction for your desires. Jesus gives sinners who believe in him the truth which they need to know; the assurance of sin forgiven through his blood, favour ensured by his righteousness, and heaven secured by his eternal life.

Moreover, Jesus has power over his people because *he testifies not to symbols, but to the very substance of truth.* The Scribes and Pharisees were very fluent upon sacrifices, offerings, oblations, tithes, fastings, and the like; but what influence could all that exert over aching hearts? Jesus has imperial power over contrite spirits, because he tells them of his one real sacrifice and of the perfection which he has secured to all believers. The priests lost their power over the people because they went no further than the shadow, and sooner or later all will do so who rest in the symbol. The Lord Jesus retains his power over his saints because he reveals the substance, for grace and truth are by Jesus Christ. What a loss of time it is to debate upon the fashion of a cope, or the manner of celebrating communion, or the colour suitable for the clergyman's robes in Advent, or the precise date of Easter. Vanity of vanities, all is vanity! Such trifles will never aid in setting up an everlasting kingdom in men's hearts. Let us take care lest we also set great store by externals, and miss the essential, spiritual life of our holy faith. Christ's kingdom is not meat and drink, but righteousness and peace, and joy in the Holy Ghost!

The power of King Jesus in the hearts of his people lies much in the fact that *he brings forth unalloyed truth, without mixture of error.* He has delivered to us pure light and no darkness; his teaching is no combination of God's word and man's inventions; no mixture of inspiration and philosophy; silver without dross is the wealth which he gives his servants. Men taught of his Holy Spirit to love the truth, recognize this fact and surrender their souls to the royal sway of the Lord's truth, and it makes them free, and sanctifies them; nor can anything make them disown such a sovereign, for as the truth lives and abides in their hearts, so Jesus, who is the truth, abides also. It you know what truth is, you will as naturally submit yourselves to the teachings of Christ as ever children yield to a father's rule.

The Lord Jesus taught that *worship must be true, spiritual, and of the heart, or else it would be nothing worth.* He would not take sides with the temple at Gerizim or that on Zion, but he declared that the time was come when those who worshipped God would worship him in spirit and in truth. Now, regenerate hearts feel the power of this, and rejoice that it emancipates them from the beggarly elements of carnal ritualism. They accept gladly the truth that pious words of prayer or praise are vanity, unless the heart has living worship within it. In the great truth of spiritual worship, believers possess a Magna Charta, dear as life itself. We refuse to be again subject to the yoke of bondage, and cleave to our emancipating king.

Our Lord taught, also, that *all false living was base and loathsome*. He poured contempt on the phylacteries of hypocrites and the broad borders of the garments of oppressors of the poor. With him, ostentatious alms, long prayers, frequent fasts, and the tithe of mint and cummin, were all nothing when practiced by those who devoured widows' houses. Ho cared nothing for whitewashed sepulchres and platters with outsides made clean, he judged the thoughts and intents of the heart. What woes were those which he denounced upon the formalists of his day! It must have been a grand sight to have seen the lowly Jesus roused to indignation, thundering forth peal on peal his denunciations of hypocrisy. Elijah never called fire from heaven one half so grandly. 'Woe unto you Scribes and Pharisees, hypocrites,' is the loudest roll of heaven's artillery! See how, like another Samson, Jesus slays the shams of his age, and piles them heaps upon heaps to rot for ever. Shall not he who teaches us true living be king of all the sons of truth? Let us even now salute him as Lord and King.

Besides, beloved, our Lord came *not only to teach us the truth,* but a mysterious power goes forth from him, through that Spirit which rests on him without measure – which subdues chosen hearts to truthfulness, and *then guides truthful hearts into fullness of peace and joy*. Have you never felt when you have been with Jesus, that a sense of his purity has made you yearn to be purged of all hypocrisy and every false way? Have you not been ashamed of yourself when you have come forth from hearing his word, from watching his life, and, above all, from enjoying his fellowship – quite ashamed that you have not been more real, more sincere, more true, more upright, and so a more loyal subject of the truthful King? I know you have. Nothing about Jesus is false or even dubious; he is transparent – from head to foot he is truth in public, truth in private, truth in word, and truth in deed. Hence it is that he has a kingdom over the pure in heart, and is vehemently extolled by all those whose hearts are set upon righteousness.

IV. And now, in the fourth place, our Lord DISCLOSED THE METHOD OF HIS CONQUEST. 'To this end was I born, and for this cause came I into the world, *that I should bear witness for the truth.*' Christ never yet set up his kingdom by force of arms. Muhammad drew the sword, and converted men by giving them the choice of death or conversion; but Christ said to Peter, 'Put up thy sword into its sheath.' No compulsion ought to be used with any man to lead him to receive any opinion, much less to induce him to espouse the truth. Falsehood requires the rack of the Inquisition, but truth needs not such unworthy aid; her own beauty, and the Spirit of God, are her strength. Moreover, Jesus used no arts of priestcraft, or tricks of superstition. The foolish are persuaded of a dogma, by the fact that it is promulgated by a learned doctor of high degree, but our Rabboni wears no sounding titles of honour; the vulgar imagine that a statement must be correct if it emanates from a person who wears wide sleeves of fine linen, or from a place where the banners are of costly workmanship, and the music of the sweetest kind: these things are arguments with those who are amenable to no other; but Jesus owes nothing to his apparel, and influences none by artistic arrangements. None can say that he reigns over men by the glitter of pomp, or the fascination of sensuous ceremonies. His battle-axe is the truth; truth is both his arrow and his bow, his sword and his buckler. Believe me, no kingdom is worthy of the Lord Jesus but that which has its foundations laid in indisputable verities; Jesus would scorn to reign by the help of a lie.

True Christianity was *never promoted by policy or guile, by doing a wrong thing, or saying a false thing.* Even to exaggerate truth is to beget error, and so to pull down the truth we would set up. There are some who say, 'Bring out one line of teaching, and nothing else, lest you should seem inconsistent.' What have I to do with that? If it be God's truth, I am bound to deliver it all, and to keep back none of it. Policy, like a sailing vessel, dependent on the wind, tacks about hither and thither; but the true man, like a vessel having its motive power within, goes straight onward in the very teeth of the hurricane. When God puts truth into men's souls, he teaches them never to tack or trim, but to hold to truth at all hazards. This is what Jesus always did. He bore witness to the truth, and there left the matter; being guileless as a lamb.

Here it will be fit to answer the question, 'What truth did he witness to?' Ah, my brethren what truth did he *not* witness to? Did he not mirror all truth in his life? See how clearly he set forth the truth that God is love. How melodious, how like a peal of Christmas bells, was his witness to the truth that 'God so loved the world, that he gave his only begotten Son, that whosoever believeth in him might not perish but have everlasting life.' He also bore witness that God is just. How solemnly he proclaimed that fact! His flowing wounds, his dying agonies rang out that solemn truth, as with a knell which even the dead might hear. He bore witness to God's demand for truth in the inward parts; for he often dissected men and laid them bare, and opened up their secret thoughts and discovered them to themselves, and made them see that only sincerity could bear the eye of God. Did he not bear witness to the truth that God had resolved to make for himself a new people and a true people? Was he not always telling of his sheep who heard his voice, of the wheat which would be gathered into the garner, and of the precious things which would be treasured up when the bad would be thrown away? Therein he was bearing witness that the false must die, that the unreal must be consumed, that the lie must rust and rot; but that the true, the sincere, the gracious, the vital, shall stand every test, and outlast the sun. In an age of shams, he was always sweeping away pretences and establishing truth and right by his witness.

And now, beloved, this is the way in which Christ's kingdom is to be set up in the world. For this cause was the church born, and for this end came she into the world, that she might set up Christ's kingdom by bearing witness to the truth. I long, my beloved, to see you all witness-bearers. If you love the Lord, bear witness to the truth. You must do it personally; you must also do it collectively. Never join any church whose creed you do not entirely and unfeignedly believe, for if you do you act a lie, and are, moreover, a partaker in the error of other men's testimonies. I would not for a moment say anything to retard Christian unity, but there is something before unity, and that is, 'truth in the inward parts' and honesty before God. I dare not be a member of a church whose teaching I knew to be false in vital points. I would sooner go to heaven alone than belie my conscience for the sake of company. You may say, 'But I protest against the error of my church.' Dear friends, how can you consistently protest against it when you profess to agree with it, by being a member of the church which avows it? If you are a minister of a church, you do in effect say before the world, 'I believe and teach the doctrines of this church;' and if you go into the pulpit and say you do not believe them, what will people conclude? I leave you to judge that. I saw a church tower the other day, with a clock upon it, which startled me by pointing to half past ten when I thought it was only nine; I was, however, quite relieved when I saw that another face of the clock indicated a quarter past eight. 'Well,' thought I, 'whatever time it may be, that clock is wrong, for it contradicts itself.' So if I hear a man say one thing by his church membership and another by his private protest, why, whatever may be right, he certainly is not consistent with himself.

Let us bear witness to the truth, *since there is great need of doing so just now, for witnessing is in ill repute.* The age extols no virtue so much as 'liberality', and condemns no vice so fiercely as bigotry, *alias* honesty. If you believe anything and hold it firmly, all the dogs will bark at you. Let them bark: they will have done when they are tired! You are responsible to God, and not to mortal men. Christ came into the world to bear witness to the truth, and he has sent you to do the same; take care that you do it, offend or please; for it is only by this process that the kingdom of Christ is to be set up in the world.

Now, the last thing is this. Our Saviour, having spoken of his kingdom and the way of establishing it, DESCRIBED HIS SUBJECTS: 'Everyone that is of the truth heareth my voice.' That is to say, wherever the Holy Spirit has made a man a lover of truth, he always recognizes Christ's voice and yields himself to it. Where are the people who love the truth? Well, we need not enquire long. We need not Diogenes' lantern to find them, they will come to the light; and where is light but in Jesus? Where are those that would not seem to be what they are not? Where are the men who desire to be true in secret and before the Lord? They may be discovered where Christ's people are discovered; they will be found listening to those who bear witness to the truth. Those who love pure truth, and know what Christ is, will be sure to fall in love with him and hear his voice. Judge ye, then, this day, brethren and sisters, whether ye are of the truth or not; for if you love the truth, you know and obey the voice which calls you away from your old sins, from false refuges, from evil habits, from everything which is not after the Lord's mind. You have heard him in your conscience rebuking you for that of the false which remains in you; encouraging in you that of the true which is struggling there. I have done, when I have urged on you one or two reflections.

The first is, beloved, *Dare we avow ourselves on the side of truth at this hour of its humiliation?* Do we own the royalty of Christ's truth when we see it every day dishonoured. If gospel truth were honoured everywhere, it would be an easy thing to say 'I believe it;' but now, in these days, when it has no honour among men, dare we cleave to it at all costs? Are you willing to walk with the truth through the mire and through the slough? Have you the courage to profess unfashionable truth? Are you willing to believe the truth against which science, falsely so-called, has vented her spleen? Are you willing to accept the truth although it is said that only the poor and uneducated will receive it? Are you willing to be the disciple of the Galilean, whose apostles were fishermen? Verily, verily, I say unto you, in that day in which the truth in the person of Christ shall come forth in all its glory, it shall go ill with those who were ashamed to own it and its Master.

In the next place, if we have heard Christ's voice, *do we recognize our life-object?* Do we feel, 'For this end were we born, and for this cause came we into the world, that we might bear witness to the truth?' I do not believe that you, my dear brother, came into the world to be a linen draper, or an auctioneer, and nothing else. I do not believe that God created you, my sister, to be merely and only a seamstress, a nurse, or a housekeeper. Immortal souls were not created for merely mortal ends. For this purpose was I born, that, with my voice in this place, and everywhere else, I might bear witness to the truth. You acknowledge that: then I beg you, each one, to acknowledge that you have a similar mission. 'I could not occupy the pulpit,' says one. Never mind that: bear witness for the truth where you are, and in your own sphere. O waste no time or energy, but at once testify for Jesus.

And now, last of all, *do you own Christ's superlative dignity, beloved?* Do you see what a King, Christ is? Is he such a King to you as none other could be? It was but yesterday a prince entered one of our great towns, and they crowded all their streets to welcome him – yet he was but a mortal man. And then at night they illuminated their city, and made the heavens glow as though the sun had risen before his appointed hour. Yet what had this prince done for them? Loyal subjects were they, and that was the reason of their joy. But O, beloved, we need not ask, 'What has Christ done for us?' – we will ask, 'What has he not done for us?' Emmanuel, we owe all to thee! Thou art our new creator, our Redeemer from the lowest pit of hell! In thyself resplendent and altogether lovely, thy beauties command our adoration! Thou hast lived for us, thou hast bled for us, thou hast died for us; and thou art preparing a kingdom for us, and thou art coming again to take us to be with thee where thou art! All this commands our love. All hail! all hail! Thou art our King, and we worship thee with all our soul!

Beloved, I beseech you love Christ, and live for him while you can. Work while opportunity serves. While I have been laid aside, and able to do nothing, the great sorrow of my heart has been my inability to do him service. I heard my brethren shouting in the battle-field, and I saw my comrades marching to the fight, and I lay like a wounded soldier in the ditch, and could not stir, save that I breathed a prayer that you might all be strong in the Lord and in the power of his might. This was my thought: 'Oh, that I had preached better while I could preach, and lived more for the Master while I could serve him!' Don't incur such regrets in the future by present sluggishness, but live now for him who died for you!

If any present in this assembly have never obeyed our King, may they come to trust in him tonight; for he is a tender Saviour, and is willing to receive the biggest and blackest sinner who will come to him. Whosoever trusts in him, will never find him fail; for he will save to the uttermost them that come unto God by him. May he bring you to his feet, and reign over you in love. Amen.

10

OUR LORD'S FIRST APPEAR-
ANCE BEFORE PILATE[1]

Pilate saith unto them, I find in him no fault at all.
JOHN 18:38

I SHOULD LIKE, if God spares us, to present to you on Sabbath mornings the full story of our Saviour's sufferings. We began last Lord's day by going with him to the hall of Caiaphas, and it was a sadly solemn time when we beheld the Prince of Peace a prisoner, heard him falsely accused and unjustly condemned, and then saw him abused, till servants and abjects did spit in his face and make a mockery of him. I hope that you will not be wearied with this subject. If so, it will be the fault of the preacher, for the subject is ever full and fresh: or if the preacher be not to blame, there will be something of censure due to his hearers. If we do grow tired of the story of the cross it will be a sad indication of secret soul-sickness, and it will be well to observe the symptom and hasten to the great Physician for healing. To true saints in a healthy condition there is no place more attractive than the place of our Lord's passion, where he accomplished the glorious work of our redemption. They love to linger along that *Via Dolorosa* which leads from Gethsemane to Golgotha; let us linger with them.

When I stand and view my Lord, like the bush in Horeb, burning but not consumed, I hear a voice saying unto me, 'The place whereon thou standest is holy ground.' Nothing is more holy than the person of our divine Master; it is, therefore, well to be with

---

[1] Sermon No. 1,644. Preached at the Metropolitan Tabernacle on Sunday morning, 12 February 1882.

him. The anguish which he endured when he devoted his person as a sacrifice for us is holy too, and so it is well to be with him in his sufferings. His sorrows have a most sanctifying influence upon all who consider them with believing love. I am persuaded that if we lived more in the atmosphere of the cross sin would lose its power, and every grace would flourish. When we draw very near to him and have fellowship with him in his sufferings we raise a hue and cry against the sin which slew him, and resolve to be revenged upon it by departing from it ourselves, and by warring against it whenever we see it in others. The cross is that holy implement with which we make war with sin till it be utterly destroyed. Blessed and holy, then, are the thoughts which are aroused by our great sacrifice.

Nor is it only so; but the medicine which brings us health is in itself a joy.

> Sweet the moments, rich in blessing,
>   Which before the cross I spend,
> Life, and health, and peace possessing,
>   In the sinner's dying Friend.

Here is no noise as of them that make merry over their wine, no shout of them that triumph, no song of them that feast; but here is a grave, sweet melody as of hearts that have found rest. At the cross we find a substantial joy, a far-reaching satisfaction, 'the peace of God, which passeth all understanding'. Here, ye restless ones, is the cure of restlessness here shall you say, 'O God, my heart is fixed, my heart is fixed. I will sing and give praise.' I shall not, therefore, make any excuse, even if for weeks to come I should lead you to the place of dragons where your Lord was sore broken, and help you to drink of his cup, and to be baptized with his baptism. May the Spirit of God come upon and open our eyes to read the sacred heart of him whose sorrows are unrivalled – sorrows borne for love of us.

Let us go to the narrative at once with loving and lowly carefulness. Our Lord was condemned by the chief priests for blasphemy, because he declared himself to be the Son of God, and told them that they should hereafter see him coming in the clouds of heaven to be their judge. Rending his garments, the high priest said, 'What need have we of any further witness? Ye have heard his blasphemy.' When the morning light had come, andthey had gone through the formality of a set trial by daylight, having really condemned him in the night, they led Jesus away to Pilate. According to tradition, he was led with a rope about his neck, and his hands bound; and I can fully believe in the tradition when I remember the words of Isaiah: 'He was led as a sheep to the slaughter.' It was a strangely sad procession which moved through Jerusalem a little after six in the morning. Those men of the Sanhedrin in all their pomp and power surrounding this one poor victim, whom they were about to deliver to the Gentiles with the one design that he might be put to death! Those wicked men of pride were as the dogs of whom the Psalmist sang when the hind of the morning was his tender theme.

When they came to the house of the Roman governor, they would not themselves enter within its doors. It is said to have been one of the many magnificent palaces which Herod the Great built for himself; the architecture was gorgeous, the floors were inlaid with choice marbles, and all the chambers were richly gilded and furnished with oriental splendour. Into the great hall these scrupulous hypocrites would not enter because they must by no means be defiled by the touch of a Gentile, for they had already commenced to keep the Passover. So they waited in the courtyard, and Pilate condescended to come out to them and learn the pressing business which brought them there so early in the morning. The Roman governor was proud, and cruel, and abhorred the Jews; but still, knowing their fanaticism and the readiness with which they broke loose at Passover times, he stood at his palace gate and heard their demands, he soon ascertained that they had brought him a prisoner, evidently a poor man, and in personal appearance emaciated, weary, and suffering. About him there was a mysterious dignity combined with singular gentleness, and Pilate for this and other reasons evidently took a singular interest in him. Fixing his gaze first upon the extraordinary prisoner, he turned to the angry priests and demanded, 'What accusation bring ye against this man?'

The one object of the priests in bringing Jesus to Pilate was to get him put to death; for when Pilate told them to go and judge him according to their law, they replied that they would gladly do so, but that the power of life and death had been taken from them, implying that nothing but his death would content them. They were, however, very anxious at this stage to lay the responsibility of his death upon the Romans, for the fear of the people was still upon them, and if they could secure his death by Pilate, then they might in after days protest that they merely handed him over to the Roman governor and could not foresee that he would be handled so roughly. They had not yet bribed the populace to cry, 'Crucify him,' and they were willing to be on the safe side should the people make an uproar on his behalf. Humanly speaking, they could have put him to death themselves, for he was entirely in their power, and they frequently forgot the Roman law and slew men in riotous fury, as when they stoned Stephen. They had frequently attempted to stone our Lord himself, so that they were not always so mindful of Roman law. They might have taken his life on this occasion, but they were led by a mysterious impulse to desire that the actual responsibility of the deed should rest on Pilate. Further on they were willing to join with the fickle throng in sharing the guilt of his blood, but as yet they would fain throw it upon others. During their great festivals if they took innocent blood, their hypocrisy made them wish to do it by forms of law and by an alien hand. To do this they must bring an accusation, for no Roman ruler would condemn a man till an accusation had been made.

We shall, this morning, consider *the two accusations that they brought,* and after that we shall hear *the verdict of acquittal* which Pilate gave in the language of the text 'I find in him no fault at all.'

I. The first accusation, if you will turn to the chapter and read the thirtieth verse, was that he was A MALEFACTOR. 'They answered and said unto him, If he were not a malefactor, we would not have delivered him up unto thee.' He was said to be a factor, or doer of that which is evil; a person of such a mischievous life that he ought not to live.

Upon which we remark, first, that *it was a novel charge.* It was hot from their mint; for when he stood before Caiaphas nothing was said of any evil that he had *done*, but only of evil that he had spoken. They charged him with saying this and that, but not with doing any evil deed. The accusation of evil speaking had broken down, and they did not venture upon it a second time, because they knew very well that Pilate did not care what the man had said; all he would attend to would be some actual breach of law by act and deed. The Romans were a practical people, and so when Pilate led our Lord into the audience chamber he said to him, 'What hast thou *done?*' He did not say to him, 'What hast thou taught or preached?' but, 'What hast thou done?' For this reason, the priests brought forward this newly invented accusation and totally unfounded charge that he was a bad doer, which might mean little or much, as the hearer chose to interpret it – malice is seldom specific in its charges. The accusation of being a malefactor grew out of their malevolence, and not out of any action of our Lord's perfect life. One is surprised that even hate should be so blind as to assail his perfections. Whatever men may think of our Lord as a teacher, candour demands that they admire his example and award it the highest meed of honour.

Observe, the priests herein brought against our Lord *a charge which they did not attempt to sustain.* How craftily they evaded the task of supplying proof! They brought no witnesses, their suborned perjurers were left behind; they even forbore from specific charges, but the general statement that he was a malefactor was supported only by their reputation. 'If he were not a malefactor, we would not have delivered him up unto thee,' as much as to say, 'You must take it for granted that he is guilty, or we would not say so. Here is our high priest: can it be supposed that such a gem of an individual would bring a false accusation? We also are the chief priests and the scribes, and teachers of Israel: can it be imagined that persons of our station and sanctity could by any possibility have brought an innocent person before you to be condemned!' This style of argument I have heard even in these days: we are expected to give up the faith because scientists condemn it, and they are such eminent persons that we ought to accept their dicta without further delay. I confess I am not prepared to accept their infallibility any more than that which hails from Rome. The Roman governor was not to be overridden by priests, neither are we to be led by the nose by pretendedly learned men. 'If he were not a malefactor, we would not have delivered him up unto thee.' Oh, the hypocrisy of this speech! They had tried to bring witnesses, and no witness had been found. They had suborned false witnesses, but these had so differed in their testimony that the whole thing broke down. They, therefore, go upon another tack, and put their own names at the back of the indictment, as if that were quite enough, and enquiry need go no further. I think I see the scornful glance of Pilate as he bade them judge him themselves if that was their style of justice; as for him, he must hear an accusation or dismiss them to do their own pleasure if they dare. He knew that through envy they had brought Jesus unto him, and he loathed the hypocrites as he heard the wretched syllables sibillating from their sanctimonious lips.

They could not have sustained the charge, and so far they were wise in not attempting the impossible. They might be foolhardy enough to wrest his words, but they hesitated before the task of attacking his deeds. Before his awful holiness they were for the moment out of heart, and knew not what slander to invent. O Lord, we marvel that any men should find fault with thee, for thou art altogether lovely, and there is in thee no spot for falsehood to light upon. But I want to call your attention to this remarkable fact, that although this charge of being a malefactor was a grievous one, a trumped up one, and unsustained by any evidence, yet *it was never denied by the Lord Jesus Christ.* It was useless to deny it before the priests. He had already challenged them to find fault with his life, saying, 'I spake openly to the world; I ever taught in the synagogue, and in the temple, whither the Jews always resort; and in secret have I said nothing. Why askest thou me? ask them which heard me, what I have said unto them: behold, they know what I said.' His appeal had been unavailing, for it was as useless to argue with them as for a lamb to enter into controversy with a pack of wolves eager to devour. But there might have been some use, one would think, in his answering to Pilate, for Pilate was evidently very favourably impressed with his prisoner; and if the Saviour had deigned to give a full account of his life, and to prove that instead of being a malefactor he had gone about doing good, might he not have escaped? The answer is this: our Lord had come on earth on purpose to be the substitute for guilty men, and so when he was called a malefactor, although it was not a truthful charge, yet he patiently bore the shame of it, as it is written, 'He was numbered with the transgressors.' He was willing to stand in the transgressor's place, and when they put him there he did not stir from it. He is dumb; he openeth not his mouth. He says nothing because, though in him is no sin, he has taken our sin upon himself. The question that Pilate put, 'What hast thou done?' was one which Jesus might have grandly answered – 'What have I done? I have fed the hungry, I have healed the sick, I have raised the fallen, I have restored the dead. What have I done? I have lived a self-sacrificing life, caring nothing for myself or my own honour. I have been the vindicator of God and the friend of man. What have I done? Certainly nothing wherefore they could put me to death, but everything why they should accept me as their Leader and their Saviour.' We hear not a word of this. The exculpation would have been complete, but it was not spoken. He might have baffled his enemies as he had aforetime vanquished those who came to take him, so that they went back to their masters, saying, 'Never man spake like this man.' He might have cleared himself before the Roman procurator and by coming forth in triumph, he might have escaped from their teeth; but because he would stand in our stead, therefore when men imagined mischievous things against him he was as a deaf man, and as a dumb man he opened not his mouth. Let us adore and bless him for his gracious condescension, his matchless grace in standing in our stead.

Yet further, *our Lord willed that by being counted as a transgressor by Pilate he might die the death appointed for malefactors by the Roman law.* If the Jews had put our Lord to death for blasphemy, it would have been by stoning; but then, none of the prophecies that went before concerning the Messiah spoke of his being dashed to the ground by stones. The death ordained for him was crucifixion. John says in the eighteenth chapter at the thirty-second verse, 'That the saying of Jesus might be fulfilled, which he spake, signifying what death he should die.' What was that saying? Is it not the saying in the twelfth chapter of John's gospel at the thirty-second verse, 'I, if I be lifted up from the earth, will draw all men unto me. This he said, signifying what death he should die.' Being lifted up from the earth on the cross was death which could only come from the Romans; the Jews, as I have said before, executed men by stoning: therefore he must be condemned by the Romans that his own words may be fulfilled. He had spoken even more expressly in a passage recorded by Matthew, in the twentieth chapter at the seventeenth verse, where he had declared how he should die. 'And Jesus going up to Jerusalem took the twelve disciples apart in the way, and said unto them, Behold, we go up to Jerusalem, and the Son of man shall be betrayed unto the chief priests and unto the scribes, and they shall condemn him to death, and shall deliver him to the Gentiles to mock, and to scourge, and to crucify him: and the third day he shall rise again.' In order that the word which he had spoken might be fulfilled, our blessed Master refused to plead before Pilate anything in answer to the question, 'What hast thou done?' He stands as a transgressor, to die a transgressor's death; wherefore for ever blessed be his adorable name for his voluntary endurance of penalty for our sakes.

When I think of that word 'malefactor', another word leaps to my lips directly. Call him not malefactor, but BENEFACTOR. What a benefactor must he be who in order to benefit us allows himself to be branded as a 'malefactor'! Only think that he who at this moment sits in the centre of adoring angels should have been called 'malefactor'; that he from whose inexhaustible store of goodness all the saints in heaven and on earth are fed should yet be called 'malefactor'; that he who never thought of harm to men, but whose very soul is love, whose every word and thought has been kindness towards this fallen race, should yet be called 'malefactor'. O earth, how couldst thou bear so grave a lie against the infinite goodness of the Son of God! And yet, for ever blessed be his name, he does not hurl back the charge, for that would have been to ruin us. He meekly bears the scandal for our sakes.

Should not this sweeten every title of reproach that can ever fall upon us? What if they call us ill names! They called the Master of the house 'malefactor', can they call us anything worse? Shall we look for honour where our Captain found nothing but shame? Wherefore let it be our glory to bear shame and reproach for Jesus' sake. So much for the first accusation.

II. Secondly, when the priests and scribes found that merely calling him a malefactor was not sufficient, these wretched men changed their tactics, and, according to Luke, they charged him with setting up to be A KING. They said that he wrought sedition, that he forbade to pay tribute unto Caesar, and made himself out to be a king. These were three great lies, for Jesus had preached peace, and not sedition; his example was submission, not rebellion; his spirit was that of a servant, not that of a turbulent party leader. He had never said that men were not to pay tribute to Caesar; on the contrary, he had said, 'Render unto Caesar the things that are Caesar's,' and submitted himself to every ordinance of authority. He had never in their sense set himself up to be a king; if he had done so, many who were now his accusers might have been his partisans. The charge against Jesus of setting up to be a king in the sense in which they desired Pilate to understand them *was utterly false,* for when the multitude had been fed, they would have taken him and made him a king, but he hid himself. Nay, so far from wishing to be a king, when one said to him, 'Master, speak to my brother that he divide the inheritance with me,' he said, 'Who made me a judge or a divider over you?' He put aside any approach to interference with the reigning powers. His accusers must have known that if he had willed he had power at his back to have supported his claims, even as he said to Pilate, that, if he had been a king of a worldly dominion, his servants would have fought for him. His followers had been brave and courageous, and enthusiastic, and they would, no doubt, have given no end of trouble both to the Jews and to the Romans if their lender had claimed a temporal sovereignty. But our Lord had made Peter put up his sword into its sheath, and healed the wound which he had given. All his life long he had preached peace and love, and a kingdom which is righteousness and peace. He was no rival to Caesar, and they knew it.

And please to notice that this charge of Christ being a king *did not come from the governing power.* When Pilate asked our Lord, 'Art thou the King of the Jews?' our Saviour wisely replied, 'Sayest thou this of thyself, or did another tell thee it of me? Have you any reason to think that I am a leader of sedition? As the governor of this nation you have to watch carefully, for the people are seditious; have you ever seen or heard anything of me that looks like an attack on your authority? Have you anything of your own knowledge that would lead you to bring a charge against me?' Pilate, knowing nothing whatever against him, and indeed scorning the idea that he knew anything about the Jewish people, whom he detested, replied haughtily, 'Am I a Jew? Your own nation and your own rulers have brought this charge against you, not I.' A great point was gained when Pilate said this; the charge was shown to be a mere invention, since the eagle eye of the Roman procurator had never seen the slightest ground for it.

It was a frivolous charge on the very face of it. How could that harmless, forsaken man be a peril to Caesar? What had the Roman legions to fear from that solitary sufferer? He was too meek and pure to threaten warfare and strife in the domain of Tiberias. Look at him, and realize the absurdity of the situation. Moreover, it would seem a strange thing that the Jewish people should bring before the Roman governor their own king. Is this the way that subjects treat their monarchs? If he be a leader of sedition he does not seem to have succeeded with his countrymen, for the heads of the people are seeking his death. There could be upon the face of it no chance of danger whatever from rebellion which was so summarily put down by the Jews themselves. If they had not been besotted by their rage, they would themselves have shrunk from so absurd a position.

But yet I want you to note very carefully that *the Lord never denied this charge* in the sense in which he chose to understand it. He first explained what he meant by his being a king, and when he had explained it then he openly confessed that it was even so.

First, I say, *he explained what he meant by being a king,* and notice carefully that he did not explain it away. He said, 'My kingdom', and also when Pilate said, 'Art thou a king then?' he said, 'Thou sayest that I am a king.' He was there and then a real king, and he avowed it without reserve. We are constantly told that the kingdom of Christ is a spiritual kingdom, and this saying is true; but I would have you take heed that you do not spirit away his kingdom as if it were only a pious dream. Spiritual or not, the kingdom of Christ on earth is real and powerful. It is real none the less, but all the more, because it may fitly be called spiritual.

Jesus is even now a king. He said, 'I am a king.' Some say that his kingdom is not yet, but is reserved for the latter days; but I aver that he is a king today, and that even now Jehovah hath set him as king upon the holy hill of Zion. I bless God that he hath translated us 'Into the kingdom of his dear Son.' 'Thou art the king of glory, O Christ.' When I say, 'Thy kingdom come,' I do not mean that it may begin to be set up on earth, but that it may continue to be set up in new places, may be extended and grow, for Jesus has at this very moment a kingdom upon the face of the earth, and they that know the truth belong to it, and recognize him as the royal witness by whom the kingdom of truth has been founded and maintained.

You remember the remarkable saying which is attributed to Napoleon Bonaparte in his later days at St Helena: 'I have founded a kingdom by force, and it has passed away; but Jesus founded his empire upon love, and therefore it will last for ever.' Verily, Napoleon spoke the truth – Jesus, the right royal Jesus, is Master of innumerable hearts today. The world knoweth him not, but yet he has a kingdom in it which shall ere long break in pieces all other kingdoms. True and loyal hearts are to be found among the sons of men, and in them his name still wakes enthusiasm, so that for him they are prepared to live and die. Our Lord is every inch a king, he has his throne of grace, has his sceptre of truth, his officers who, like himself, witness to the truth, and his armies of warriors who wrestle not with flesh and blood, and use no carnal weapons, but yet go forth conquering and to conquer. Our Lord has his palace wherein he dwells, his chariot in which he rides, his revenues, though they be not treasures of gold and silver, and his pro-clamations, which are law in his church. His reigning power affects the destiny of the world at this present moment far more than the counsels of the five great powers: by the preaching of the truth his servants shape the ages, and set up and cast down the thrones of earth. There is no prince so powerful as Jesus, and no empire so mighty as the kingdom of heaven.

Our Lord also said that his kingdom came not from this world; for that, I take it, is the more correct translation of the passage 'My kingdom is not of this world.' It came not from this world; it is a substantial kingdom, but it did not spring from the same sources as the kingdoms of the world, neither is it supported, maintained, or increased by the same power as that which the kingdoms of the world depend upon. Christ's kingdom does not depend upon the force of arms: he would have his followers lay these weapons all aside. Christ's kingdom does not depend, as earthly kingdoms too often do, upon craft, policy, and duplicity. It used to be said that an ambassador was a gentleman who was sent abroad to lie for the good of his country, and I fear it might still describe full many an ambassador. What is the science of diplomacy but the art of deceit? When statesmen are thoroughly honest, and are guided by principle, they are generally suspected, and an outcry is raised that the interests of the country will be sacrificed. But there is no diplomacy in Christ's rule; everything like crooked policy is of the devil, and not of Christ. He comes to bear witness to the truth, and it is by the truth, not by force nor by craft, that his throne is established among the sons of men, and therefore it is not from this world.

To be a king is indeed so little wrong in the sight of Jesus that it is the ultimate purpose of his coming to earth. He came to save men, did he not? Yes, but still he says, 'For this purpose was I born, and for this cause came I into the world, that I should bear witness unto the truth;' which is another way of saying, 'that I might be a king.' This is his ultimatum. Christ is a teacher that he may be a king; Christ is an exemplar that he may be a king; Christ is a Saviour that he may be a king; this is the great end and object that he hath in his life, his death, his resurrection, and his second coming – that he may set up a kingdom among the sons of men to the glory of God. Oh that this great object of his mission might be furthered in our time, and consummated speedily in the long promised age of gold.

The Master tells us that the main force and power of his kingdom lies in the truth. He came to be a King, but where is his sceptre? The truth. Where is his sword? It cometh out of his mouth; he bears witness to the truth. Where are his soldiers? They are men of truth. Jesus Christ leads on a band of whom he says, 'And ye are my witnesses.' His kingdom consists in witnessing to the truth, and who are they that become his subjects? Why, those that are of the truth, men who, hearing the truth, know the joyful sound and accept it, and feel its power.

Dear hearers, let each one of us ask himself, 'Do I belong to his kingdom? Will I have this man to reign over me? Do I desire to get rid of everything in myself that is not true? Am I anxious to put down around me everything that is false and wicked? Do I wish to uphold God's laws, for they are truth? Do I desire to spread the principles of love and kindness, for they are truth? Am I willing to learn, and so become the disciple of the greatest of all teachers, and then, am I willing to bear witness to what I have learned, and so spread the sway of truth? If so, then I am of his kingdom. I know that I address many who desire in their hearts today that Christ and his truth may triumph, and they little mind what becomes of themselves. Let but his gospel spread and the principles of righteousness prevail; and as for us, let us live or die, it shall be a matter of small concern. O King, live for ever, and we shall find our life in thy life, and glory in promoting thy glory, world without end. Such a spirit is of the truth, and we may assure ourselves that Jesus is our King.

Our Lord having explained his meaning, confessed that he was a King. This is that to which Paul refers when he says, 'The Lord Jesus, who before Pontius Pilate witnessed a good confession.' He did not draw back and say, 'I am no King.' Pilate might have delivered him then; but he spake boldly concerning his blessed, mysterious, and wonderful kingdom, and therefore it was not possible that he should be set free. This, indeed, was his accusation written over his cross, 'This is Jesus the King of the Jews.'

Poor Pilate, he did not understand our Lord, even as the men of this world understand not the kingdom of Christ. He said to him, 'What is truth?' and without waiting for a reply he went out to the Jews. Ah, brethren, let us never ourselves deny that Jesus is a king; but we shall deny it if we do not live according to his bidding. Oh you that claim to be Christ's, but do not live according to Christ's laws, you practically deny that he is a king. I dread the men who say, 'We believe, and therefore we are saved,' and then do not live in holiness; for these divide our Lord's offices, setting up his priesthood and denying his kingship. Half a Christ is no Christ – a Christ who is a priest but never a king is not the Christ of God. Oh brethren, live as those who feel that every word of Jesus is law, and that you must do what he bids you, as he bids you, and because he bids you; and so let all men know that unto you Jesus is both Lord and God.

III. I conclude by noticing THE ACQUITTAL which Pilate gave to our Lord Jesus. He had heard the charge of being a malefactor, to which the prisoner pleaded nothing; he had heard the charge of his being a king, which the prisoner had most satisfactorily explained; and now Pilate coming out to the people said, 'I find in him no fault at all.' Pilate, thou hast well spoken. Thy verdict is typical of the verdict of all who have ever *examined* Christ. Some have examined him with an unfriendly eye, but in proportion as they have been candid in the observation of facts, they have been struck with his life and spirit. It is a very rare thing to hear even the infidel rail at the character of Jesus; in fact, some of the foremost sceptics as to our Lord's teaching have been remarkably impressed with admiration of his life. No character like that of Jesus is to be seen in history, nay not even in romance. If anyone says the four gospel are forgeries, let him try to write a fifth, which shall be like the other four. Why, you cannot add an incident to the life of Christ; its details are unique; the fancy cannot imagine a fresh incident which could be safely joined on to that which is recorded. Every critic would cry out, 'This is not genuine.' The life of Jesus is a roll of cloth of gold, of the manufacture of which the art is utterly lost. His spotless character stands alone and by itself, and all true critics are compelled to say they find no fault at all in him.

Let me add that this verdict of Pilate is the verdict of all that have ever *associated* with Christ. One disciple who was with Christ betrayed him, but he spoke nothing against him. Nay, the last witness of Judas before he hanged himself was this, 'I have sinned in that I have betrayed the innocent blood.' If there had been a fault in Jesus, the traitor would have spied it out; his unquiet conscience would have been glad enough to find therein a sedative, but even he was compelled to say, 'I have betrayed the innocent blood.' 'Which of you convinceth me of sin?' is the challenge of Jesus, to which there is no reply.

Some of us have *lived with Christ spiritually.* In the course of his providence he has brought some of us very low by sickness, or by bereavement, or loss. Everyone saved by our Lord has come under the discipline of his house, for 'whom the Lord loveth he chasteneth, and scourgeth every son whom he receiveth.' Now, what is the verdict of all here present who know Jesus, our king? For my part, I find no fault at all in him. He is everything that is lovely. He is all my salvation and all my desire. Do you not think that out of the millions of Christians who have lived hoping in Christ some one would have told us if it is his habit to disappoint his people? Out of so many believers who dwell with him surely some one or other of them, when they came to die, would have told us if he is not all that he professes to be. Would not some one or other have confessed, 'I trusted in Christ and he has not de-livered me; it is all a delusion'? Surely, out of the many we have seen depart we should have found some one or two that would have let out the secret, and have said, 'He is a deceiver. He cannot save, he cannot help, he cannot deliver.' But never one dying believer throughout the ages has spoken ill of him, but all have said, 'We find no fault at all in him.'

Mark you, that will be the verdict of everyone among you all. If any of you reject Christ, when you shall stand at his judgment seat to be condemned because you believe not on him, and when that withering word, 'Depart, ye cursed!' shall consign you to your everlasting portion, you shall then be obliged to say, 'I find no fault at all in *him*.' There was no failure in his blood, the failure was in my want of faith; no failure in his Spirit – the failure was in my obstinate will; no failure in his promise – the failure was that I would not receive him; there was no fault at all in him. He never spurned me. He never refused to hear my prayers. If my Sabbaths were wasted, it was no fault of his; if I defied the gospel, it was no fault of his; if I have perished, my blood is at my own door. I find no fault at all in him.' From all parts of creation shall go up one general attestation to his perfection. Heaven and earth and hell shall all join the common verdict, 'We find no fault at all in him.'

I will send you away when I give you three practical words to think of. The first is this: *beware of an external religion*, for the men that called Jesus malefactor and falsely accused him were very religious people, and would not go into Pilate's hall for fear of polluting themselves. They were strong in rituals, but weak in morals. None are so inveterate against the principles of the gospel as those whose religion consists in form and ceremony but does not affect their hearts. I charge you rend your hearts and not your garments. Follow Christ spiritually; follow Christ in your very souls, or else sacraments will be your ruin, and even in trying to keep yourselves from ceremonial defilement you will be defiling yourselves with hypocrisy.

The next thing is to charge you, dear friends, and to charge myself also, to *shun all proud worldliness like that of Pilate.* Pilate treats the whole matter cavalierly; he is a proud and haughty Roman; he hates the people whom he governs, and though he has a conscience, and at the first he shows a tenderness towards his prisoner, yet his chief end and aim was to keep his office and amass money, and therefore innocent blood must be spilt. He must please the Jews, even if he murder the 'Just One'. This selfish worldliness in which a man makes his gold and himself his god always treats religion with contempt. The man minds the main chance, and sneeringly cries, 'What is truth?' He knows what money is and what power is, but what is truth? It is a dream, a folly to him, and he despises it. There are persons around us now, clever time-serving men, with grand notions of their own abilities, and to them Jesus and his gospel are matters for old women, servant girls, and what they call a Puritan crew. Such topics are not for gentlemen of thought, culture, and understanding, like their high and mighty selves. 'What is truth?' say they. They are rather favourably inclined to religion, that is to say, they do not persecute, but they despise, which in some respects is worse. They say, 'We are agnostics; we have no particular views; we are large-hearted, and let every man think as he chooses, but still there is nothing in it; it is all matter of opinion. One man says this is the truth, and another says that is the truth, and how are we to know? The fact is, there is no such thing as fixed truth at all.

> For differing creeds let graceless zealots fight;
> He can't be wrong whose life is in the right.

This is this great man's conclusion of the matter, and yet it so happens that this gentleman's life is not in the right at all, and therefore on his own showing he has not much joy of his pretty rhyme. I think I see him as he turns on his heel with, 'What is truth?' Let him be a warning to you. Come not near to such arrogant trifling. Be always foolish enough to be willing to judge candidly. Be so little clever as to be willing still to learn. Be so little certain of your own infallibility that you will at least hear reason, and will enquire whether these things be so. Alas, I fear that through worldly pride many will have it said of them, as it is said of the Roman governor every day in the creed: 'Suffered under Pontius Pilate'. Oh, how many times has Christ suffered under just such people as Pontius Pilate!

Last of all, *let us all submit ourselves to Jesus our King.* Wayworn and weary, emaciated and broken down, with his face more marred than that of any man, yet let us bow before him and say, 'All hail, thou King of the Jews. Thou art our King for ever and ever.' If we are willing thus to acknowledge him as our King in his shame and derision, he will by-and-by honour us when he cometh in the glory of the Father, and all his holy angels with him. Then shall he cause it to be seen that he hath made us who follow him to be kings and priests unto God, and we shall reign with him for ever and ever. Amen.

I I

BARABBAS PREFERRED TO JESUS[1]

Then cried they all again, saying,
Not this man, but Barabbas.
Now Barabbas was a robber.
JOHN 18:40

THE CUSTOM of delivering a prisoner upon the day of the Passover was intended no doubt as an act of grace on the part of the Roman authorities towards the Jews, and by the Jews it may have been accepted as a significant compliment to their Passover. Since on that day they themselves were delivered out of the land of Egypt, they may have thought it to be most fitting that some imprisoned person should obtain his liberty. There was no warrant however in Scripture for this, it was never commanded by God, and it must have had a very injurious effect upon public justice, that the ruling authority should discharge a criminal, some one quite irrespective of his crimes or of his repentance; letting him loose upon society, simply and only because a certain day must be celebrated in a peculiar manner. Since some one prisoner must be delivered on the paschal day, Pilate thinks that he has now an opportunity of allowing the Saviour to escape without at all compromising his character with the authorities at Rome. He asks the people which of the two they will prefer, a notorious thief then in custody, or the Saviour. It is probable that Barabbas had been up, till that moment, obnoxious to the crowd; and yet,

[1] Sermon No. 595. Preached at the Metropolitan Tabernacle on Sunday morning, 16 October 1864.

notwithstanding his former unpopularity – the multitude, instigated by the priests, forget all his faults, and prefer him to the Saviour. Who Barabbas was, we cannot exactly tell. His name, as you in a moment will understand, even if you have not the slightest acquaintance with Hebrew, signifies 'his father's son', '*Bar*' signifying 'son', as when Peter is called Simon Bar-jonas, son of Jonas; the other part of his name '*Abbas*', signifying 'father' – 'abbas' being the word which we use in our filial aspirations, 'Abba Father'. Barabbas, then, is the 'son of his father'; and some mysticists think that there is an imputation here, that he was particularly and specially a son of Satan. Others conjecture that it was an endearing name, and was given him because he was his father's darling, an indulged child; his father's boy, as we say; and these writers add that indulged children often turn out to be imitators of Barabbas, and are the most likely persons to become injurious to their country, griefs to their parents, and curses to all about them.

If it be so, taken in connection with the case of Absalom, and especially of Eli's sons, it is a warning to parents that they err not in excessive indulgence of their children. Barabbas appears to have committed three crimes at the least: he was imprisoned for murder, for sedition, and for felony – a sorry combination of offences, certainly; we may well pity the sire of such a son. This wretch is brought out and set in competition with Christ. The multitude are appealed to. Pilate thinks that from the sense of shame they really cannot possibly prefer Barabbas; but they are so bloodthirsty against the Saviour, and are so moved by the priests, that with one consent – there does not appear to have been a single objecting voice, nor one hand held up to the contrary – with a marvellous unanimity of vice, they cry, 'Not this man, but Barabbas,' though they must have known, since he was a *notable* well-known offender, that Barabbas was a murderer, a felon, and a traitor.

This fact is very significant. There is more teaching in it than at first sight we might imagine. Have we not here, first of all, in this act of the deliverance of the sinner and the binding of the innocent, a sort of type of that great work which is accomplished by the death of our Saviour? You and I may fairly take our stand by the side of Barabbas. We have robbed God of his glory; we have been seditious traitors against the government of heaven: if he who hateth his brother be a murderer, we also have been guilty of that sin. Here we stand before the judgment-seat; the Prince of Life is bound for us and we are suffered to go free. The Lord delivers us and acquits us, while the Saviour, without spot or blemish, or shadow of a fault, is led forth to crucifixion. Two birds were taken in the rite of the cleansing of a leper. The one bird was killed, and its blood was poured into a basin; the other bird was dipped in this blood, and then, with its wings all crimson, it was set free to fly into the open field. The bird slain well pictures the Saviour, and every soul that has by faith been dipped in his blood, flies upward towards heaven singing sweetly in joyous liberty, owing its life and its liberty entirely to him who was slain. It comes to this, Barabbas must die or Christ must die; you the sinner must perish, or Christ Immanuel, the Immaculate, must die. He dies that we may be delivered.

Oh! have we all a participation in such a deliverance today? And though we have been robbers, traitors, and murderers yet can we rejoice that Christ has delivered us from the curse of the law, having been made a curse for us?

The transaction has yet another voice. This episode in the Saviour's history shows that in the judgment of the people, Jesus Christ was a greater offender than Barabbas; and, for once, I may venture to say, that *vox populi* (the voice of the people), which in itself was a most infamous injustice, if it be read in the light of the imputation of our sins to Christ, was *vox Dei* (the voice of God). Christ, as he stood covered with his people's sins, had more sin laid upon him than that which rested upon Barabbas. In him was no sin; he was altogether incapable of becoming a sinner: holy, harmless, and undefiled is Christ Jesus, but be takes the whole load of his people's guilt upon himself by imputation, and as Jehovah looks upon him, he sees more guilt lying upon the Saviour, than even upon this atrocious sinner, Barabbas.

Barabbas goes free – innocent – in comparison with the tremendous weight which rests upon the Saviour. Think, beloved, then, how low your Lord and Master stooped to be thus *numbered with the transgressors*. Watts has put it strongly, but, I think, none too strongly –

> His honour and his breath
> Were taken both away,
> Join'd with the wicked in his death,
> And made as vile as they.

He was so in the estimation of the people, and before the bar of justice, for the sins of the whole company of the faithful were made to meet upon him. 'The Lord hath laid upon him the iniquity of us all.' What that iniquity must have been, no heart can conceive, much less can any tongue tell. Measure it by the griefs he bore, and then, if you can guess what these were, you can form some idea of what must have been the guilt which sunk him lower before the bar of justice than even Barabbas himself. Oh! what conde-scension is here! The just One dies for the unjust. He bears the sin of many, and makes intercession for the transgressors.

Yet, again, there seems to me to be a third lesson, before I come to that which I want to enforce from the text. Our Saviour knew that his disciples would in all ages be hated by the world far more than outward sinners. Full often the world has been more willing to put up with murderers, thieves, and drunkards, than with Christians; and it has fallen to the lot of some of the best and most holy of men to be so slandered and abused that their names have been cast out as evil, scarcely worthy to be written in the same list with criminals. Now, 'Christ has sanctified these sufferings of his people from the slander of their enemies, by bearing just such sufferings himself, so that, my brethren, if you or I should find ourselves charged with crimes which we abhor, if our heart should be ready to burst under the accumulation of slanderous venom, let us lift up our head and feel that in all this we have a comrade who has true fellowship with us, even the Lord Jesus Christ, who was rejected when Barabbas was selected. Expect no better treatment than your Master. Remember that the disciple is not above his Lord. If they have called the Master of the house Beelzebub, much more will they call them of his household; and if they prefer the murderer to Christ, the day may not be distant when they will prefer even a murderer to you.

These things seem to me to lie upon the surface; I now come to our more immediate subject. First, we shall consider *the sin as it stands in the Evangelical history;* secondly, we shall observe that *this is the sin, of the whole world;* thirdly, that *this sin we ourselves were guilty of before conversion;* and fourthly, that *this is, we fear, the sin of very many persons who are here this morning:* we shall talk with them and expostulate, praying that the Spirit of God may change their hearts and lead them to accept the Saviour.

I. A few minutes may be profitably spent in CONSIDERING, THEN, THE SIN AS WE FIND IT IN THIS HISTORY.

They preferred Barabbas to Christ. The sin will be more clearly seen if we remember that *the Saviour had done no ill.* No law, either of God or man, had he broken. He might truly have used the words of Samuel – 'Behold, here I am: witness against me before the Lord, and before his anointed: whose ox have I taken? or whose ass have I taken? or whom have I defrauded? whom have I oppressed? or of whose hand have I received any bribe to blind mine eyes therewith? and I will restore it you.' Out of that whole assembled crowd there was not one who would have had the presumption to accuse the Saviour of having done him damage. So far from this, they could but acknowledge that *he had even conferred great temporal blessings upon them.* O ravening multitude, has he not fed you when you were hungry? Did he not multiply the loaves and fishes for you? Did he not heal your lepers with his touch? cast out devils from your sons and daughters? raise up you paralytics? give sight to your blind, and open the ears of your deaf? For which of these good works do ye conspire to kill him? Among that assembled multitude, there were doubtless some who owed to him priceless boons, and yet, though all of them were his debtors if they had known it, they clamour against him as though he were the worst trouble of their lives, a pest and a pestilence to the place where he dwelt. *Was it his teaching that they complained of?* Wherein did his teaching offend against morality? Wherein against the best interests of man? If you observe the teaching of Christ there was never any like it, even judged of by how far it would subserve human welfare. Here was the sum and substance of his doctrine, 'Thou shalt love the Lord thy God with all thy heart, and thy neighbour as thyself.' His precepts were of the mildest form. Did he bid them draw the sword and expel the Roman, or ride on in a ruthless career of carnage, and rapine? Did he stimulate them to let loose their unbridled passions? Did he tell them to seek first of all their own advantage and not to care for their neighbour's weal? Nay, every righteous state must own him to be its best pillar, and the commonwealth of manhood must acknowledge him to be its conservator; and yet, for all this, there they are, hounded on by their priests, seeking his blood, and crying, 'Let him be crucified! let him be crucified!' *His whole intent evidently was their good.* What did he preach for? No selfish motive could have been urged. Foxes had holes, and the birds of the air had nests, but he had not where to lay his head. The charity of a few of his disciples alone kept him from absolute starvation. Cold mountains and the midnight air witnessed the fervour of his lonely prayers for the multitudes who now are hating him. He lived for others: they could see this; they could not have observed him during the three years of his ministry without saying, 'Never lived there such an unselfish soul as this;' they must have known, the most of them, and the rest might have known, had they enquired ever so little, that he had no object whatever in being here on earth, except that of seeking the good of men.

For which of these things do they clamour that he may be crucified? For which of his good works, for which of his generous words, for which of his holy deeds will they fasten his hands to the wood, and his feet to the tree? With unreasonable hatred, with senseless cruelty, they only answer to the question of Pilate, 'Why, what evil hath he done?' 'Let him be crucified! let him be crucified!' The true reason of their hate, no doubt, lay in the natural hatred of all men to perfect goodness. Man feels that the presence of goodness is a silent witness against his own sin, and therefore he longs to get rid of it. To be too holy in the judgment of men is a great crime, for it rebukes their sin. If the holy man has not the power of words, yet his life is one loud witness-bearing for God against the sins of his creatures. This inconvenient protesting led the wicked to desire the death of the holy and just One. Besides, the priests were at their backs. It is a sad and lamentable thing, but it is often the case that the people are better than their religious teachers. At the present moment the laity of the Church of

England, as a whole, have honest consciences, and would have their Prayer Book revised tomorrow if their voices could be heard. But their clerics care far too little about truth, and are not very particular how they swear, or with whom they associate. So long as their Church can be kept together, Father Ignatius shall be heard in their assemblies, although Christ's call to the Church to purify herself, awakens only resentment and ill-will. No matter that the throats of certain clergymen were exercised in hissing for a moment at the apparition of the bold Anglican monk, he is one of themselves, a brother of their own order, and their Church is responsible for all that he does. Let them come out and separate themselves, and then we shall know that they abhor this modern popery; but so long as they sit in the same assembly and are members of the same Church, the sin is theirs, and we shall not cease to denounce both it and them. If Evangelical clergymen remain in communion with Papists, now that they come out in their full colours, I will cease to say that they violate their consciences, but I shall doubt whether they have any consciences at all.

Brethren, it is still the case that the people are better than their teachers. This people would not have crucified Christ had not the clergy of the day, the priests, the endowed ministers, cried out, 'Let him be crucified!' He was the Dissenter, the heretic, schismatic, the troubler in Israel. He it was who cried aloud against the faults of their Establishment. He it was who could not be put down, the *ignorant* man from Galilee, who would continue to clamour against them, the mischief-maker, and therefore 'Let him be crucified! Let him be crucified!' Anything is good enough for the man who talks about reform, and advocates changes in established rules.' No doubt bribery also was used in this case. Had not Rabbi Simon paid the multitude? Was there not a hope of some feast after the Passover was over to those who would use their throats against the Saviour? Beside, there was the multitude going that way; and so if any had compassion they held their tongue. Often they say that 'Discretion is the better part of valour;' and truly there must be many valorous men, for they have much of valour's better part, discretion. If they did not join in the shout, yet at least they would not incommode the others, and so there was but one cry, 'Away with him! away with him! It is not fit that he should live.' What concentrated scorn there is this fortieth verse. It is not 'this Jesus', they would not foul their mouths with his name, but this *fellow* – 'this devil', if you will. To Barabbas they give the respect of mentioning his name; but 'this . . .' whom they hate so much, they will not even stoop to mention. We have looked, then, at this great sin as it stands in the history.

II. But now let us look, in the second place, AT THIS INCIDENT AS SETTING FORTH THE SIN WHICH HAS BEEN THE GUILT OF THE WORLD IN ALL AGES, AND WHICH IS THE WORLD'S GUILT NOW.

When the apostles went forth to preach the gospel, and the truth had spread through many countries, there were severe edicts passed by the Roman Emperors. Against whom were these edicts framed? Against the foul offenders of that day? It is well known that the whole Roman Empire was infested with vices such as the cheek of modesty would blush to hear named. The first chapter of the Epistle to the Romans is a most graphic picture of the state of society throughout the entire Roman dominions. When severe laws were framed, why were they not proclaimed against these atrocious vices? It is scarcely fit that men should go unpunished who are guilty of crimes such as the Apostle Paul has mentioned, but I find no edicts against these things – I find that they were borne with and scarcely mentioned with censure; but burning, dragging at the heels of wild horses, the sword, imprisonment, tortures of every kind, were used against whom think you? Against the innocent, humble followers of Christ, who, so far from defending themselves, were willing to suffer all these things, and presented themselves like sheep at the shambles, willing to endure the butcher's knife. The cry of the world, under the persecutions of Imperial Rome, was 'Not Christ, but Sodomites and murderers, and thieves – we will bear with any of these, but not with Christ; away with his followers from the earth.'

Then the world changed its tactics; it became nominally Christian, and Antichrist came forth in all its blasphemous glory. The Pope of Rome put on the triple crown, and called himself the Vicar of Christ; then came in the abomination of the worship of saints, angels, images, and pictures; then came the mass, and I know not what, of detestable error; and what did the world say? 'Popery for ever!' Down went every knee, and every head bowed before the sovereign representative of Peter at Rome. The Church of Rome was equal in sin to Barabbas; nay, I do but compliment Barabbas when I mention him in the same breath with many of the popes, for their character was foul and black right through and through, till even those who superstitiously looked upon them as infallible in their office, could not defend their personal characters. The world chose the harlot of Rome, and she who was drunk with the wine of her abominations had every eye to gaze upon her with admiration, while Christ's gospel was forgotten, buried in a few old books, and almost extinguished in darkness.

Since that day the world has changed its tactics yet again; in many parts of the earth Protestantism is openly acknowledged, and the gospel is preached, but what then? Then comes in Satan, and another Barabbas, the Barabbas of mere ceremonialism, and mere attendance at a place of worship is set up. 'Yes, we are orthodox; so orthodox, so sound. Yes, we are religious, strictly religious; we attend our meeting-house, or go to our church. We are never absent. We attend every form, but we have no vital godliness; we have not been born again; we have not passed from death unto life.'

However, this will do; so long as we are as good as our neighbours, and keep the outward rite, the inward does not matter. This which is a foul robbery of God's glory, this which murders men's souls, is the Barabbas of the present age. An outward name to live is set up, and is received by those who are dead; and many of you now present are quite easy and content, though you have never felt the quickening Spirit of God: though you have never been washed in the atoning blood, yet you are satisfied because you take a seat in some place of worship; you give your guinea, your donation to an hospital, or your subscription to a good object, forgetting and not caring to remember that all the making clean of the outside of the cup and the platter will never avail, unless the inward nature be renewed by the Spirit of the living God. This is the great Barabbas of the present age, and men prefer it before the Saviour.

That this is true, that the world really loves sin better than Christ, I think I could prove clearly enough by one simple fact. You have observed sometimes Christian men inconsistent, have you not? The inconsistency was nothing very great, if you had judged them according to ordinary rules of conduct. But you are well aware that a worldly man might commit any sin he liked, without much censure; but if the Christian man commits ever so little, then hands are held up, and the whole world cries, 'Shame!' I do not want to have that altered, but I do want just to say this: 'There is Mr So-and-So, who is known to live a fast, wicked, dissipated life; well, I do not see that he is universally avoided and reprobated, but on the contrary, he is tolerated by most, and admired by some.' But suppose a Christian man, a well-known professor, to have committed some fault which, compared with this, were not worth mentioning, and what is done? 'Oh! publish it! publish it! Have you heard what Mr So-and-So did? have you heard of this hypocrite's transgression?' 'Well, what was it?' You look at it: 'Well, it is wrong, it is very wrong, but compared with what you say about it is nothing at all.'

The world therefore shows by the difference between the way in which it judges the professedly religious man, and that with which it judges its own, that it really can tolerate the most abandoned, but cannot tolerate the Christian. Of course, the Christian never will be altogether free from imperfections; the world's enmity is not against the Christian's imperfections evidently, because they will tolerate greater imperfections in others; the objection must therefore be against the man, against the profession which he has taken up, and the course which he desires to follow. Watch carefully, beloved, that ye give them no opportunity; but when ye see that the slightest mistake is laid hold of and exaggerated, in this you see a clear evidence that the world prefers Barabbas to the followers of the Lord Jesus Christ. Now the world will change its various modes of dealing, but it will never love the church better than it does now. We do not expect to see the world lifted up to become more and more absorbed into the church, The union of the world with the church was never the object of our religion. The object of Christ is to gather to himself a people from among men; it is not the lifting up of all, but the calling out of the some, the making of men to differ, the manifestation of his special and discriminating grace, the gathering together of a people whom he has formed for himself. In this process morality is promoted, men are civilised and improved, but this is only indirectly God's object, and not his immediate end; the immediate end of the gospel being the salvation of the people whom he has ordained unto eternal life, and who, therefore, in due season arc led to believe in him. The world, to the end of the chapter, will be as much at enmity with true believers as ever it was. Because 'ye are not of the world, therefore the world hateth you,' this will be as true when Christ shall come as at the present moment. Let us expect it; and when we meet with scorn and persecution, let us not be surprised as though some strange thing had happened unto us.

III. I come in the third place, and O for some assistance from on high, to observe that THE SIN OF PREFERRING BARABBAS TO CHRIST WAS THE SIN OF EVERY ONE OF US BEFORE OUR CONVERSION.

Will you turn over the leaves of your diary, now, dear friends, or fly upon the wings of memory to the hole of the pit whence you were digged. Did you not, O you who live close to Christ, did you not once despise him? What company did you like best? Was it not that of the frivolous, if not that of the profane? When you sat with God's people, their talk was very tedious; if they spoke of divine realities, and of experimental subjects, you did not understand them, you felt them to be troublesome. I can look back upon some whom I know now to be most venerable believers, whom I thought to be a gross nuisance when I heard them talk of the things of God. What were our thoughts about? When we had time for thinking, what were our favourite themes? Not much did we meditate upon eternity; not much upon him who came to deliver us from the misery of hell's torments, Brethren, his great love wherewith he loved us was never laid to heart by us as it should have been; nay, if we read the story of the crucifixion, it had no more effect upon our mind than a common tale. We knew not the beauties of Christ; we thought of any trifle sooner than of him. And what were our pleasures? When we had what we called a day's enjoyment, where did we seek it? At the foot of the cross? In the service of the Saviour? In communion with him? Far from it; the further we could remove from godly associations the better pleased we were. Some of us have to confess with shame that we were never more in our element than when we were without a conscience, when conscience ceased to accuse us and we could plunge into sin with riot. What was our reading then? any book sooner than the Bible: and if there had lain in our way anything that would have exalted Christ and extolled him in our understandings, we should have put by the book as much too dry to please us. Any three-volume heap of nonsense, any light literature; nay, perhaps, even worse would have delighted our eye and our heart; but thoughts of *his* eternal delight towards us – thoughts of his matchless passion and his glory now in heaven, never came across our minds, nor would we endure those who would have led us to such meditations. What were our aspirations then? We were looking after business, aiming at growing rich, famous for learning or admired for ability. Self was what we lived for. If we had some regard for others, and some desire to benefit our race, yet self was at the bottom of it all.

We did not live for God – we could not honestly say, as we woke in the morning, 'I hope to live for God today;' at night, we could not look back upon the day, and say, 'We have this day served God.' He was not in all our thoughts. Where did we spend our best praise? Did we praise Christ? No; we praised cleverness, and when it was in association with sin, we praised it none the less. We admired those who could most fully minister to our own fleshly delights, and felt the greatest love to those who did us the worst injury. Is not this our confession as we review the past? Have I not read the very history of your life? I know I have of my own. Alas! for those dark days, in which our besotted soul went after any evil, but would not follow after Christ. It would have been the same today with us, if almighty grace had not made the difference. We may as well expect the river to cease to run to the sea, as expect the natural man to turn from the current of his sins. As well might we expect fire to become water, or water to become fire, as for the unrenewed heart ever to love Christ. It was mighty grace which made us to seek the Saviour. And as we look back upon our past lives, it must be with mingled feelings of gratitude for the change, and of sorrow that we should have been so grossly foolish as to have chosen Barabbas, and have said of the Saviour, 'Let him be crucified!'

IV. And now I shall come to the closing part of the sermon, which is THAT THERE ARE DOUBTLESS MANY HERE WHO THIS DAY PREFER BARABBAS TO OUR LORD JESUS CHRIST.

Let me first state your case, dear friends. I would describe it honestly, but at the same time so describe it that you will see your sin in it; and while I am doing so, my object will be to expostulate with you, if haply the Lord may change your will. There are many here, I fear, who prefer sin to Christ. I may say, without making a guess, I know that there are those here who would long ago have been followers of Christ, but that they preferred *drunkenness*. It is not often, it is not every day, it is not even every week, but there are occasions when they feel as if they must go into company, and as a sure result they return home intoxicated. They are ashamed of themselves – they have expressed as much as that; they have even gone so far as to pray to God for grace to overcome their habit; but after being the subject of convictions for years, they have hitherto made no advance. It did seem once as if they had conquered it. For a long time there was an abstinence from the fault, but they have gone back to their folly. They have preferred the bestial degrading vice – shall I say bestial? I insult the beasts, for they are not guilty of such a vice as this – they prefer this degrading vice to Christ Jesus. There stands drunkenness, I see it mirrored before me with all its folly, its witlessness, its greed and filth; but the man chooses all that, and though he has known by head knowledge something concerning the beauty and excellency of Christ, he virtually says of Jesus, 'Not this man, but drunkenness.'

Then there are other cases, where a favourite *lust* reigns supreme in their hearts. The men know the evil of the sin, and they have good cause to know it; they know also something of the sweetness of religion, for they are never happier than when they come up with God's people; and they go home sometimes from a solemn sermon, especially if it touches their vice, and they feel, 'God has spoken to my soul today, and I am brought to a standstill.' But for all that, the temptation comes again, and they fall as they have fallen before. I am afraid there are some of you whom no arguments will ever move; you have become so set on this mischief, that it will be your eternal ruin. But oh! think you, how will this look when you are in hell – 'I preferred that foul Barabbas of lust to the beauties and perfections of the Saviour, who came into the world to seek and to save that which was lost!' and yet this is the ease, not of some, but of a great multitude who listen to the gospel, and yet prefer sin to its saving power.

There may be some here, too, of another class, who prefer *gain*. It has come to this: if they become truly the Lord's people, they cannot do in trade what they now think their trade requires them to do; if they become really and genuinely believers, they must of course become honest, but their trade would not pay, they say, if it were conducted upon honest principles; or it is such a trade, and there are some few such, as ought not to be conducted at all, much less by Christians. Here comes the turning point. Shall I take the gold, or shall I take Christ? True, it is cankered gold, and gold on which a curse must come. It is the fool's pence; may be it is gain that is extorted from the miseries of the poor; money that would not ever stand the light because it is not fairly come by; money that will burn its way right through your souls when you get upon your deathbeds; but yet men who love the world, say, 'No, not Christ, give me a full purse, and away with Christ.' Others, less base or less honest, cry, 'We know his excellence, we wish we could have him, but we cannot have him on terms which involve the renunciation of our dearly beloved gain.' 'Not this man, but Barabbas.'

Others say, 'I fain would be a Christian, but then I should *lose so many of my acquaintances and friends.* For the matter of what it comes to, my friends are not much good to me; they are such friends as are fondest when I have most money to spend with them; they are friends who praise me most when I am oftenest at the alehouse, when I am seen plunging deepest into their vices. 'I know they do me mischief, but,' says the man, 'I could not venture to oppose them. One of them has such a glib tongue, and he can make such telling jokes, I could not bear to have him down upon me; and there is another, I have heard him give Christians such stinging names, and point at their faults in such a sarcastic manner, I could not run the gauntlet of his tongue; and therefore, though I fain would be a Christian, yet I will not.' That is the way you prefer to be a serf, a slave to the tongue of the scorner, sooner than be a free man, and take up the cross and follow Christ. You prefer, I say, not merely by way of allegory, but as matter of fact, you prefer Barabbas to the Lord Jesus Christ.

I might thus multiply instances, but the same principle runs through them all. If anything whatever keeps you back from giving your heart to the Lord Jesus Christ, you are guilty of setting up an opposition candidate to Christ in your soul, and you are choosing 'not this man, but Barabbas'.

Let me occupy a few minutes with pleading Christ's cause with you. Why is it that you reject Christ? Are you not conscious of the many good things which you receive from him? You would have been dead if it had not been for him; nay, worse than that, you would have been in hell. God has sharpened the great axe; justice, like a stern woodman, stood with the axe uplifted, ready to cut you down as a cumberer of the ground. A hand was seen stopping the arm of the avenger. and a voice was heard saying, 'Let it alone, till I dig about it and dung it.' Who was it that appeared just then in your moment of extremity? It was no other than that Christ, of whom you think so little that you prefer drunkenness or vice to him! You are this day in the house of God, listening to a discourse which I hope is sent from him. You might have been in hell – think one moment of that – shut out from hope, enduring in body and soul unutterable pangs. That you are not there, should make you love and bless him, who has said, 'Deliver him from going down into the pit.' Why will you prefer your own gain and self-indulgence to that blessed One to whom you owe so much. Common gratitude should make you deny yourself something for him who denied himself so much that he might bless you.

Do I hear you say that you cannot follow Christ, because his precepts are too severe? In what respect are they too severe? If you yourself were set to judge them, what is the point with which you would find fault? They deny you your sins – say, they deny you your miseries. They do not permit you, in fact, to ruin yourself. There is no precept of Christ which is not for your good, and there is nothing which he forbids you which he does not forbid on the

principle that it would harm you to indulge in it. But suppose
Christ's precepts to be ever so stern, is it not better that you should
put up with them than be ruined? The soldier submits implicitly
to the captain's command, because he knows that without discipline there can be no victory, and the whole army may be cut in
pieces if there be a want of order. When the sailor has risked his
life to penetrate through the thick ice of the north, we find him
consenting to all the orders and regulations of authority, and bearing all the hardships of the adventure, because he is prompted by
the desire of assisting in a great discovery, or stimulated by a large
reward. And surely the little self-denials which Christ calls us to
will be abundantly recompensed by the reward he offers; and when
the soul and its eternal interests are at stake, we may well put up
with these temporary inconveniences if we may inherit eternal life.
I think I hear you say that you would be a Christian, but there is
no happiness in it. I would not tell you a falsehood on this point, I
would speak the truth if it were so, but I do solemnly declare that
there is more joy in the Christian life than there is in any other
form of life; that if I had to die like a dog, and there were no hereafter, I would prefer to be a Christian. You shall appeal to the very
poorest among us, to those who are most sick and most despised,
and they will tell you the same. There is not an old country woman
shivering in her old ragged red cloak over a handful of fire, full of
rheumatism, with an empty cupboard and an aged body, who
would change with the very highest and greatest of you if she had
to give up her religion; no, she would tell you that her Redeemer
was a greater comfort to her than all the luxuries which could be
heaped upon the table of Dives. You make a mistake when you
dream that my Master does not make his disciples blessed; they
are a blessed people who put their trust in Christ.

Still I think I hear you say, 'Yes, this is all very well, but still I
prefer *present* pleasure.' Dost thou not in this talk like a child;
nay, like a fool, for what is present pleasure? How long does that
word 'present' last? If thou couldst have ten thousand years of
merriment I might agree with thee in a measure, but even there I
should have but short patience with thee, for what would be ten
thousand years of sin's merriment compared with millions upon
millions of years of sin's penalty. Why, at the longest, your life will

be but very short. Are you not conscious that time flies more hurriedly every day? As you grow older, do you not seem. as if you had lived a shorter time instead of longer? till, perhaps, if you could live to be as old as Jacob, you would say, 'Few and evil have my days been, for they appear fewer as they grow more numerous.' You know that this life is but a span, and is soon over. Look to the graveyards, see how they are crowded with green mounds. Remember your own companions, how one by one they have passed away. They were as firm and strong as you, but they have gone like a shadow that declineth. Is it worth while to have this snatch space of pleasure, and then to lie down in eternal pain? I pray you to answer this question. Is it worth while to choose Barabbas for the sake of the temporary gain he may give you, and give up Christ, and so renounce the eternal treasures of joy and happiness which are at his right hand for evermore? I wish that I could put these questions before you as they ought to be put. It needs the earnest seraphic voice of Whitefield, or the pleading tongue of Richard Baxter, to plead with you, but yet I think I talk to rational men; and if it be a matter of arithmetic, it shall need no words of mine. I will not ask you to take your life at the longest that you expect it to be – at eighty, say – crowd it full of all the pleasures you can imagine; suppose yourself in good health; dream yourself to be without business cares, with all that heart can wish; go and sit upon the throne of Solomon if you will, and yet what will you have to say when it is all over? Looking back upon it, can you make more of it than Solomon did, when he said, 'Vanity of vanities, all is vanity' – 'All is vanity and vexation of spirit'? When you have cast up that sum, may I ask you to calculate how much you will have gained, if, in order to possess this vanity, you have renounced eternal happiness, and have incurred everlasting woe?

Do you believe the Bible? You say, 'Yes.' Well, then, it must be so. Many men profess to be believers in Scripture, and yet, when you come to the point as to whether they do believe in eternal woe and eternal joy, there is a kind of something inside which whispers, 'That is in the Book – but still it is not real, it is not true to us.' Make it true to yourselves, and when you have so done it, and have clearly proved that you must be in happiness or woe, and that you must here either have Barabbas for your master, or have Christ for your Lord, then, I say, like sane men, judge which is the better choice, and may God's mighty grace give you spiritual sanity to make the right choice; but this I know, you never will unless that mighty Spirit who alone leads us to choose the right, and reject the wrong, shall come upon you and lead you to fly to a Saviour's wounds.

I need not, I think, prolong the service now, but I hope you will prolong it at your own houses by thinking of the matter. And may I put the question personally to all as you separate, whose are you? On whose side are you? There are no neuters; there are no betweenites: you either serve Christ or Belial; you are either with the Lord or with his enemies. Who is on the Lord's side this day? Who? Who is for Christ and for his cross; for his blood, and for his throne? Who, on the other hand, are his foes? As many as are not for Christ, are numbered with his enemies. Be not so numbered any longer, for the gospel comes to you with an inviting voice – 'Believe in the Lord Jesus Christ, and thou shalt be saved.' God help thee to believe and cast thyself upon him now; and if thou trustest him, thou art saved now, and thou shalt be saved for ever. Amen.

12

OUR LORD BEFORE HEROD[1]

And when Herod saw Jesus, he was exceeding glad:
for he was desirous to see him of a long season,
because he had heard many things of him; and
he hoped to have seen some miracle done by
him. Then he questioned with him in many words;
but he answered him nothing.
LUKE 23:8–9.

AFTER PILATE HAD DECLARED to the chief priests and scribes
that he found no fault at all in Jesus, they were afraid that their
victim would escape, and therefore their fury was raised to the
highest pitch, and they cried out the more vehemently against him.
In the course of their outcries they made use of the word 'Galilee';
going, as it seems to me, a little out of their way in order to drag
in the name: 'He stirreth up the people, teaching throughout all
Jewry, beginning from Galilee to this place.' Galilee was a region
held in very great contempt, and they mentioned it to cast a slur
upon our Lord, as if he were a mere boor from among the clowns
of Galilee.

To Pilate they thought that the mention of the name would,
perhaps, act like the proverbial red rag held before an infuriated
bull; for he appears to have been troubled by seditious persons from
that province. We all remember that they were Galileans whose
blood Pilate had mingled with their sacrifices. The Galileans were
reputed to be an ignorant people, apt to be led astray by impostors,

[1] Sermon No. 1,645. Preached at the Metropolitan Tabernacle on Sunday
morning, 19 February 1882.

and so enthusiastic that they ventured their lives against the Romans. The priests would not only cast contempt upon Jesus, whom they were wont to call the Galilean, but also excite the prejudices of Pilate, so that he might condemn him to die as one of a nest of rebels.

They were mistaken, however, in the consequences of their device, for Pilate caught at the word 'Galilee' directly. That province was not immediately under his rule; it was under the sway of the tetrarch Herod Antipas, and therefore he thought within himself, 'I can kill two birds with one stone: I can get rid of this troublesome business by sending this prisoner to Herod, and I can also greatly gratify the king by showing him this attention.' Pilate had quarrelled with Herod, and now for some purpose of his own he resolved to patch up a friendship by pretending great deference to his sovereign powers by sending one of his subjects to be tried by him. Pilate, therefore, asked, 'Is this man a Galilean?' and when they told him that he was so – for he was so by repute, his birth at Bethlehem having been wilfully ignored – then Pilate at once commanded that he be led to Herod, for Herod was in his palace at Jerusalem attending the Passover festival.

See, then, my brethren, our divine Master conducted in his third march of sorrow through Jerusalem. First, he was led from the garden to the house of Annas, then he was conducted through the streets from the hall of Caiaphas to the judgment hall of Pilate, and now by Pilate's orders he is led a third time by the angry crowd of priests through the streets to the palace of Herod, there to await his fourth examination. Certain of the old writers delight to remark that as there were four evangelists to do honour to our Lord, so were there four judges to do him shame. Annas and Caiaphas, Pilate and Herod. We are on safer ground when we observe with the early church the coalition of the heathen and the Jews: 'For of a truth against thy holy child Jesus, whom thou hast anointed, both Herod, and Pontius Pilate, with the Gentiles, and the people of Israel, were gathered together, for to do whatsoever thy hand and thy counsel determined before to be done.'

This morning I shall endeavour to set forth this portion of the sad narrative under two heads, which will be these: *Herod before Jesus, and Jesus before Herod.*

I. I call your attention first to HEROD BEFORE JESUS, because you must know something of his character, something of the meaning of his questions, before you can rightly understand the sorrow which they caused to Jesus our Lord and Master.

This Herod Antipas was the son of the old Herod the Great, who had put to death the babes at Bethlehem in the hope of destroying the King of the Jews. He was a chip off the old block, but still he was several degrees baser than his sire. There was nothing of the grandeur of his father about him: there was the same evil disposition without the courage and the decision. He did not in some things out-Herod Herod, for in certain points he was a more despicable person. Herod the Great may be called a lion, but our Lord very descriptively called this lesser Herod a fox, saying, 'Go and tell that fox.' He was a man of dissolute habits and frivolous mind; he was very much under the sway of a wicked woman, who destroyed any little good there might have been in him: he was a lover of pleasure, a lover of himself, depraved, weak, and trifling to the last degree. I almost grudge to call him a man, therefore let him only be called a tetrarch.

This petty tetrarch had once been the subject of religious impressions. These Herods all more or less felt the influence of religion at times, though they were by no means benefited thereby. The impressions made upon his conscience by John did not last with Herod. They were at first powerful and practical, for we are informed that 'Herod feared John, knowing that he was a just man and an holy, and observed him; and when he heard him, he did many things, and heard him gladly.' I suppose he reformed many matters in his kingdom, and cast off perhaps some of his grosser vices; but when at last John began to denounce him for having taken his brother's wife to be his paramour, while yet the brother lived, he cast his reprover into prison, and then you remember how, with reluctance, Herod, to please his mistress, beheaded John in prison. Mark this: probably there is no more dangerous character living than a man who has once come under religious influences so as to be materially affected by them, and yet has broken loose and cast off all fear of God. He has done despite to his conscience so violently that henceforth he will know few qualms. In such a man is fulfilled the saying of our Lord 'When the unclean spirit is

179

gone out of a man, he walketh through dry places, seeking rest, and findeth none. Then he saith, I will return into my house from whence I came out; and when he is come, he findeth it empty, swept, and garnished. Then goeth he, and taketh with himself seven other spirits more wicked than himself, and they enter in and dwell there: and the last state of that man is worse than the first.' The mind of Herod Antipas was in the condition of the chamber which has been swept and garnished, for his life had been somewhat reformed, but the unclean spirit with the terrible seven had come back to his old den, and now he was a worse man by a great deal than he had ever been before. The dog returned to his vomit, and the sow that was washed to her wallowing in the mire. This Herod was an Idumaean, that is to say, one of the descendants of Esau, an Edomite, and though he had professedly become a Jew, yet the old blood was in him, as it is written concerning Edom, 'He did pursue his brother with the sword, and cast off all pity.' The true Jacob stood before one of the seed of Esau, a tetrarch, profane and worldly like his ancestor, and scant was the pity which he received. Esau was descended from Abraham according to the flesh, but with Jacob was the covenant according to the spirit: it bodes no good to the spiritual seed when it comes even for a moment under the power of the carnal seed. We see how the child of the flesh takes to mocking, while the child according to promise is called to patience.

Herod was in such a state of mind that he furnishes me with a typical character which I would use for the instruction and admonition of you all. He is a type of some who frequently come to this Tabernacle, and go to other places of worship occasionally – people who were once under religious impressions, and cannot forget that they were so, but who will never be under any religious impressions again. They are now hardened into vain curiosity: they wish to know about everything that is going on in the church and kingdom of Christ, but they are far enough from caring to become part and parcel of it themselves. They are possessed with an idle curiosity which would lift the golden lid of the ark, and intrude behind the veil. They like to gather together all the absurd stories which are told about ministers and to repeat in detail all the odd remarks that were ever made by preachers for centuries. All the gossip of the churches is sure to be known to them, for they eat up the sins of God's people as they eat bread. It is not likely that their knowledge of religious things will be of any use to them, but they are ever eager after it; the church of God is their lounge, divine service is their theatre, ministers are to them as actors, and the gospel itself so much play-house property. They are a sort of religious Athenians, spending their time in nothing else than in hearing some new thing: hoping that perhaps some singular and unexpected discourse may be delivered in their hearing which they can repeat in the next company where they would raise a laugh. To them preaching is all a farce, and, worked up with a few falsehoods of their own, it makes excellent fun for them, and causes them to be regarded as amusing fellows. Let them look at Herod, and see in him their leader, the type of what they really are or may soon become.

First, let us see *idle curiosity at its best*. Look here, sirs, and then look in a glass and trace the likeness.

To begin with, we find that Herod's curiosity had been created in him by his having heard many things concerning Jesus. How did he come to hear of him? His great deeds were common talk: all Jerusalem rang with the news of his miracles and wondrous words. Herod, a convert to the Jewish faith, such as he was, took interest in anything that was going on among the Jews, and all the more so if it touched upon the kingdom, for the jealousy which set his father in a rage was not altogether absent in his son. No doubt also he had heard of Christ from John. John would not long have preached to Herod without using his own grand text, 'Behold the Lamb of God, which taketh away the sin of the world.' I am sure that, though he was a preacher of righteousness, he had not left off being the herald of the coming Saviour, and so from the stern lips of the great Baptist Herod had heard concerning the King of the Jews, and something concerning his kingdom. When John was dead Herod heard still more of Christ, so that, astonished with what was being done, he said, 'This is John the Baptist whom I have beheaded: he is risen from the dead.' Jesus became a kind of nightmare to his conscience: he was disturbed and alarmed by what he heard that the prophet of Nazareth was doing. Besides that, there was one in his household who doubtless knew a great deal about the Saviour; for in Herod's court was the husband of a woman who ministered unto the Lord of her substance. The lady's name was Joanna, and her husband was Chuza, Herod's steward – I suppose Herod's butler and manager of his household. From Chuza he could readily have learned concerning Jesus, and we may be sure that he would enquire, for the fear of the great prophet was upon him. Thus Herod's curiosity had been excited about our Lord Jesus Christ for a considerable time, and he longed to see him. I am not sorry when this happens to any of my hearers: I am right glad that they should hear something about the Lord from his friends, something about him from his ministers, and from those of us whose highest glory it is that, though we are not worthy to unloose the latchets of his shoes, yet it is all our business here below to cry, 'Behold the Lamb!' So these rumours, this talk, these admonitions, had begotten in Herod's mind the desire that his eyes should light on Jesus; so far, so good. Often men at this day come up to the house of prayer that they may hear the preacher; not because they want to be converted, not because they have any idea of ever becoming followers of Jesus, but because they have heard something about true religion which excites their curiosity, and they would know what it is all about; they are fond of curiosities of literature, and so they would study curiosities of religion, oddities of oratory, and things remarkable of a theological kind.

It is said of Herod, in consequence of this curiosity, that he rejoiced to see Jesus. It is said that he was 'exceeding glad'. What a hopeful state to be in! May we not expect great things when a man sees Jesus and is exceeding glad? As I read this passage to myself, I thought, Why, the language might well describe a child of God; our text might fitly be spoken concerning ourselves; let me read it line by line, and remark upon it. 'When Herod saw Jesus, he was exceeding glad;' so were the apostles when Jesus manifested himself to them; for it is written, 'Then were the disciples glad when they saw the Lord.' What other sight could bring to a true believer such joy? 'For he was desirous to see him.' Are we not? Are not all his people longing for that blessed vision which will make their heaven throughout eternity? 'For he was desirous to see him of a long season.' This is also true of us: our hearts are weary with watching, and our eyes fail for the sight of his face.

'Why tarries he?' we cry. 'Make haste, my beloved, and be thou like to a roe or to a young hart upon the mountains of spices.' 'Because he had heard many things of him; and he hoped to have seen some miracle done by him.' This, also, is our hope: we would both see and feel some gracious miracle – upon our eyes, that they may be opened; or upon our hands, that we may have greater power in the Master's work; or upon our feet, that we may run in the ways of obedience; and especially upon our hearts, that we may be ever soft and tender, pure and gracious, to feel the mind of God. Yes, these words read very prettily indeed; but yet, you see, the meaning was not the high and spiritual one which we could put into them, but the low and grovelling one, which was all that Herod could reach. He was 'exceeding glad'; but it was a frivolous gladness, because he hoped that now his curiosity would be satisfied. He had Jesus in his power, and he hoped now to hear some of the oratory of the prophet of whom men said, 'Never man spake like this man.'

He hoped to see him work a miracle, even he, of whom the record was, 'He hath done all things well.' Could not the great prophet be induced to multiply loaves and fishes? Might he not persuade him to heal a blind beggar, or make a lame man leap as a hart? Would not a miracle make rare mirth in Herod's palace, and cause a new sensation in the mind of the worn-out debauchee? If, for instance, a corpse were dug up, and Jesus would restore it to life, it would be something to tell of when next the king sat down to a drinking bout with Herodias and her like. When each was trying to exceed the other in telling strange tales Herod would match them all! In this style many people come to hear the gospel. They want to have an anecdote of their own about a notorious preacher, and if they do see something ludicrous, or hear something striking, they will invent a tale, and swear that they heard it and saw it, though the lie might well choke them. They act thus because they come to hear for nothing but to feed their hungry curiosity. None carry this to such an extreme as those who did at one time feel a measure of the power of the word of God, but have shaken it off. These are the mockers whose bands are made strong; these are the idlers who turn even the testimony of the Lord into food for mirth. Still, at the first blush, there is something that looks very hopeful about them, and we are pleased that they exhibit such gladness when Christ is set forth before them.

One ill sign about Herod was the fact that his conscience had gone to sleep after having for awhile troubled him. For a little he had been afraid of Jesus, and trembled lest John had risen from the dead; but that fear had subsided, and superstition had given way before his Sadducean scepticism. He hoped that Jesus would perform some wonderful thing in his presence; but he had lost all dread of the Just and Holy One. He was a man of vain mind: the man whom he feared one day he murdered the next, and he whom he welcomed with gladness, he hurried off with derision. There was left to Herod no feeling towards Jesus but the craving after something new, the desire to be astonished, the wish to be amused. I think I see him now, sitting on his throne, expectant of wonders, like the trifler that he was. 'Now we shall see,' saith he, 'now we shall see what we shall see! Perhaps he will deliver himself by sheer force; if he walked the sea, he will probably fly away in the air. Perhaps he will render himself invisible, and so pass away through the midst of the chief priests. I have heard that many a time when they would have stoned him or cast him down from the brow of a hill, he departed, gliding through their midst: perhaps he will do the same this morning.' There sits the cunning prince, divining what the wonder will be; regarding even displays of divine power as mere showman's tricks, or magician's illusions.

When Jesus was set before him he began to ask him questions 'Then he questioned with him in many words.' I am glad the questions are not recorded: they could have done us no good; and, besides, our modern Herods nowadays are great masters of the art, and need not that any man teach them. We need not to be furnished with the old-fashioned quibbles and questions; for the supply is quite equal to our requirements. Fools can ask more questions in ten minutes than wise men are able to answer in fifty years. I say we do not want the old questions, but I daresay they would run somewhat in this line, 'Are you that King of the Jews whom my father strove to slay? How came you to be a Nazarene? Have you been a miracle-worker, or is it all legerdemain or necromancy? John told me something about you; did you deceive him, or is it true? Have you raised the dead? Can you heal the sick?'

Trying all the while to excite him to work a miracle, he raised doubts and chopped logic volubly, for the text suggestively mentions his 'many words'. The curious in religion are generally very apt at question-asking; not that they want Christ, not that they want heaven, not that they want pardon of sin, not that they want any good thing; but still they would like to know everything that is dark and mysterious in theology; they would like to have a list of the difficulties of belief, a catalogue of the curiosities of spiritual experience. Some men collect ferns, others are learned upon beetles, and these persons pry into church life, its doctrines, pursuits, aims, and infirmities – especially the latter. They could write a book upon orthodox England and unorthodox England, and dwell with unction upon mental vagaries. It furnishes them with something new, and adds to their store of information, and so they spare no prying questions; for they would analyse manna from heaven, and distil the tears of Christ: nothing is sacred to them; they put Scripture on the rack, and cavil at the words of the Holy Ghost.

Thus have I set forth idle curiosity in its better stage. Now let us pass on and see how Jesus treated this curiosity, considering it under the head of IDLE CURIOSITY DISAPPOINTED. 'He questioned with him in many words, but he answered him nothing'! If Herod had wanted to believe, Jesus would have been ready enough to instruct; if Herod had possessed a broken heart, Jesus would have hastened with tender words to bind it up; if Herod bad been a candid enquirer, if his doubts had been sincere and true, the faithful and true Witness, the Prince of the kings of the earth, would have been delighted to speak with him. But Jesus knew that Herod would not believe in him and would not take up his cross and follow him and therefore he would not waste words on a heartless, soulless profligate. Had he not said to his own disciples, 'Give not that which is holy unto the dogs, neither cast ye your pearls before swine'? He saw in this man one so mean, cunning, cowardly, and heartless, that he viewed him as a fox to be let alone rather than a lost sheep to be sought after. He was a tree twice dead, and plucked up by the roots. All the Master did was to maintain an absolute silence in his presence; 'and, let him question as he might, he answered him nothing.'

Observe, my brethren, that our Lord Jesus Christ came not into this world to be a performer: he did not leave his glory to earn the wondering approbation of men; and as Herod regarded him as a mere wonder-worker, and would have turned his court into a theatre wherein Jesus should be the chief actor, our Lord very wisely held his peace and did nothing at all. And sometimes his ministers might be wise if they were silent too. If they know that men have no desire to learn, no spiritual wish or aspiration, I say they might be wise if they held their tongue altogether. I have sometimes admired George Fox, who, on one occasion, when the crowd had gathered round him, expecting him to deliver some fiery address, stood still by the space of two hours while they clamoured that he would speak. Never a word did they get from him. He said he would famish them of words; for words were all they wanted, and not the power of the Spirit. Probably they recollected his silence better than they would have remembered his most vehement discoursing. Sometimes silence is all that men deserve, and the only thing which in any probability will impress them. As the Lord Jesus was no performer, he did not gratify Herod, but answered him not a word.

Moreover, be it recollected that Herod had already silenced the Voice, and no marvel that he could not hear the Word. For what was John? He said, 'I am the voice of one crying in the wilderness.' What was Jesus but the Word? He that silences the Voice may well be denied the Word. Had not his shallow soul been moved – I was about to say, to its depths, such depths as they were? Had he not been admonished by one of the greatest of the children of men? For among them that were born of women there had not then been a greater than John the Baptist. Had not a burning and shining light shone right into his very eyes? And if he refused to hear the greatest of the sons of men, and to see the brightest light that God had then kindled, it was but right that the Saviour should refuse him even a ray of light, and let him perish in the darkness which he had himself created. Ah, sirs, you cannot trifle with religious impressions with impunity. God thinks it no trifle. He who has once been moved in his soul and has put away the heavenly word from him, may fear that it will be said of him, 'My Spirit shall not always strive with man. Ephraim is joined to idols: let him alone.'

May not some conscience here, if it has but a little life in it, be alarmed at the memory of former rejections of the gospel, frequent quenchings of the Spirit, repeated tramplings upon the blood of Jesus? If God never speaks to you again in the way of mercy, you have no right to expect that he should do so; and if from this day to the day of judgment the Lord should never give you another word of mercy, who shall say that you have been treated harshly? Have you not deserved it at his hands as Herod had done?

Furthermore, recollect that Herod might have heard Christ hundreds of times before if he had chosen to do so. Jesus was always to be found by those who desired to listen to him. He did not go sneaking about Galilee, or holding secret conventicles in holes and corners. He ever spake in the synagogue, and Herod might have gone there; he spake in the street or by the seashore, or on the mountain side, and Herod might have gone there. Jesus stood out boldly before the people, and his teaching was public and free; if Herod had wished to hear him, he might have done so times beyond number: therefore now, having despised all these opportunities, the Saviour will not furnish him with another, which he would have treated in the same manner. He answers him nothing, and by so doing answered him terribly. Beware how you waste opportunities. Dear hearers, beware how you waste your Sabbaths. There may come a day when you would give a thousand worlds for another Sabbath, but it shall be denied you. There may come a day when you would count out all your wealth to have another invitation to Christ, but it will be denied you; for you must die, and the voice of mercy will never ring in your ears again. They that will not when they may, shall not when they would. Many will knock after the Master of the house has risen up and shut to the door; but when he shutteth, no man openeth. The door was shut on Herod.

Observe, that our Master had good reason for refusing to speak to Herod this time, over and above what I have mentioned; because he would not have it supposed that he yielded to the pomp and dignity of men. Jesus never refused an answer to the question of a beggar; but he would not gratify the curiosity of a king. Herod dreams that he has a right to ask whatever impertinent questions he may choose to invent but Jesus knows nothing of men's rights in such a matter: it is all grace with him, and to him the prince upon the throne is not an atom better than the peasant in the cottage, and so when Herod in all his pride and glory thinks full sure that Christ will pay deference to him and, perhaps, will pay him court to win his favour, Jesus disregards him. He wants nothing of the murderer of John the Baptist. Had Herod been the poorest and most loathsome leper throughout all Judea, had he been the meanest mendicant in the street, who was lame or blind, his voice would at once have been heard by the Lord of mercy; but he will not answer the prince who hopes for homage at his hands, nor feed the idle wishes of a crafty reprobate. What favour did he want at Herod's hand? He had not come to be set free; he had come to die, and therefore his face is set like a flint, and, with heroic courage, he answers him not a word.

Now, then, you have seen frivolous curiosity at its best, and you have seen it disappointed, as it generally is to this day. If people come to hear the gospel out of this frivolous curiosity, they usually retire saying, 'Really, I do not see anything in it. We have heard nothing eloquent, nothing profound, nothing outrageous.' Just so; there is nothing in the gospel to please the luxurious, though everything to bless the poor. Jesus answered Herod nothing, and he will answer you nothing if you are of Herod's order. It is the doom of triflers that they should get no answer from the gospel: neither the Scriptures, nor the ministry, nor the Spirit of God, nor the Lord Jesus will speak with them.

What was the result of this disappointment upon Herod? *Idle curiosity curdles into derision.* He thinks the man is a fool, if not an idiot, and he says so, and begins to deride him. With his men of war he mocks him, and 'set him at nought,' which signifies to make nothing of him. He calls his soldiers and says, 'Look at this creature: he will not answer a word to what I have to say: is he bereft of his senses? Rouse him up, and see.' Then they mock and laugh and jest and jeer. 'Here,' says Herod, 'he calls himself a king! Bring out one of my shining white robes, and put it on him we will make a king of him.' So they put it about his blessed person, and again heap contumely upon him. Was it not strange – this decking him in a gorgeous robe of dazzling white? The mediaeval writers delight to dwell on the fact that Herod arrayed our Lord in white and afterwards Pilate clothed him in red. Is he not the Lily of the valley and the Rose of Sharon? Is he not matchlessly white for innocence, and then gloriously red in his atoning blood? Thus, in their very mockery, they are unconsciously setting forth to us both his spotless holiness and his majestic royalty. When they had insulted to their full, they sent him back to Pilate, kicking him from foot to foot at their pleasure, as if he were a football for their sport. Then our Lord made his fourth sorrowful march through the streets of the city over which he had wept.

That is what idlers in the long run do with Christ; in their disappointment they grow weary of him and his gospel, and they cry, 'Put him away; there is nothing in him, nothing of what we looked for, nothing to satisfy curiosity, nothing sensational; take him away.' Away goes Jesus, never to return; and that is the end of Herod, and the end of a great many more.

II. My time is nearly gone; but bear with me while for a few minutes I try to set forth JESUS IN THE PRESENCE OF HEROD. Although no blows are recorded, I greatly question whether our Divine Master suffered anywhere more than he did in the palace of Herod. You and I, perhaps, apprehend most easily the woe of the coarser sufferings when they scourged him and when they plaited the crown of thorns and put it upon his head, but the delicate and sensitive mind of our Master was, perhaps, more touched by what he suffered in the palace of Herod than by the rougher torture. For, first, here is a man fully in earnest for the salvation of our souls, and in the midst of his grievous passion he is looked upon as a mountebank and a mere performer, who is expected to work a miracle for the amusement of an impious court. How it cuts an earnest man to the quick when he finds that, let him do what he may, people do not sympathise with him in earnestness, but are coolly criticizing his style, or imitating his mannerisms, or admiring his expressions as matters of literary taste. It is heart-breaking when your ardour makes you self-forgetful to find others pecking at trifles, or making your efforts into a kind of show. The Christ must have been wounded in his very soul when he was treated as a mere performer, as if he had left the Father's bosom and was about to give himself to death, and yet

was aiming to amuse or to astonish. I know how it saddens my
Lord's servants when they preach their very hearts out to bring
men to repentance, and the only result is to elicit the remark that
'his arguments were very telling, and that pathetic passage was
very fine.' There is a thorn in such chill words to pierce deeper
than the crown of thorns: horrible indifference smites like the
Roman scourge.

Then to think of our Lord's being questioned by such a fop as
Herod! A man of earnest and intense soul, living for one thing
only, and that the redemption of mankind, is here worried by the
foolish questions of a man of the world. Were you ever in an agony
of bodily pain yourself, and did some frivolous person call upon
you and begin to torture you with the veriest inanities and
absurdities? Have you not felt that his chatterings were worse than
the pain? It must have been so with Jesus, When the ridiculous
must needs question the sublime the result is misery. With the
bloody sweat yet damp upon his brow, and with the accursed spittle
still defacing his blessed countenance, the Man of Sorrows must
be tortured by the drivellings of a heartless idler. With his heart
all bowed down under a sense of the awful penalty of sin, the great
Substitute for sinners must be molested by the petty small talk and
ribald jests of the meanest of mankind. Solving eternal problems,
and building up an everlasting temple unto the living God, he must
be twitted by a vainglorious tetrarch, tormented and tortured by
foolish questions fit only to be asked of a mountebank. We think
the cross itself was not a worse instrument of torture than the
haughty tongue of this debauched monarch.

Then the ribaldry of the whole thing must have tortured our
Lord. The whole of them gathered round about him with their
hoarse laughter and coarse jests. He has become a by-word and a
proverb to them. When you are merry you can enjoy merriment;
but when the heart is sad laughter is wretchedly discordant, and
embitters your grief. Now this one laughs, and then another sneers;
while a third thrusts out the tongue, and they are all uproariously
jovial. In harmony they are all making nothing of him, though
with awful earnestness he is lifting the world out of the slough of
despair, and hanging it in its place again among the stars of glory.
Jesus was performing more than Herculean labours, and these little

beings, like so many gnats and flies, were stinging him. Small things are great at torturing, and these worthless beings did their utmost to torment our Lord. Oh, the torture of the Master's spirit!

Remember, it was no small sorrow to our Lord to be silent. You tell me that he appears majestic in his silence. It is even so; but the pain of it was acute. Can you speak well? Do you love to speak for the good of your fellow men, and do you know that when you speak full often your words are spirit and life to those who hear you? It will be very hard to feel compelled to refuse them a good word. Do not imagine that the Lord despised Herod as Herod despised the Lord. Ah, no! The pity of his soul went out to this poor frivolous creature who must needs make sport of the Saviour's sufferings, and treat the Son of the Highest as though he were a court fool, who must play before him.

The Saviour's infinite love was breaking his heart; for he longed to bless his persecutor, and yet he must not speak, nor give forth a warning word. True, there was little need for words, for his very presence was a sermon which ought to have melted a heart of stone; but yet it cost the Saviour a mighty effort to keep down the flood-gates and hold in the blessed torrents of his holy speech, which would have flowed out in compassionate pleadings. Silent he must be; but the anguish of it I can scarcely tell. Sometimes to be permitted to speak a word is the greatest comfort you can have. Have you never been in such a state that if you could cry out, it would have been a relief to you? What anguish, then, to be forced to be as a dumb man! What woe to be forced to be silent with all these mockers about him, and yet to be pitying them all! As a man might pity a moth that flies into the flame of the candle, and will not be delivered, so did our Lord pity these creatures. How sad that they could make sport of their own damnation, fling the salvation of God to the ground, and tread it down as swine tread down their husks. Oh, it grieved the Master's heart: it moved his soul to its very centre.

Think of the utter contempt that was poured upon him. I do not judge that this was the bitterest of his woes, for their contempt was an honour to him; but yet it was one ingredient of his cup of mingled wormwood and gall, that they should so despise him as to clothe him in a white robe, and mock his kingship, when on that kingship their only hope was hung. They 'set him at nought', that is, put him down as nothing, jeered and jested at him, and if there was nothing even about his manhood which they could respect, they invented ways by which they could pour scorn upon him. Luke is the gospel of the man; if you want to read about Jesus in his manhood, read Luke; and here you will see how his very manhood was trampled in the mire by these inhuman creatures, who found their joy in despising him.

See, then, your Lord and Master, and let me put two or three questions to you. Do you not think that this peculiar silence of Jesus was a part of his anguish, in which he was bearing the punishment for your sins of the tongue? Ah me, ah me! Redeemed of the Lord, how often have you misused your speech by wanton words! How often have we uttered murmuring words, proud words, false words, words of despite to holy things; and now our sins of the tongue are all coming upon him, and he must stand silent there and bear our penalty.

And is it not possible that when they put the gorgeous robe upon him, he was bearing your sins of vanity, your sins of dress and pride, when you made yourselves glorious to behold, and arrayed yourselves in gorgeous robes and glittering apparel? Know ye not that these things are your shame? For had you had no sin, you would have needed none of these poor rags; and may not the Christ in white and red be bearing your sins of folly? And do you not think that when they were making him nothing, and despising him, he was then bearing our sins, when we set him at nought – our words of despite and derision when, perhaps, in our ungodly days we, too, made sport of holy things, and jested at the word of God? Ah me, I think it was so, and I ask you to look at him, and say as you see him there, 'It is not Herod after all; it is my tongue, my vanity, my trifling with holy things, which caused him this exquisite torture. Lord Jesus, substitute for me, let all these transgressions of mine be put away once for all by thy meritorious passion.'

Finally, we read that Herod and Pilate were made friends from that day, and I do hope if there are any here that are true-hearted Christians if they have had any ill-will towards one another they will think it a great shame that Herod and Pilate should be friends, and that any two followers of Jesus should not be friends at the sight of the suffering Master. As for those two foxes, Pilate and Herod, they were tied tail to tail that day by our great Samson. Our Lord has often been a point of union for wicked men, not by his intent and purpose, but because they have joined together to oppose him. I have often smiled in my heart to see how superstition and scepticism will march together when they are anxious to oppose the gospel. Then the Sadducee says, 'Give me your hand, dear Pharisee; we have a common interest here, for this man would overturn us all.' The gospel is the mortal enemy both of the sceptical Sadducee and the superstitious Pharisee, and so they lay aside their differences to assail it. Now, then, if the wicked unite before our Lord Jesus when he wears the white robe, should not his people much more be united, especially when they remember that he said, 'A new commandment give I unto you, that ye love one another'? I charge you by your homage to him you call Master and Lord, if you have any difference of any sort with any Christian brother, let not yon sun go down till you have ended it by hearty love for Jesus' sake. Let it be seen that Christ is the great uniter of all those who are in him. He would have us love one another even as he has loved us, and his prayer is that we may be one.

May the Lord hear that prayer, and make us one in Christ Jesus. Amen.

13

SETTING JESUS AT NOUGHT[1]

And Herod with his men of war set him at nought.
LUKE 23:11

IT IS YOUR LORD whom Herod set at nought! Once worshipped of angels and all the heavenly host, he is made nothing of by a ribald regiment. In himself 'the brightness of his Father's glory, and the express image of his person'; but now set at nought by men not worthy of the name. Soon to reassume all his former glory with the Father, and to descend in infinite splendour to judge the earth in righteousness, and reign as King of kings; and yet here he is set at nought! It is a sight of horror and of shame. How could angels bear to see it? This paltry prince and his rough retinue made nothing of him who is All in all; they treated him as beneath their contempt. The veriest abjects flouted him. The meanest soldier in the petty army of a petty princelet made unholy mirth of heaven's high Lord and earth's Redeemer.

What a sorrowful and shameless business! May we be helped to sorrow over it! These wretches were of our race. May we mourn because of him! When the thorns of grief and repentance are at our breast, may God grant that they may act as lancets to let out the foul blood of our pride, for we, too, are partakers in this tremendous crime, since our sin involved our Saviour in the necessity of bearing this barbarous scorn.

Herod himself set him at nought. In this loathsome being I see the most likely person to think nothing of the Lord Jesus. Let me

[1] Sermon No. 2,051. Preached at the Metropolitan Tabernacle on Sunday evening, 2 September 1888.

just say a word or two about this member of a detestable family, that I may see whether his like can be found here tonight. I will not give you any history of this Herod. It is not worthwhile. This 'fox' is not worth unearthing. The page of history is stained by the Herodian name. I will give you enough concerning him to help you to answer the question – Are you like him? Have you set Christ at nought?

I. This shall be our first enquiry: WHO IS THE MOST LIKELY PERSON TO SET OUR LORD AT NOUGHT?

Herod was a man who had once heard the Word of God; yes, heard it with a measure of attention, and apparent benefit. We read, 'Herod feared John, knowing that he was a just man and an holy, and observed him; and when he heard him, he did many things, and heard him gladly.' According to the margin, Herod 'kept him or saved him' – preserving him from those who would have laid violent hands upon him. But he broke away from his respectful regard of John, and now that Jesus stands before him, his memory of the Baptist does not restrain him from mocking the Baptist's Lord. He had silenced that eloquent tongue, and now he had no care to listen to anything which might further bestir his conscience.

We often find that the greatest despisers of Christ are those who formerly were hearers and readers of his Word, but have turned from it. An apostate Methodist is a scoffer: a runaway Baptist is an infidel. It looks as if men must have some knowledge of the truth to be able to fight against it in the most malicious way. The viper must be warmed in the man's bosom that he may have strength to bite him. Is not this a wretched business? Am I talking to any here who, not so many years ago, were regular attendants upon a faithful ministry, but who have grown weary of it, and given it up? I do not know what reason you give; but I suppose the real reason is, that you love the world better than Christ, and so you have left his people and his Word. It troubles your conscience that you have done so, and now you try to conceal your uneasiness by picking holes in your former minister, and finding fault with the truths which he preached to you. I know the tricks and manners of apostates. Wanting an opiate for your consciences, you invent a fault in the gospel, or try to disbelieve it altogether. What an unhappy thing that the hopeful hearer should decline into a hopeless despiser! Herod heard John, but he ridiculed Jesus. See to what unconverted hearers may come!

If I look at Herod again, I see in him a man who, after hearing the Word faithfully preached, *had distinctly done violence to his conscience.* He heard John until John came home to him about the woman with whom he was living in an incestuous union. Herodias would have killed John at once; and though Herod did not dare to go so far as that, yet he shut him up in prison. A filthy lust must not be rebuked: Herod imprisons his reprover. He knew that John was right, and he trembled at his rebuke; but he could not give up his sin, and so he put the servant of God in a dungeon. He was held fast, as many a man before and since has been held fast, by an evil woman. She demanded of him that at the very least the man of God should be cast into prison. How dare he speak against what the prince chose to do? How dare a peasant censure so great a man as Herod about his personal life? So, instead of bowing before the supreme authority of right, and listening to the voice of truth as uttered by the Lord's Elijah, he must needs exercise his royal power, and lay his reprover by the heels.

The man who could do this was in training for the more daring act of setting the Lord Jesus at nought. First despise the man, and then the Master. First do violence to your better self, and then scoff at godliness. My friend, do you remember that night when you distinctly decided for the devil? Do you recollect when, after having the evil set before you, and seeing it, and counting the cost, you decided to continue in it? Then you turned with bitterness upon the honest reprover whose rebuke you had aforetime endured. Perhaps it was your wife upon whom you turned with anger. What hard words you said to her for the gentle remark she ventured to make! It was an effort for you. You gave conscience an awful wrench; and therefore you put yourself into a passion, and talked like an injured man. Or was it your brother? It may be you quitted his society in order to be free from his remarks. Was it your child, or your friend? You could not put them in prison; but you were determined that you would not bear any more of their protests. You abused and silenced them; not because you thought they were wrong, but because they made you feel that *you* were wrong. By all this you have prepared yourself to set the Lord at nought; and we cannot wonder that you do so.

This man also *had yielded to sinful companions, and had committed a gross sin as the result of it,* for when Herodias danced, and he promised to give her whatsoever she desired, she asked the head of John the Baptist in a charger; and he, not liking to break his word in the presence of the assembled guests, and not willing to stand out against the woman with whom he lived in unhallowed intercourse, yielded, and the Baptist's head was taken from his shoulders. Ah, well! you may not have sinned quite in that way; but you, too, once had better thoughts and higher aims. Your companions were too many for you, and drove all good out of you. I do not mention this that you may dare to cast the blame upon others of that which was really your own act and deed. If there had been a spark of true manhood in you, you would have resisted the suggestion of those enemies in the garb of friends. But you are soft and plastic, like wax, in the hand of evil; instead of being, as you ought to be, like granite towards evil, and like wax towards good. You now feel as if you had gone too far to turn back. You are now fixed in an evil estate. A black sin seems to bar the way to repentance.

Truly, even now you will be welcomed to the bosom of mercy, but you are not anxious enough for it. It is a long lane that has no turning, but you seem to have got into such a lane, and you are driven along it by evil forces. This is the man that thinks nothing of Christ – the man who thinks so much of drinking and dancing, and of the companions which such things have brought around him. Of course he does not think anything of Christ, for his ways would take from him these vile associates. How should he value the holy Jesus? Will swine ever think much of pearls? It is vain that we set before you beauties for which you have no eyes, hopes for which you have no heart. Jesus cannot be valued by a man of Herod's sort, who puts so high a value upon the opinion of those who sit with him at his banquets.

Once more: the man who thinks nothing of Christ is the man that *means to go on in sin,* even as Herod did. The die was cast; his mind was made up for evil. He would be very glad to hear

Christ: he has no objection still to go to a place of worship and listen to a preacher. He would be very pleased to see a miracle: he would join in a revival, for he would be glad to enjoy something sensational, but he does not mean to give up the sin in which he lives, nor the company which eggs him on in it. He does not mean to cut off the right hand, and pluck out the right eye. Not he! He is too fond of the vice, too much ensnared and bird-limed by his passions; and so, as he gives his heart to his lust, he takes away his heart from Christ; nay, he treats religion with derision, because it is opposed to his bent and inclination.

What a sad thing! I generally find, when man speaks against the Lord Jesus, that if you follow him home, he would rather not have you go indoors, for fear his inner life should be known. He does not want you to see the skeleton in the cupboard. I have so often met with this fact in actual life, that when I have heard a man speak bitterly of my Master, I have formed my opinion, and have not been wrong. A little enquiry has revealed so much that I have said, 'It is not at all surprising that such a man should speak evil of Christ. It is as natural to such a man to talk against Christ as for a dog to bark.' When a bad fellow once praised Socrates, that philosopher said, 'I wonder what I can have been doing amiss, that such a man should speak well of me.' If lustful lips praised the Saviour, one might begin to be afraid; but when they denounce and deride him, we feel that it is the only homage which vice can pay to purity.

This, then, is the man who sets Jesus at nought. I wonder whether he is here tonight! Possibly it is a woman who is doing this. Women fall into precisely the same evils as men from their own side of the house, and the same remarks apply to both sexes. You who once were hearers, you who once were impressed, you who did wilful violence to conscience, you who persist in sin, you who are the slaves of evil company, and dare not do right for the life of you, for fear of ridicule – you are the kind of people of whom Herod was a sad specimen: you set Jesus at nought.

II. Having tried to find out Herod, let us now answer a second question – ON WHAT GROUND DID HE SET OUR LORD AT NOUGHT?

Men have some reason or other for their acts, although often those reasons are most unreasonable. Before we consider the unhallowed reasons for this great crime, let us do homage to the name of the Son of God. O Lord Jesus, even in thy lowest humiliation thou art worthy of all reverence. To thy friends thou art all the more dear and the more honoured because thou wast greatly despised. Thou, bound and brought a prisoner before the tetrarch, art free to rule our hearts. Thou wert charged with sedition, but we fall at thy blessed feet, and proclaim thee King of kings! Herod sets him up as the butt of his ridicule, and makes nothing of him. As Herbert puts it –

> Herod and all his bands do set me light,
> Who teach all hands to war, fingers to fight,
> And only am the Lord of hosts and might.
>   Was ever grief like mine?

I suppose that part of the reason why he and his men of war made nothing of our Lord was *because of his gentleness and patience.* Our Lord had no sword, and none of the temper of men who wear weapons. His visage was not like the face of a man of war: it was marred with grief, but not with anger; worn with sorrow, but not with battle. He was the lamb and not the lion, the dove and not the eagle, and therefore the fighting men despised him. If he had any weapons they were his tears and his almighty love; but these the Herodian ruffians utterly despised. All unarmed he stood before them, and when he was reviled he reviled not again. You know how men of muscular strength and physical bravado value men by their muscles and bones, and think nothing of those who are feeble in arm and body. The Saviour, in his emaciation and faintness, must have seemed a poor creature to these hectors. The Christian religion teaches us to be meek and gentle, to forgive injuries, and even to give up our own rights rather than to inflict wrong. Such precepts savour of cowardice to the blustering world. Non-resistance they cannot hear of. They do not like the word 'Forgive'. 'Surely,' say they, 'a worm will turn?' Thus they think so little of Christ that they prefer an earthworm's example to that of the Lord. The sweet savour of gentle forbearance, which the spirit of Jesus breathes into the hearts of his people, is by many held in contempt. They call it cant and hypocrisy, because it is so alien to their nature, so inconsistent with their ideas of manly conduct.

Furthermore, our Lord was ridiculed by Herod because *he refused to gratify his curiosity and amuse his love of sensation.* The wicked Herod virtually said to the holy Jesus, 'Come, work us a miracle. We hear that thou didst deliver from death, now release thyself from our hands. We hear that thou didst multiply loaves and fishes, and feed multitudes, give us a banquet here. Thou canst do all things, so report says of thee – come, do some little thing that we may see and believe. Did not Moses work miracles before Pharaoh? Work a miracle before us.' There stands our Lord, with all power in his hands, but he will not lift a finger for his own deliverance and Herod's amusement. O blessed Jesus, it is the same still, thou wilt not dazzle nor amuse, and therefore men prefer any charlatan to thee.

Herod then begins to question him. He asks him this, and that, and the other, with many a jest rolled in between; but he receives no answer. He who answered blind beggars when they cried for mercy is silent to a prince who only seeks to gratify his own irreverent curiosity. Then the men-at-arms laugh at their silent victim. 'Why,' they say, 'the man is dumb. Either he can say nothing for himself, or he is obstinate and ill-mannered. He speaks not when he is spoken to. Has he lost his wits?' Thereupon they multiply their profane jests, and make nothing of the silent One. I do not doubt that often men turn away from the faith because their curiosity is not gratified, and they see nothing marvellous in it. A gospel for the age! A brand new gospel every year might suit them; but the old is stale: they know all about it, and sneer at it. Plain gospel is too plain for them. They desire adornment, or at least mystery, and the pomp which veils the unknown. They would rather go where there are gorgeous ceremonies, and mutterings in an unknown tongue amid the smoke of incense and the harmony of music. The simple gospel of 'Believe and live' does not suit them; for it seems fit only for the poor and unintellectual: thus they set Jesus at nought.

Moreover, the royal claims of Jesus excited their scorn. I think I hear the 'Aha! aha! aha!' of Herod as he said, 'Call *him* a King?

You could find such kings as this in every street of Jerusalem. Talk of a kingdom for him! Go to the pool of Bethesda, and fetch up some poor wretch who lies waiting there for the moving of the water, and call him a king! King? What hosts art at thy command? What kingdom dost thou govern? What laws canst thou make? Here! Put the white robe upon him. Let him at least look like a monarch. Yes, that old robe will do! Is he not every inch a King?' Then the soldiery took up the jest! How bitterly, how derisively did they make his royalty the football of contempt! Thus today the world makes nothing of the royalty of King Jesus. A nominal king he may be, but as a real king they will not have him. Those who would be in the dust before the meanest princelet have no esteem for him. There is no pomp about the pure religion of Jesus; there is no glory of philosophy about his teaching; and so they set him and his cause at nought. Ah, me! what will a rebellious people do in the day when he appeareth to claim his throne and punish sedition?

Then, too, *they denied his prophetic office.* 'Look!' said Herod, 'he will not speak. I have asked him twenty questions, and he will not answer one of them. This is a pretty prophet! John was the voice of one crying in the wilderness, but this man has no voice at all. A dumb prophet! Why, he is mute as a fish, and has nothing to say for himself.' With such unhallowed merriment did Herod and his men of war set the Lord at nought. How they provoked him! But he stands in the majesty of his self-government, quiet to the end. Here was an omnipotence which restrained the lips of omnipotence. It was a wondrous power, that Godlike patience which enabled indignant holiness to withhold its word of condemnation. The prophet proved his commission by his silence; and yet he provoked their scorn, so that they set him at nought. At this time, because the Christian faith is silent upon a great many questions, certain men deride it. When men come to it with captious questions they receive no answer, and they are irritated thereby. When they idly demand a miracle, and it does not yield to their desires, they have fresh jeers for it. 'You preach up the faith of Christ as the only true and divine religion: let us see it work wonders. Where are your miracles? We have asked you fifty questions about the past and the future, and you do not reply; where is the ground for your boastings?' Thus they make nothing of Christ, and disdain his claim to teach with authority.

Those, I suppose, were the grounds upon which Herod, and such as Herod, make light of Christ. Poor grounds they are, and such as will fail to justify them before the bar of God.

III. Now, dear friends, let us consider, now DO MEN NOW SET OUR LORD AT NOUGHT? Herod is dead and buried, and there is no sort of reason why we should not let him rot into oblivion. I therefore speak to you, and try to discover whether you are setting Christ at nought. I fear there are such. Who are they?

Some set him at nought, for *they will not even consider his claims.* 'Oh,' say they, 'we have plenty else to think about besides religion. What is there in it which will fill our pockets? There is nothing at all in it worth a moment's attention.' How do they know? They do not know. Nothing in it? God gives his own Son to die for guilty men, and there is nothing in it! The highest thoughts of God are set forth in the person of the Lord Jesus Christ, and you do not think it worth while even to consider what God has therein revealed? A man goes to a bookstall, and turns over a book. It is a novel: he reads a page, and would like to buy it. But suppose it is a book upon the glories of Christ. Does he read then? Does he wish to buy it? No, it is one of those dry theological books, and he shuts it up. He will make no bid for a volume on so dull a subject. He would like to know of Alexander the Great or even of Tom Thumb, but for the world's Redeemer he cares nothing. He makes nothing of Christ. Do I not convict some here present tonight? They have never set apart one solitary hour in their lives to the honest and candid consideration of the claims of Jesus, the divine Saviour. If it be so, you have indeed made Christ very cheap; and if you perish for lack of him, your blood be on your own heads! If this be the medicine that will heal your disease, and you huff at it, and will not even hear of the cures it has wrought, who is to blame if you perish? Who is to save the man who will not listen when salvation is put before him? Yet the great mass of our fellow citizens are of this kind. In London there are millions who make so little of Christ that they will not even come to hear what his ministers have to say about him, nor read their Bibles, nor show the least interest in the matter. In many a house in London Muhammad is practically as much esteemed as Jesus. Ah me!

There are *many others who prefer their business to Jesus.* They would not mind giving some little attention to the Lord Jesus, but then they are too busy just now. They say that they really cannot afford the time. O my busy hearer! you will have to find time to die before long: why not think of that solemn certainty? You are very busy, and yet you find time to eat. Have you no time to feed your soul? You find time to put on your dress, have you no time to dress your souls? You seek out the surgeon when you are ill; have you no time to seek out a Saviour for your sin-sick soul? Ah! it is not that: you have the time, but you have not the heart.

Others prefer amusements to the Lord Jesus. 'Well,' says one, 'we must have recreation. In my spare time I like a game.' I know that. I am not for denying you healthy recreation, but everything should be in order, and I claim first place for Jesus Christ and his salvation. What! is it not worth while to give up a sport to seek Jesus? Do you think a game of cards more important than seeking the pardon of your sin? An evening at the theatre or the music-hall; do you really think so little of Jesus that you can live without him, and satisfy your mind with these poor things? Can you suffer the paltry amusements of the world to stand before the Lord Jesus? Yet it is so with some of you: I wish it were not. My Master's blood and righteousness, the salvation of a soul from hell, the preparing of a heart for heaven – these are laid away in the lumber-room, to allow the childish pleasures of a vain world to engross your thoughts. You will know better one day. God grant you may learn wisdom while yet it may be of use to you. Too late! What awful words! May you even now feel that if the Son of God has lived and died for men, it is of the first importance that you put business and pleasure in their proper places, and seek first the kingdom of God and his righteousness.

Another sort of persons make nothing of Christ, because *they profess to see nothing profound and philosophical in the faith* which he has revealed. These are the Greeks, to whom the doctrine of the cross is foolishness. O foolish Greeks! These wise men will not hear some of us because we can be understood of the people.

'Anybody can understand you,' say they, 'you speak after the manner of the crowd, and what you say is simple enough to be clear to the most ignorant. We like something deeper, something too profound to be readily grasped. We are above commonplace people, and need something more intellectual and philosophical.' A man of note once said to me, 'Why do you keep on preaching to those thousands at Newington? Preach so that the mob will leave you, and the *élite* will support you.' To whom I answered, that if one man's soul was of less value than another, his was of the least value who could talk so slightingly of others. Those who make no pretence to culture, are often far more sensible people than those who affect superiority. The man who thinks that he is intellectual, and talks in that fashion, is a miserable snob, and has scarcely a soul at all. When a man despises the multitude, he deserves to be despised himself. But, my dear sir, if the salvation of Christ be very simple, and very plain, is it not so much the better? Have you not enough of philanthropy to make you feel that if you could have a gospel only for the *élite*, it would be a matter of deep regret? Is not a gospel for the multitude the thing to be desired? Do you not desire the vast mass to be saved? I hope you do. But I fear you make nothing of Christ when you despise his gospel because you imagine that it is not deep enough and philosophical enough for you. The most profound science in the world is the science of the cross! Christ himself is the highest wisdom, for he is the wisdom of God.

Others make nothing of the Lord because *they confide in themselves*. They think themselves quite good enough without a Saviour. If they are not quite perfect, they believe that they can make themselves so, and be saved without an atoning sacrifice, or a new heart, or union to Christ. They are doing their best, and they make no doubt whatever that they will find their way to heaven as well as others. Do you thus think? You are in grave error. There was a learned Romanist who once ventured to say that if salvation could only be had on terms of free grace, he would not have it. Do you know what happened? Why, he did not have it: that was all. And that is what will happen to you. If you will not have salvation as a free gift of grace, without any merit wherewith to purchase it, then you must go without it, and perish in your sin;

for the terms of free grace will never be altered to suit the pride of the human heart. If any man sets up his righteousness in the place of Jesus Christ, the sin-removing Lamb, why then he has made nothing of Christ, and the Lord will make less than nothing of him. Alas! that any man should be so profane as to think himself so good that he does not need God's grace and the atoning blood! Such pride insults the Lord Christ, and will bring sure destruction upon the man who is guilty of it.

I have no doubt that there are many also who make nought of Christ because they *have no conscience whatever as to his present claims upon them*. O dear sirs, if you did but know his kindness to the sons of men, even to his enemies, and how he sought them with his tears, and then bought them with his blood, you would feel forced to love him.

> Sure Christ deserves the noblest place
> In every human heart.

Truly know Jesus, and you must love him. But some men do not think that they owe him anything, or are in any need of him. It is nothing to such that he died, for they did not require his death to save them: in their judgment they are not lost. Those who are of this mind will leave this Tabernacle tonight, and will go back to the world just as they came in, practically saying, 'Whether Jesus lived or whether he died, and whatever he did or was, I care nothing, for I owe him nothing.' And yet you owe him everything. You had not been here tonight if it were not for the mercy which has spared you, and which has come to you through him. The axe would have had you down long ago but for his intercession. There had been no gospel to set before you tonight if it had not been for the death agony of the Lord Jesus. You owe the very opportunity of hearing the gospel, and the opportunity of accepting it to his dying love. Oh, that you had a conscience which would make you just towards Jesus! Oh, that you felt that you were bound to love him and live for him, because of all that he has done for guilty men!

As they have no conscience of his claims upon them, so many *have no fears concerning the day of his appearing*. Whether you believe it or not, Jesus, as your Judge, is at the door. He said, years ago, 'Behold, I am coming quickly.' He is still coming, and must soon arrive to commence the last dread session of justice. What matters it how many more years may elapse? They will fly like the wind. The day will come when heaven and earth shall be ablaze. The thick darkness will lower down,

> And, withering from the vault of night,
> The stars shall pale their feeble light.

The hour will come when the earth and sky will rock and reel, and pass away, rolled up like a worn-out vesture. Then shall the trumpet ring out exceeding loud and long – 'Awake, ye dead, and come to judgment!' How will you endure that voice which shall disturb the stillness of the sepulchre? 'Come to judgment! Come to judgment! Come to judgment!' How it will peal forth! None of you will be able to resist the call. From your beds of dust you will start up amazed to a terrible awakening. From the sea, from the land, from the teeming cemetery, from the lonely grave, men will rise, and all of them stand before Christ! In that day you will see nothing but the great white throne, and him that sits upon it. You will be unable to close your eyes, or to turn your gaze elsewhere. There will he sit, and you will know him by his scars.

> How resplendent shine the nail-prints!
> Every eye shall see him move.

Still shall the trumpet thrill out the summons, 'Come to judgment! Come to judgment! Come away!' And you must come, whether you will or not; and if you have despised the Lord as Saviour, you will tremble before him as Judge. You will then hear his voice, which in itself is sweeter than the harps of heaven, but to the ungodly it will be more full of thunder than the crash of tempest – 'Depart! Depart! Depart!' O my hearer, what will then become of you? The prospect is terrible: but you have no concern about it. To die, to rise, to be judged, to be condemned: you take no account of it. Like Herod, you set him at nought. How dare you do so? How dare you despise the great Judge? Ah, my Lord, have mercy upon them! Have mercy upon them now, and turn them from doing to thee and to themselves this grievous wrong of making nothing of the Lord of all. They set him at nought!

This is very heavy preaching to me. If it is as painful to you to hear as to me to speak, you will be glad when I have done. I pray that these solemn words may long remain upon your hearts. Oh, that they might bring you to Jesus at once by the power of the Holy Ghost!

IV. But I close with this: WHAT DO BELIEVERS SAY ABOUT THEIR LORD? Herod made nothing of him: what do we make of him?

Well, we say, first, that *we mourn and lament that there ever was a time when we ourselves made nothing of the glorious One.* It is many years ago with some of us; but we cannot forget it, nor cease to bewail it. There were a certain number of years in our lives in which it was nothing to us that Jesus should die. O my dear hearers, perhaps some of you have been lately converted after forty, or fifty, or sixty years of sin. Repent with all your hearts that you were Herods so long. Christ has forgiven you; but can you forgive yourselves? No; I think that you still smite on your breast, and say, 'Lord, I grieve that ever I lived a moment without acknowledging my Lord – that I ever ate a meal or drew in a breath without bowing before him.' Lord, bury those years in forgetfulness which we spent in forgetfulness of thee!

Next, *it is now our grief that any others should set the Lord Jesus at nought.* It must be a great grief to any man here if she who lies in his bosom sets the Lord at nought. Dear woman, I know what your daily burden must be if the husband who is so dear to you does not love your Saviour, whom you love with a higher love. What an anguish it is to nourish and bring up children, and see them refuse our Lord! 'I have no greater joy than to hear that my children walk in the truth;' and no greater sorrow than to see them running into evil ways. Could we really see the heart of an unregenerate man or woman it would cause us the utmost distress. If we felt as we ought to feel, if there were only one unconverted person in this Tabernacle, we should make a Bochim of it till that heart was yielded to Christ. If there existed only one man or woman who did not love the Saviour, and if that person lived amongst the wilds of Siberia, and if it were necessary that all the millions of believers on the face of the earth should journey thither, and every one of them plead with him to come to Jesus, before he could be converted; it would be well worth all the zeal, and labour, and expense of all that effort. One soul would repay the travail in birth of myriads of zealous Christians. Lord, we cannot bear it that there should go on existing men and women who make nothing of the bleeding Son of God! It is an awful thing: as awful as hell itself! Out in that street tonight think of the thousands who will be hunting for the precious life. Walk along our crowded thoroughfares, and think of the myriads even of this city who live and die without God, and without hope, making nothing of Jesus, and you will feel a heartbreak which will make life a burden. I could wish that you felt that heartbreak for their sakes, and for Christ's sake.

But then, dear friends, what do we make of Christ ourselves now? Well, that I cannot tell you, except it be in one word – *Christ is all*. Herod made nothing of him; we make everything of him.

> All my capacious powers can wish,
>   In thee doth richly meet;
> Nor to my eyes is light so dear,
>   Nor friendship half so sweet.

Could any of you who love my Lord tell me what you think of him? I am sure that you would break down in the attempt. For my own part, I always fail in the glad endeavour.

> When my tongue would fain express
>   All his love and loveliness,
> Then I lisp and falter forth
>   Broken words not half his worth.

If we could give every drop of our blood for Jesus; if we could be burnt at a slow fire for a century for him, he deserves all our suffering and all our life. Could our zeal no respite know, a whole eternity of service would not adequately set forth what we think of him.

I close with this practical thought. Sometimes believers show their love and their appreciation of their Master by special acts of homage. Herod, you see, when he made nothing of him, said, 'Here, bring out that glittering white robe of mine, and put it on him, that we may heap contempt upon him. He calls himself a King! Let us pay him homage!' They mocked him, and they put the robe upon him, and then sent him back to Pilate. Now, I want you to imitate Herod in the opposite direction. Let us do our Lord special honour tonight. Let us crown him. As soon as we have opportunity, let us make some special offering of our substance to his cause. Let us set apart a season for adoration and reverent worship. Let us resolve that for his sake we will speak well of his name to somebody to whom we have not yet spoken. It may be that some of you can sing a hymn to Jesus with choice music, or write a glorious verse for his dear sake. Go, take your pen, and dip it in your heart, and write a fresh tract in honour of his blessed name. Herod set him at nought, but let us set him on high in our best manner. Set him at the highest figure that your thought and your imagination can reach. It may be that some brother here could preach about his Lord, and yet he has not opened his mouth from timidity. Come, try, my friend. Shake off your bashfulness. It may be that some sister here might teach women, or get together a class of youngsters, and glorify Christ by instructing them. I long to undo what Herod did, and pay the Well-beloved a recompense for his shame. Oh, how would I honour him! But what am I? What can one person do? Come, all of you, my brethren, and help to cry 'Hosanna!' Alas! what are we all together? The music has no volume in it, compared with what he deserves. Come, all ye saints, and worship him! And what are all the saints on earth? Come, ye in heaven, who bear the palm, redeemed, perfected, and white-robed as ye are; come, worship him who washed your robes in his own blood! And what are all they? Even the armies of the redeemed suffice not. Come, all holy ones and praise him!

> Angels, assist our mighty joys!
> Strike all your harps of gold!
> But when you raise your highest notes,
> His love can ne'er be told.

Therefore do I summon all things that are to praise the Lord, without whom was not anything made. I charge all living things to adore him who is the resurrection and the life. Let space become one great mouth for song. Let time unceasingly flow with hallelujahs. Let eternity become an orchestra to the praise of Jesus, who was mocked of Herod and his men of war.

Glory be to his name! Hallelujah! Hallelujah! Amen.

14

ECCE REX[1]

He saith unto the Jews, Behold your King.
JOHN 19:14

PILATE SAID MUCH MORE than he meant, and, therefore, we shall not restrict our consideration of his words to what *he* intended. John tells us considering Caiaphas, 'and this spake he not of himself,' and we may say the same of Pilate. Everything said or done in connection with the Saviour during the day of his crucifixion was full of meaning, far fuller of meaning than the speakers or actors were aware. Transformed by the cross, even the commonplace becomes solemn and weighty. When Caiaphas said that it was expedient that one man should die for the people, that the whole nation perish not, he little thought that he was enunciating the great gospel principle of substitution. When the Jewish people cried out before Pilate 'His blood be on us and on our children,' they little knew the judgment which they were bringing upon themselves, which would commence to be fulfilled at the siege of Jerusalem, and follow them, hanging like a heavy cloud over their race, for centuries. When the soldier with a spear pierced his side he had no idea that he was bringing forth before all eyes that blood and water which are to the whole church the emblems of the double cleansing which we find in Jesus, cleansing by atoning blood and sanctifying grace. The fullness of time had come, and all things were full. Each movement on that awful day was brimming with mystery, neither could the Master or those

[1] Sermon No. 1,353. Preached at the Metropolitan Tabernacle on Sunday morning, 6 May 1877.

around him stir or speak without teaching some gospel, or enforcing some lesson. Whereas on certain days frivolity seems to rule the hour, and little is to be gathered from much that is spoken; on the day of the passion even the most careless spake as men inspired. Pilate, the undecided spirit, with no mind of his own, uttered language as weighty as if he too had been among the prophets. His acquittal of our Lord, his mention of Barabbas, his writing of the inscription to be fixed over the head of Jesus, and many other matters, were all fraught with instruction.

It was to the Jews that Pilate brought forth Jesus arrayed in garments of derision, and to them he said, '*Ecce rex*'– 'Behold your King!' It was by the seed of Abraham that he was rejected as their King; but we shall not think of them in order to blame that unhappy nation, but to remind ourselves that we also may fall into the same sin. As a nation favoured with the gospel we stand in many respects in the same privileged condition as the Jews did. To us is the word of God made known, to our keeping the oracles of God are committed in these last days, and we, though by nature shoots of the wild olive, are engrafted into that favoured stock from which Israel have for a while been cut off. Shall we prove equally unworthy? Shall any of us be found guilty of the blood of Jesus? We hear of Jesus this day; are we rejecting him? The suffering Messiah will be brought forth again this morning, not by Pilate, but by one who longs to do him honour, and when he stands before you, and is proclaimed again in the words, 'Behold your King!' will you also cry, 'Away with him, away with him'? Let us hope that there will not be found here hearts so evil as to imitate the rebellious nation and cry, 'We will not have this man to reign over us.' Oh that each one of us may acknowledge the Lord Jesus to be his King, for beneath his sceptre there is rest and joy. He is worthy to be crowned by every heart. Let us all unite in beholding him with reverence and receiving him with delight. Give me your ears and hearts while Jesus is evidently set forth as standing among you, and for the next few minutes let it be your only business to 'Behold your King.'

I. Come with me, then, to the place which is called the Pavement, but in the Hebrew Gabbatha, and there 'behold your King.' I shall first ask you to BEHOLD YOUR KING PREPARING HIS THRONE, yea, and making himself ready to sit thereon. When you look in answer to the summons, 'Behold your King,' what do you see? You see the 'Man of sorrows and acquainted with grief;' wearing a crown of thorns and covered with an old purple cloak, which had been thrown about him in mockery; you can see, if you look narrowly, the traces of his streaming blood, for he has just been scourged, and you may also discover that his face is blackened with bruises and stained with shameful spittle from the soldiers' mouths.

> Thus trimmed forth they bring him to the rout,
> Who, 'Crucify him', cry with one strong shout,
> God holds his peace at man, and man cries out.

It is a terrible spectacle, but I ask you to gaze upon it steadily and see the establishment of the Redeemer's throne. See how he becomes your mediatorial King. He was setting up a new throne on Gabbatha, whereon he would reign as the King of pardoned sinners and the Prince of Peace. He was King before all worlds as Lord of all by right of his eternal power and Godhead; he had a throne when worlds were made, as King of all kings by creation; he had also always filled the throne of providence, upholding all things by the word of his power. On his head were many crowns, and to Pilate's question, 'Art thou a king then?' he did fitly answer, 'Thou sayest that I am a king.'

But here before Pilate and the Jews, in his condition of shame and misery, he was about to ascend, and first of all to prepare the throne of the heavenly grace, which now is set up among the sons of men, that they may flee to it and find eternal salvation. Mark how be is preparing this throne of grace, it is *by pain and shame endured in our room and stead*. Sin was in the way of man's happiness, and a broken law, and justice requiring a penalty: and all this must be arranged before a throne of grace could be erected among men. If you look at our suffering Lord you see at once the ensigns of his *pain*, for he wears a crown of thorns which pierce his brow. Pain was a great part of the penalty due for sin, and the great Substitute was therefore sorely pained. When Pilate brought forth our martyr Prince he was the very mirror of agony, he was majesty in misery, misery wrought up to its full height and stature. The cruel furrows of the scourge, and the trickling rivulets of his blood adown his face were but the tokens that he was about to die in cruel pangs upon the cross, and these together were incumbent upon him because there could be no throne of grace till first there had been a substitutionary sacrifice. It behoved him to suffer that he might be a Prince and a Saviour. Behold your King in his pains, he is laying the deep foundations of his kingdom of mercy. Many a crown has been secured by blood, and so is this, but it is his own blood; many a throne has been established by suffering, and so is this, but he himself bears the pain. By his great sacrificial griefs our Lord has prepared a throne whereon he shall sit till all the chosen race have been made kings and priests to reign with him. It is by his agony that he obtains the royal power to pardon: by his stripes and bruises he wins the right to absolve poor sinners. We shall have no cause to wonder at the greatness of his mediatorial power if we consider the depth of his sacrificial sufferings: as his misery is the source of his majesty, so the greatness of his pains has secured to him the fullness of power to save. Had he not gone to the end of the law, and honoured justice to the highest degree, he had not now been so gloriously able to dispense mercy from his glorious high throne of mediatorial grace. Behold your King, then, as he lays deep in his own pain and death the basis of his throne of grace.

Nor is it only pain, for he wears also the tokens of *scorn*. That crown of thorns meant mainly mockery: the soldiers made him a mimic monarch, a carnival king, and that scarlet robe, too, was cast upon his shoulders in bitter scorn: thus did this world deride its God. The Evangelists give you the description in brief sentences, as if they stopped between each line to cover their faces with their hands and weep. So there he stands before the crowd, helpless, friendless, with none to declare his generation or give him a good word. He is deserted by all who formerly called him Master, and he has become the centre of a scene of rioting and ridicule. The soldiers have done their worst, and now the chief men of the nation look at him with contempt, and are only kept back from the most ribald scorn by a hate too furiously eager for death to afford them leisure for their scoffs. His enemies had done everything in their power to clothe him with scorn, and they were asking for permission to do more, for they cried, 'Let him be crucified.' Behold ye, how he has left all the honour of his Father's house, and his own glory among the angels, and here he stands with a mock robe, a mimic sceptre, and a thorny crown, the butt of ridicule, scoffed at by all! Yet this must be, because sin is a shameful thing, and a part of the penalty of sin is shame, as they will know who shall wake up in the day of judgment to everlasting contempt. Shame fell on Adam when he sinned, and then and there he knew that he was naked; and now shame has come down in a tremendous hail upon the head of the Second Adam, the substitute for shameful man, and he is covered with contempt. 'All they that see me laugh me to scorn.'

It is hard to say whether cruelty or mockery had most to do with the person of our Lord at Gabbatha; but by enduring these two things together he laid on an immovable foundation the cornerstone of his dominion of love and grace. How could he have been the king of a redeemed people if he had not thus redeemed, them? He might have been Lord over a people doomed to die, the stern ruler of a people who continued in sin, and would so continue till they perished for ever from his presence; but no such a kingdom did he seek; he sought a kingdom over hearts that should eternally be under obligation to him, hearts that, being redeemed from the lowest hell by his atoning death, would for ever love him with the utmost fervency. His sorrow secured his power to save, his shame endowed him with the right to bless.

'Behold your King.' Look at him with steady eye and see what a King he now is *by right of benefit conferred*. Behold, he hath put away sin for ever by the sacrifice of himself, and therefore all the ransomed ones agree that he should be king who smote the great dragon which devoured the nations. Behold by his stooping to shame he hath dethroned Satan, who was the prince of this world; and who should occupy the throne but he who has won it, and cast out the strong one who ruled aforetime. Christ has done more for men than the prince of darkness could or would, for he has died for them, and so he has earned a just supremacy over all grateful hearts. As for death, Jesus, by yielding to death, has conquered it. Let him be crowned with the victor's wreath who has destroyed the world's destroyer. In his shame you also see the Lord Jesus Christ fulfilling the law and making it honourable. He who could honour that law, which else would have cursed us, deserveth to have all honour and homage paid to him by the sons of men, whom he has rescued from the curse. You see, then, our Lord, when he put on the old red cloak, and submitted his brows to be environed with thorns, was really establishing for himself an empire the foundations of which shall never be shaken: he was performing that saving work which has made him king among sinners whom he saves, and Lord of the kingdom of grace, which through his death is bestowed upon men.

Note this, too, that men are kings among their fellows when they can show *deep sympathy, and give substantial succour.* He who can sympathise wins power of the best sort, not coarse force, but refined spiritual influence. For this cause our Lord was afflicted, as you see him afflicted, that he might have sympathy with you in your direst grief, and in your most grievous dishonour. As the children were partakers of flesh and blood, he himself also took part of the same, and as they must suffer, so the Captain of their salvation was made perfect by suffering. This gives him his glorious power over us. He is a faithful high priest, for he can be touched with the feeling of our infirmities, and this ability to enter into our infirmities and sorrows makes him supreme ins our hearts. Look at your King in pain and mockery, and see how royal he is to your heart! How sovereignly he commands your heart to rejoice. With what regal power he commands your fears to lie still, and how obediently your despondency yields to his word. Now, as it is with you, so is it on a larger scale in the world. The suffering nations will yet see their true deliverer in their suffering Lord. That sceptre of a reed will secure him power far greater than a rod of iron. His love to man is proved by his suffering to the death on their behalf, and this, when the Holy Spirit hath made men wise, shall be to the myriads of our race the reason for proclaiming him Lord of all. The kings and princes who rule mankind by reason of their descent or by the force of arms have but the names of kings, the true kings are the great benefactors. The heroes are our kings after all. We look upon those as royal who can risk their lives for their fellow men, to win them liberty, or to teach them truth. The race forgets its masters, but it remembers its friends. Earth, but for Jesus, had been a vast prison, and men a race of condemned criminals, but he who stands before us in Gabbatha, in all his shame and grief, hath delivered us from our lost estate, and therefore he must be King. Who shall say him nay? If love must ultimately triumph; if disinterested self-sacrifice must obtain homage, then Jesus is and shall be King. If eventually when the morning breaketh and man's heart is purged from the prejudice and injustice occasioned by sin, the might shall be with the right, and truth must prevail; then Jesus must reign. The eternal fitness of things demands that the best should be highest, that he who does men most service should be most honoured among them; in a word, that he who was made nothing of for man's sake should become everything to him. See you, then, how the crown of thorns is mother to the crown which Jesus wears in his church! The scarlet robe is the purchase price of the vesture of universal sovereignty, and the mock sceptre of reed is the precursor of the rod of nations wherewith the whole earth will yet be ruled. 'Behold your King,' and see the sources of his mediatorial power.

II. O you who see in your bleeding and rejected Lord 'the king in his beauty,' come ye hither yet again and BEHOLD HIM CLAIMING YOUR HOMAGE. See in what way he comes to win your hearts.. What is his right to be King over you? There are many rights, for on his head are many crowns, but the most commanding right which Jesus has over any of us is signified by that crown of thorns: it is *the right of supreme love:* he loved us as none other could have loved. If we put all the loves of parents and of wives and children all together, we can never rival even for a moment the love of Christ to us, and whenever that love touches us, so that we feel its power, we crown him King directly. Who can resist his charms? One look of his eyes overpowers us. See with your heart those eyes when they are full of tears for perishing sinners, and you are a willing subject. One look at his blessed person subjected to scourging and spitting for our sakes will give us more idea of his crown rights than anything besides. Look into his pierced heart as it pours out its life-flood for us, and all disputes about his sovereignty are ended in our hearts. We own him Lord because we see how he loved. How could we do otherwise? Love in action, or rather love suffering, carries an omnipotence about it. Behold what his love endured, and so 'Behold your King.'

Jesus in the garb of mockery, marred with traces of his pain, also reminds us of *his complete purchase of us by his deeds and death.* 'Ye are not your own, ye are bought with a price.' Behold your King, and see the price. It is the price of suffering immense, of shame most cruel. It is an incalculable price, for the Lord of all is set at nought. It is an awful price, for he who only hath immortality yields himself to die. It is the price of blood. It is the scourging and bleeding and woe of Jesus; nay, it is himself. If you would see the price of your redemption, 'Behold your King.' 'Tis he that hath redeemed us unto God by his blood, he that 'made himself of no reputation, and took upon him the form of a servant; and being found in fashion as a man, humbled himself; and became obedient unto death, even the death of the cross.' You own that claim, the love of Christ constraineth you; you feel that henceforth you live for him alone, and count it joy that in all respects he should reign over you with unlimited sway.

Jesus, because he suffered, hath acquired a power over us which is far superior to any which could be urged in courts of law, or enforced by mere power, for our hearts have voluntarily surrendered to him and given him *the right of our free submission,* charmed to own allegiance to such imperial love. Is it possible for a believer to look at the Lord Jesus Christ without feeling that he longs to be more and more his servant and disciple? Do you not thirst to serve him? Can you behold him in the depth of shame without pining to lift him up to the heights of glory? Can you see him stooping thus for you without pleading with God that a glorious high throne may be his, and that he may sit upon it and rule all the hearts of men? There is no need to argue out the right of King Jesus, for you feel it; his love has carried you by storm, and it holds fast its capture. You cannot have a Saviour without his being your King, and seeing such a Saviour in such a condition, you cannot even think of him without delighting to ascribe to him all power and dominion. Could we escape his sway it would be bondage to us, and when we at any time fail to own it, it is our worst affliction.

'Behold your King,' then, for he himself is his own claim to your obedience. See what he suffered for you, my brethren, and henceforth never draw back from any labour, shame, or suffering for his dear sake. 'Behold your King,' and reckon to be treated like him. Do you expect to be crowned with gold where he was crowned with thorns? Shall lilies grow for you and briars for him? Never again be ashamed to own his glorious name, unless indeed you can be so vile as to prove a traitor to such a Lord. See to what shame he was put, and learn from him to despise all shame for his truth's sake. Shall the disciple be above his master, or the servant above his lord? If they have thus maltreated the master of the house, what shall they do to the household? Let us reckon upon our share of this treatment, and by accepting it prove to all men that the despised and rejected of men is really the King over us, and that the subjects blush not to be like their monarch. Even though the cost be all the shame the world can possibly pour upon us, or all the suffering that flesh and blood can in any condition endure, let us be faithful in our loyalty, and cry, 'Who shall separate us? Shall persecution, or distress, or tribulation divide us from our King? Nay, in all these things we are more than conquerors. King of griefs, thou art King of my soul! O King of shame, thou art absolute monarch of my heart. Thou art King by right divine, and King by mine own voluntary choice. Other lords have had dominion over us, but now, since thou hast revealed thyself after this fashion, thy name only shall govern our spirit.' Do you not see, then, that Jesus before Pilate reveals his claim in the appearance which he wears. 'Behold your King.'

III. 'Behold your King,' for a third time, that you may see him SUBDUING HIS DOMINIONS. Dressed in robes of scorn, and with a visage marred with pain, he comes forth conquering and to conquer. This is not very apparent at a superficial glance, for he is not arrayed like a man of war. You see no sword upon his thigh, nor bow in his hand. No fiery threatenings fall from his lips, nor does he speak with eloquent persuasion. He is unarmed, yet victorious; is silent, but yet conquering. In this garb he goeth forth to war. His shame is his armour, and his sufferings are his battle axe. How say you? How can it be so? I speak no fiction, but sober fact, and it shall be proved.

Missionaries have gone forth to win *the heathen* for Christ, and they have commenced with the uncivilized sons of sin by telling them that there is a God, and that he is great and just: the people have listened unmoved, or have only answered, 'Dost thou think we know not this?' Then they have spoken of sin and its punishment, and have foretold the coming of the Lord to judgment, but still the people stirred not, but coolly said, '"Tis true,' and then went on their way to live in sin as before. At last these earnest men have let fall the blessed secret, and spoken of the love of God in giving his only begotten Son, and they have begun to tell the story of the matchless griefs of Immanuel. Then have the dry bones stirred, then have the deaf begun to hear. They tell us that they had not long told the story before they noticed that eyes were fastened on them, and that countenances were beaming with interest which had been listless before, and they have said to themselves, 'Why did we not begin with this?' Ay, why indeed? for this it is that touches men's hearts. Christ crucified is the conqueror. Not in his robes of glory does he subdue the heart, but in his vestments of shame. Not as sitting upon the throne does he at first gain the faith and the affections of sinners, but as bleeding, suffering, and dying in their stead. 'God forbid that I should glory,' said the apostle, 'save in the cross of our Lord Jesus Christ;' and though every theme that is connected with the Saviour ought to play its part in our ministry, yet this is the master theme. The atoning work of Jesus is the great gun of our battery. The cross is the mighty battering-ram wherewith to break in pieces the brazen gates of human prejudices and the iron bars of obstinacy. Christ coming to be our judge alarms, but Christ the Man of sorrows subdues. The crown of thorns has a royal power in it to compel a willing allegiance, the sceptre of reed breaks hearts better than a rod of iron, and the robe of mockery commands more love than Caesar's imperial purple. There is nothing like it under heaven. Victories ten thousand times ten thousand have been achieved by him whom Pilate led forth to the multitude – victories distinctly to be ascribed to the thorny crown and vesture of mockery, are they not written in the book of the wars of the Lord? There will be more such as he is more frequently set forth in his own fashion, and men are bidden in the Man of sorrows to behold their King.

Has it not been so *at home* as well as among the far-off heathen? What winneth men's hearts to Christ today? What but Christ in shame and Christ in suffering? I appeal to you who have been newly converted; what has bound you as captives to Jesus' chariot? What has made you henceforth vow to be his followers, rejoicing in his name? What but this, that he bowed his head to the death for your sake and hath redeemed you unto God by his blood? You know it is so.

And oh, dear *children of God*, if ever you feel the power of Christ upon you to the full, till it utterly overcomes you, is it not the memory of redeeming grief which doeth it? When you become like harps, and Jesus is the minstrel and layeth his finger amongst your heart-strings and bringeth out nothing but praise for his dear name, what is it that charms you into the music of grateful love but the fact of his condescension on your behalf? Is not this your song, that he was slain and hath redeemed you unto God by his blood? I confess I could sit me down at his cross' foot and do nothing else but weep until I wept myself away, for his sufferings make my soul to melt within me. Then if the call of duty is heard I feel intensely eager to plead with others, ready to make any sacrifice to bring others under my Lord's dominion, and full of a holy passion that even death could not quench – all this, I say, if I have but just come from gazing on the Redeemer's passion, and drinking of his cup and being baptized with his baptism. The sceptre of reed rules as nothing else ever did, for it rouses enthusiasm. The thorn-crown commands homage as no other diadem ever did, for it braces men into heroes and martyrs. No royalty is so all-commanding as that which has for its insignia the chaplet of thorn, the reed, the red cloak, and the five wounds. Other sovereignties are forced, and feigned, and hollow compared with the sovereignty of 'the despised of men': fear, or custom, or self-interest make men courtiers elsewhere, but fervent love crowds the courts of King Jesus. We do not merely say that the marred countenance is the most majestic ever seen, but we have felt it to be so on many an occasion, yea, and feel it to be so now. Do you want to make our hard hearts soft? Tell us of Jesus' grief. Would you make us, strong men, into children? Set the Man of sorrows in our midst; there is no resisting him.

Look ye also at *backsliders* if ye would see the power of the despised Nazarene. If they have gone away from Christ, if they have become lukewarm, if their hearts have become obdurate to him who once could charm them, what can bring them back? I know but one magnet which in the hands of the Holy Spirit will attract these sadly fallen ones: it is Jesus in his shame and pains. We tell them that they crucified the Son of God afresh, and put him to an open shame, and they look on him whom they have pierced, and mourn for him. O ye that after having sipped of the communion cup have gone to drink at the table of Bacchus, ye who after having talked of love to Christ have followed after the lusts of the flesh, ye who after singing his praises have blasphemed the sacred name with which ye are named – may his omnipotence of love be proved in you also. What can ever bring you back but this sad reflection, that ye also have twisted for him a crown of thorns and caused him to be blasphemed among his enemies? Still the merit of his death is available for you: the power and efficacy of his precious blood have not ceased even for you, and if you come back to him – and oh, may a sight of him draw you – he will receive you graciously as at the first. I say to you, 'Behold your King,' and may the sovereignty of his humiliation and suffering be proved this morning in some of you as you shall come bending at his feet, conquered by his great love and restored to repentance and faith by his marvellous compassion. A sight of his wounds and bruises heals us, so that we grieve at our rebellions and long to be brought home to God, never to wander more.

Ah, dear brethren, we shall always find, as long as the world standeth, that among saints, sinners, backsliders, and all classes of men Jesus Christ's power is most surely felt when his humiliation is most faithfully declared and most believingly known. It is by this that he will subdue all things to himself. If we will but preach Jesus Christ to the Hindu it will not be necessary to answer all his metaphysical subtleties – the sorrows of Jesus are as a sharp sword to cut the Gordian knot. If we will go down amongst the degraded inhabitants of Africa we shall not need first to civilize them; the cross is the great lever which lifts up fallen men: it conquers evil and establishes truth and righteousness. The most depraved and hardened learn his great love, and hearts of stone begin to beat; they see Jesus suffering to the death out of nothing else but love to them, and they are touched by it, and eagerly enquire what they must do to be saved by such a Saviour. The Holy Spirit worketh in the minds of many by setting forth the great love and grief of Jesus. May we who are his ministers have great faith in his cross, and henceforth say, as we preach the suffering Jesus, 'Behold your King.'

IV. In the fourth place I beg you to 'Behold your King' SETTING FORTH THE PATTERN OF HIS KINGDOM. When you look at him you are struck at once with the thought that if he be a king he is like no other monarch, for other kings are covered with rich apparel and surrounded with pomp, but he has none of these. Their glories usually consist in wars by which they have made others suffer, but his glory is his own suffering; no blood but his own has flowed to make him illustrious. He is a king, but he cannot be put in the list of sovereigns such as the nations of the earth are compelled to serve. When Antoninus Pius set up the statue of Jesus in the Pantheon as one of a circle of gods and heroes, it must have seemed strangely out of place to those who gazed upon its visage if the sculptor was at all true to life. It must have stood apart as one that could not be numbered with the rest. Neither can you set him among the masters of the human race who have crushed mankind beneath their iron heel. He was no Caesar; you cannot make him appear like one: call him not autocrat, emperor, or czar – he has an authority greater than all these, yet not after their kind. His purple is different from theirs, and his crown also, but his face differs more, and his heart most of all. 'My kingdom,' saith he, 'is not of this world.' For troops he has a host of sorrows, for pomp a surrounding of scorn, for lofty bearing humility, for adulation mockery, for homage spitting, for glory shame, for a throne a cross. Yet was there never truer king, indeed all kings are but a name, save this King, who is a real ruler in himself and of himself; and not by extraneous force. Right royal indeed is the Nazarene, but he cannot be likened unto the princes of earth, nor can his kingdom be reckoned with theirs. I pray that the day may soon come when none may dream of looking upon the church as a worldly organization capable of alliance with temporal sovereignties so as to be patronized, directed, or reformed by them. Christ's kingdom shines as a lone star with a brightness all its own. It standeth apart like a hill of light, sacred and sublime: the high hills may leap with envy because of it, but it is not of them nor like unto them. Is not this manifest even in the appearance of our Lord as Pilate brings him forth and cries, 'Behold your King!'?

Now as he sets before us in his own person the pattern of his kingdom, we may expect that we shall see some likeness to him in his subjects; and if you will gaze upon the church, which is his kingdom, from the first day of her history until now, you will see that it too is wearing its purple robe. The martyrs' blood is the purple vesture of the church of Christ; the trials and persecutions of believers are her crown of thorns. Think of the rage of persecution under Pagan Rome, and the equally inhuman proceedings of Papal Rome, and you will see how the ensign of Christ's kingdom is a crown of thorns; a crown and yet thorns, thorns but still a crown. The bush is burning, but it is not consumed. If you, beloved, are truly followers of Jesus, you must expect to take your measure of shame and dishonour, and you may reckon upon your allotment of griefs and sorrows. The 'Man of sorrows' attracts a sorrowful following. The lamb of God's Passover is still eaten with bitter herbs. The child of God cannot escape the rod, for the elder brother did not, and to him we are to be conformed. We must 'fill up that which is behind of the afflictions of Christ for his body's sake, which is the church' (*Col*. 1:24).

Recollect, however, that Christ's sufferings as a pattern were not for his own sins, nor brought upon him as a chastisement for his own faults, so that the sufferings which belong to his kingdom are those which are endured for his name and for his glory's sake, and for the good of others. If men lie in prison for their own crimes, that has nothing to do with his kingdom; if we suffer for our sins, that is no part of his kingdom; but when a man loseth of his substance for Christ's cause, layeth out himself to toil even unto death, beareth contempt and suffers hardness as a Christian – this is after the type of Christ's kingdom. When the missionary goeth forth with his life in his hand among the heathen, or when a believer in any way divesteth himself of comfort for the good of others, it is then that he truly copies the pattern set him in Pilate's hall by our great King. I say to you Christians who court ease, to you who are hoarding up your gold, to you who will do nothing that would bring you under the criticism of your fellow men, to you who live unto yourselves – would it not be irony of the severest kind if I were to point to Jesus before Pilate and say, 'Behold your King.' Living in undue luxury, amassing wealth, rolling in ease, living to enjoy yourselves! Is that your King? Poor subjects you, and very unlike your Lord; but if there be among us those who for his sake can make sacrifices, we may look upon our King without fear. You who are undaunted by contempt, and who would give all that you have, yea, and give yourselves to know Jesus, and are doing so, to such I say, 'Behold your King,' for you are of his king-dom and you shall reign with him. In your conquest of yourselves you have already become kings. In reigning over your own desires and carnal inclinations, for the sake of his dear love, you are already kings and priests unto God, and you shall reign for ever and ever. He who is ruled by his passions in any degree is still a slave, but he who lives for God and his fellow men hath a royal soul. The insignia of a prince unto God are still shame and suffer-ing: which adornments are readily worn when the Lord calls him so to do. In Christ's kingdom those are peers of the highest rank who are most like their Lord and are the lowest and humblest in mind, and most truly the servants of all. The secondary princes of his kingdom approximate less closely to him, and the lower you descend in the scale the less you are like him in those respects. The Christian surrounded with every comfort, who never endured hardness for Christ, who never knew what it was to be sneered at for Jesus' sake, who never made a sacrifice which went so far as to pinch him in the least, he, if indeed he be a Christian, is least in the kingdom of heaven. Proud, rich men who give but trifles to Christ's cause are pariahs in his kingdom, but they are the chief who are willing to be least of all, they are princes who make them-selves the offscouring of all things for his name's sake, such as were the apostles and first martyrs, and others whom his love has greatly constrained.

V. Our concluding remark shall be, 'Behold your King – PROVING THE CERTAINTY OF HIS EMPIRE – for if; beloved,

Christ was King when he was in Pilate's hands, after being scourged and spit upon, and while he was wearing the robe and crown of mockery, when will he not be King? If he was King at his worst, when is it that his throne can ever be shaken? They have brought him very low, they have brought him lower than the sons of men, for they have made him a worm and no man, despised of the people, and *yet he is King!* Marks of royalty were present on the day of his death. He dispensed crowns when he was on the cross – he gave the dying thief a promise of an entrance into paradise. In his death he shook the earth, he opened the graves, he rent the rocks, he darkened the sun, and he made men smite on their breasts in dismay. One voice after another, even from the ranks of his foes, proclaimed him to be King, even when dying like a malefactor.

Was he a King then? When will he not be King? and who is there that can by any means shake his throne? In the days of his flesh 'the kings of the earth stood up, and the rulers took counsel together, saying, Let us break his bonds asunder, and cast his cords from us;' but he that sat in the heavens did laugh, the Lord did have them in derision, and Christ on the cross was acknowledged, in Hebrew, and Greek, and Latin, to be still the King of the Jews. When will he not be King? If he was King before he died and was laid in the grave, what is he now that he has risen from the dead, now that he has vanquished the destroyer of our race, and lives no more to die?

What is he now? Ye angels, tell what glories surround him now! If he was King when he stood at Pilate's bar, what will he be when Pilate shall stand at his bar, when he shall come on the great white throne and summon all mankind before him to judgment? What will be his acknowledged sovereignty and his dreaded majesty in the day of the Lord? Come, let us adore him; let us pay our humble homage in the courts of the Lord's house this day; and then let us go forth to our daily service in his name, and make this our strong resolve, his Spirit helping us, that we will live to crown him in our hearts and in our lives, in every place where our lot may be cast, till the day break and the shadows flee away, and we behold the King in his beauty and the land that is very far off. None can overturn a kingdom which is founded on the death of its King;

none can abolish a dominion whose deep foundations are laid in the tears and blood of the Prince himself. Napoleon said that he founded his empire by force, and therefore it had passed away; but, said he, 'Jesus founded his kingdom upon, love, and it will last for ever.' So it must be, for whatever may or may not be, it is written – 'He *must reign.*'

As for us, if we wish to extend the Redeemer's kingdom we must be prepared to deny ourselves for Christ, we must be prepared for weariness, slander, and self-denial. In this sign we conquer. The cross will have to be borne by us as well as by him if we are to reign with Jesus. We must both teach the cross and bear the cross. We must participate in the shame if we would participate in the glory. No thorn no throne. When again shall be heard the voice, 'Behold your King,' and Jew and Gentile shall see him enthroned, and surrounded with all his Father's angels, with the whole earth subdued to his power, happy shall he be who shall then in the exalted Saviour behold his King.

The Lord grant us this day to be loyal subjects of the Crucified that we may be favoured to share his glory.

15

THE DREAM OF
PILATE'S WIFE[1]

When he was set down on the judgment seat, his wife
sent unto him, saying, Have thou nothing to do with
that just man: for I have suffered many things this
day in a dream because of him.
MATTHEW 27:19

I EARNESTLY WISHED to pursue the story of our Saviour's trials
previous to his crucifixion, but when I sat down to study the
subject I found myself altogether incapable of the exercise. 'When
I thought to know this, it was too painful for me.' My emotions
grew so strong, and my sense of our Lord's grief became so
extremely vivid, that I felt I must waive the subject for a time. I
could not watch with him another hour, and yet I could not leave
the hallowed scene. It was, therefore, a relief to meet with the
episode of Pilate's wife and her dream: it enables me to continue
the thread of my narrative, and yet to relax the extreme tension of
the feelings caused by a near view of the Master's grief and shame.
My spirit failed before the terrible sight. I thought I saw him
brought back from Herod where the men of war had set him at
nought. I followed him through the streets again as the cruel priests
pushed through the crowd and hastened him back to Pilate's hall.
I thought I heard them in the streets electing Barabbas, the robber,
to be set free, instead of Jesus, the Saviour, and I detected the first

---

[1] Sermon No. 1,647. Preached at the Metropolitan Tabernacle on Sunday
morning, 26 February 1882.

rising of that awful cry, 'Crucify, crucify,' which they shrieked out from their bloodthirsty throats: and there he stood, who loved me and gave himself for me, like a lamb in the midst of wolves, with none to pity and none to help him. The vision overwhelmed me, especially when I knew that the next stage would be that Pilate who had exculpated him by declaring, 'I find no fault in him,' would give him over to the tormentors that he might be scourged, that the mercenary soldiery would crown him with thorns and mercilessly insult him, and that he would be brought forth to the people and announced to them with that heart-rending word, 'Behold the man!' Was there ever sorrow like unto his sorrow? Rather than speak about it this day I feel inclined to act like Job's friends, of whom it is written, that at the sight of him 'they lifted up their voice, and wept; and sat down with him upon the ground seven days and seven nights, and none spake a word unto him: for they saw that his grief was very great.'

We leave the Master awhile to look at this dream of Pilate's wife, which is only spoken of once in the Scriptures, and then by Matthew. I know not why that evangelist only should have been commissioned to record it; perhaps he alone heard of it; but the one record is sufficient for our faith, and long enough to furnish food for meditation. We receive the story as certified by the Holy Spirit.

Pilate throughout his term of office had grossly misbehaved himself. He had been an unjust and unscrupulous ruler of the Jews. The Galileans and the Samaritans both felt the terror of his arms; for he did not hesitate to massacre them at the slightest sign of revolt; and among the Jews themselves he had sent men with daggers into the midst of the crowds at the great gatherings, and so had cut off those who were obnoxious to him. Gain was his object, and pride ruled his spirit. At the time when Jesus of Nazareth was brought before him a complaint against him was on the way to Tiberius the Emperor, and he feared lest he should be called to account for his oppressions, extortions, and murders. His sins at this moment were beginning to punish him: as Job would word it, 'The iniquities of his heels compassed him about.' One terrible portion of the penalty of sin is its power to force a man to commit yet further iniquity. Pilate's transgressions were now howling around him like a pack of wolves; he could not face them, and he had not grace to flee to the one great refuge; but his fears drove him to flee before them, and there was no way apparently open for him but that which led him into yet deeper abominations. He knew that Jesus was without a single fault, and yet since the Jews clamoured for his death he felt that he must yield to their demands, or else they would raise another accusation against himself, namely, that he was not loyal to the sovereignty of Caesar, for he had allowed one to escape who had called himself a king. If he had behaved justly he would not have been afraid of the chief priests and scribes. Innocence is brave; but guilt is cowardly. Pilate's old sins found him out and made him weak in the presence of the ignoble crew, whom otherwise he would have driven from the judgment seat. He had power enough to have silenced them, but he had not sufficient decision of character to end the contention: the power was gone from his mind because he knew that his conduct would not bear investigation, and he dreaded the loss of his office, which he held only for his own ends. See there with pity that scornful but vacillating creature wavering in the presence of men who were more wicked than himself and more determined in their purpose. The fell determination of the wicked priests caused hesitating policy to quail in their presence, and Pilate was driven to do what he would gladly have avoided.

The manner and the words of Jesus had impressed Pilate. I say the manner of Jesus, for his matchless meekness must have struck the governor as being a very unusual thing in a prisoner. He had seen in captured Jews the fierce courage of fanaticism; but there was no fanaticism in Christ. He had also seen in many prisoners the meanness which will do or say anything to escape from death; but he saw nothing of that about our Lord. He saw in him unusual gentleness and humility combined with majestic dignity. He beheld submission blended with innocence. This made Pilate feel how awful goodness is. He was impressed – he could not help being impressed – with this unique sufferer. Besides, our Lord had before him witnessed a good confession – you remember how we considered it the other day – and though Pilate had huffed it off with the pert question, 'What is truth?' and had gone back into the judgment-hall, yet there was an arrow fixed within him which he could not shake off. It may have been mainly superstition; but he felt an awe of one whom he half suspected to be an extraordinary personage. He felt that he himself was placed in a very extraordinary position, being asked to condemn one whom he knew to be perfectly innocent. His duty was clear enough, he could never have had a question about that; but duty was nothing to Pilate in comparison with his own interests. He would spare the Just One if he could do so without endangering himself; but his cowardly fears lashed him on to the shedding of innocent blood.

At the very moment when he was vacillating, when he had proffered to the Jews the choice of Barabbas, or Jesus of Nazareth – at that very moment, I say, when he had taken his seat upon the bench, and was waiting for their choice, there came from the hand of God a warning to him, a warning which would for ever make it clear that, if he condemned Jesus, it would be done voluntarily by his own guilty hands. Jesus must die by the determinate counsel and foreknowledge of God, and yet it must be by wicked hands that he is crucified and slain; and hence Pilate must not sin in ignorance. A warning to Pilate came from his own wife concerning her morning's dream, a vision of mystery and terror, warning him not to touch that just person; 'for,' said she, 'I have suffered many things this day in a dream because of him.' There are times in most men's lives when, though they have been wrong, yet they have not quite been set on mischief, but have come to a pause and have deliberated as to their way; and then God in great mercy has sent them a caution, and has set up a danger-signal bidding them stop in their mad career ere they plunged themselves finally into irretrievable ruin. Somewhere in that direction lies the subject of our present discourse. O that the Spirit of God may make it useful to many.

I. And, first, I call your attention to THE CO-OPERATION OF PROVIDENCE WITH THE WORK OF GOD. I call it the work of God to warn men against sin, and I call your attention to Providence working with it to bring the preventives and cautions of divine mercy home to men's minds.

For, first, observe the providence of God *in sending this dream*. If anything beneath the moon may be thought to be exempt from law, and to be the creature of pure chance, surely it is a dream. True, there were in old time dreams in which God spake to men prophetically; but ordinarily they are the carnival of thought, a maze of mental states, a dance of disorder. The dreams which would naturally come to the wife of a Roman governor would not be likely to have much of tenderness or conscience in them, and would not, in all probability, of themselves run in the line of mercy. Dreams ordinarily are the most disorderly of phenomena, and yet it seems that they are ordered of the Lord. I can well understand that every drop of spray which flashes from the wave when it dashes against the cliff has its appointed orbit as truly as the stars of heaven; but the thoughts of men appear to be utterly lawless, especially the thoughts of men when deep sleep falleth upon them. As well might one foretell the flight of a bird as the course of a dream. Such wild fantasies seem to be ungoverned and ungovernable.

Many things operate naturally to fashion a dream. Dreams frequently depend upon the condition of the stomach, upon the meat and drink taken by the sleeper before going to rest. They often owe their shape to the state of the body or the agitation of the mind. Dreams may, no doubt, be caused by that which transpires in the chamber of the house; a little movement of the bed caused by passing wheels, or the tramp of a band of men, or the passing of a domestic across the floor, or even the running of a mouse behind the wall panelling, may suggest and shape a dream. Any slight matter affecting the senses at such time may raise within the slumbering mind a mob of strange ideas. Yet whatever may have operated in this lady's case, the hand of providence was in it all, and her mind, though fancy free, wandered nowhere but just according to the will of God, to effect the divine purpose. She must dream just so, and no how else, and that dream must be of such and such an order, and none other. Even dreamland knows no god but God, and even phantoms and shadows come and go at his bidding, neither can the images of a night-vision escape from the supreme authority of the Most High. See the providence of God in the fact that the dream of Pilate's wife, however caused, should be of such a form and come at such a time as this. Certain old writers trace her dream to the devil, who thus hoped to prevent the death of our Lord, and so prevent our redemption. I do not agree with the notion; but even if it were so, I admire all the more the providence which overrules even the devices of Satan for the purposes of wisdom. Pilate must be warned, so that his sentence may be his own act and deed, and that warning is given him through his wife's dream. So doth Providence work.

Note, next, the providence of God in arranging that *with this dream there should be great mental suffering.* 'I have suffered many things in a dream concerning him.' I cannot tell what vision passed before her mind's eye, but it was one which caused her terrible agony. A modern artist has painted picture of what he imagined the dream to be, but I shall not attempt to follow that great man in the exercise of fancy. Pilate's wife may have realized in her sleep the dreadful spectacle of the thorn-crown and the scourge, or even of the crucifixion and the death-agony; and truly I know of nothing more calculated to make the heart suffer many things concerning the Lord Jesus than a glance at his death. Around the cross there gathers grief enough to cause many a sleepless night, if the soul has any tenderness left in it. Or her dream may have been of quite another kind. She may have seen in vision the Just One coming in the clouds of heaven. Her mind may have pictured him upon the great white throne, even the man whom her husband was about to condemn to die. She may have seen her husband brought forth to judgment, himself a prisoner to be tried by the Just One, who had aforetime been accused before him. She may have awoke, startled at the shriek of her husband as he fell back into the pit that knows no bottom. Whatever it was, she had suffered repeated painful emotions in the dream, and she awoke startled and amazed. The terror of the night was upon her, and it threatened to become a terror to her for all her days, and she therefore hastens to stay her husband's hand. Now, herein is the hand of God, and the simple story goes to prove that the wandering Zingari of dreamland are still under his control, and he can cause them to produce distress and anguish, if some grand end is to be served thereby.

Equally remarkable is it that *she should have sent to her husband the message,* 'Have nothing to do with this just person.' Most dreams we quite forget; a few we mention as remarkable, and only now and then one is impressed upon us so that we remember it for years. Scarcely have any of you had a dream which made you send a message to a magistrate upon the bench. Such an intention would only be resorted to in an urgent case. Though the judge were your own husband you would be very hard pressed before you would worry him with your dreams while he was occupied with important public business. Mostly a dream may wait till business is over. But so deep was the impression upon this Roman lady's mind that she does not wait until her lord comes home, but sends to him at once. Her advice is urgent – 'Have thou nothing to do with this Just One.'

She must warn him now, before he has laid a stroke on him, much less imbrued his hands in his blood. Not 'have a little to do and scourge him, and let him go,' but 'have thou nothing to do with him. Say not an unkind word, nor do him any injury! Deliver him from his adversaries! If he must die, let it be by some other hand than thine! My husband, my husband, my husband, I beseech thee, have thou nothing to do with this just person. Let him alone, I pray thee!' She words her message very emphatically. 'Have thou nothing to do with this just person: for I have suffered many things in a dream concerning him. Think of thy wife! think of thyself! Let my sufferings about this Holy One be a warning to thee. For my sake let him alone!' And yet, do you know, her message to my ear sounds rather authoritative for a woman to her husband, and he a judge! There is a tone about it that is not ordinarily in the address of wives to husbands. 'Have thou nothing to do with that just man: for I have suffered many things this day in a dream because of him.' It shows a wonderful providence of God that this lady was moved to send so strong a message to her self-willed husband, to beseech, to entreat, to implore, almost to demand of him, that he let this just man go. O Providence, how mightily canst thou work! O Lord, the seraphim obey thee, but thou findest an equally willing servitor in a wife who, at thy bidding, stands between her husband and a crime.

Once more, about this providence I want you to notice *the peculiar time in which her warning came*. It was evidently a dream of the morning: 'I have suffered many things in a dream this day.' The day had not long broken – it was yet early in the morning. The Romans had a superstition that morning dreams are true. I suppose it was after her husband had left her that she thus dreamed. If I may be allowed, not to state a fact, but to make a conjecture, which seems to me most probable, she was a dearly beloved wife, but sickly, and therefore needed to rest further into the day than her husband; and when he had left his couch she had yet another sleep, and being a sensitive person, and all the more likely to dream, she awoke from her morning sleep oppressed with a terror which she could not shake off. Pilate was gone, and she was told that he was in the judgment-hall. She asked her attendants why he was there so early, and they replied that there had been an unusual clamour in the courtyard, for the high priests and a mob of Jews had been there, and the governor had gone out to them. They might, perhaps, also tell her that Jesus of Nazareth was brought there a prisoner, and the priests were entreating Pilate to put him to death, though they had heard the governor say that he found no fault in him.

'Go,' she said to her maid, 'call to one of the guards, and bid him go at once to my husband, and say what I tell you. Let him speak aloud, that some of the cruel Jews may hear it, and be moved from their cruel purpose: let him say that I implore my husband to have nothing to do with this just person, for I have suffered many things this very morning in a dream concerning him.' Just at the moment, you see, when he had sat down on the judgment-seat, the warning came to him. When there was a little lull, and he was anxious to acquit his prisoner, at that instant of time which was the most hopeful this weight was thrown into the right side of the scale, thrown in most wisely and mercifully to keep back Pilate from his grievous sin.

The warning came in the nick of time, as we say, though, alas, it came in vain! Admire the punctuality of Providence. God never is before his time; he never is too late. It shall be seen concerning all that he doeth that on the selfsame day determined by the prophecy the fulfilment came. My soul stands trembling while she sings the glory of her God, whose providence is high, even like Ezekiel's wheels; but the wheels are full of eyes, and, as they turn, all the surroundings are observed and provided for, so that there are no slips, or oversights, or accidents, or delays. Prompt and effectual is the operation of the Lord.

Thus much concerning Providence, and I think you will all agree that my point is proven – that providence is always co-working with the grace of God. A great writer who knows but little about divine things, yet, nevertheless, tells us that he perceives a power in the world which works for righteousness. Exactly so! It is well spoken, for this is the chief of all powers. When you and I go out to warn men of sin, we are not alone, all Providence is at our back. When we preach Christ crucified, we are workers together with God; God is working with us as well as by us. Everything that happens is driving towards the end for which we work, when we seek to convince men of sin and of righteousness. Where the Spirit of God is, all the forces of nature and providence are mustered. The fall of empires, the death of despots, the uprise of nations, the making or the breaking of treaties, terrific wars and blighting famines, are all working out the grand end. Yea, and domestic matters, such as the death of children, the sickness of wives, the loss of work, the poverty of the family, and a thousand other things are working, working, ever working, for the improvement of men; and you and I, lending our poor feebleness to co-operate with God, are marching with all the forces of the universe. Have comfort, then, in this. O workers for Jesus, suffering many things for him, be of good courage, for the stars in their courses fight for the servants of the living God, and the stones of the field are in league with you.

II. Secondly, I gather from this story THE ACCESSIBILITY OF CONSCIENCE TO GOD. How are we to reach Pilate? How are we to give him warning? He has rejected the voice of Jesus and the sight of Jesus – could not Peter be fetched to expostulate with him? Alas, he has denied his Master. Could not John be brought in? Even he has forsaken the Lord. Where shall a messenger be found? It shall be found in a dream. God can get at men's hearts, however hardened they may be. Never give them up, never despair of arousing them. If my ministry, your ministry, and the ministry of the blessed Book should all seem to be nothing, God can reach the conscience by a dream. If the sword cometh not at them at close quarters, yet what seems but a stray arrow from a bow drawn at a venture shall find out the joints in their harness. We ought to believe in God about wicked men, and never say of them, 'It is impossible that they should be converted.' The Lord can wound leviathan, for his weapons are many, and they are suited to the foe. I do not think a dream would operate upon *my* mind to convince me; but certain minds lie open in that direction, and to them a dream may be a power. God may use even superstition to accomplish his beneficent purposes. Many besides Pilate have been warned by dreams.

Better still, Pilate was accessible through the dream *of his wife*. Henry Melvill has a very wonderful discourse upon this topic, in which he tries to show that probably if Pilate had dreamed this dream himself it would not have been so operative upon him as when his wife dreamed it. He takes it as a supposition, which nobody can deny, that Pilate had an affectionate and tender wife, who was very dear to him. The one brief narrative which we have of her certainly looks that way; it is evident that she loved her husband dearly, and would therefore prevent his acting unjustly to Jesus. To send a warning by her was to reach Pilate's conscience through his affections. If his beloved wife was distressed it would be sure to weigh heavily with him: for he would not have her troubled. He would fain shield his tender one from every breath of wind and give her perfect comfort, and when she pleads it is his delight to yield: it is, therefore, no small trouble to him that she is suffering, suffering so much as to send a message to him, suffering because of one who deserves her good opinion – one whom he himself knows to be without fault. If this lady was indeed the wife of Pilate's youth, tender and dearly beloved, and if she was gradually sickening before his eyes, her pale face would rise before his loving memory, and her words would have boundless power over him when she said, 'I have suffered many things in a dream.' O Claudia Procula, if that were thy name, well did the Lord of mercy entrust his message to thy persuasive lips, for from thee it would come with tenfold influence. Tradition declares this lady to have been a Christian, and the Greek Church have placed her in their calendar as a saint. For this we have no evidence; all that we know is that she was Pilate's wife, and used her wifely influence to stay him from this crime. How often has a tender, suffering, loving woman exercised great power over a coarse, rough man!

The All-wise One knows this, and hence he often speaks to sinful men by this influential agency. He converts one in a family that she may be his missionary to the rest. Thus he speaks with something better than the tongues of men and of angels, for he uses love itself to be his orator. Affection has more might than eloquence. That is why, my friend, God sent you for a little while that dear child who prattled to you about the Saviour. She is gone to heaven now, but the music of her little hymns rings in your ear even now, and her talk about Jesus and the angels is yet with you. She has been called home; but God sent her to you for a season to charm you to himself and win you to the right way. Thus he bade you cease from sin and turn to Christ. And that dear mother of yours, who is now before the throne, do you remember what she said to you when she was dying? You have heard me a great many times, but you never heard a sermon from me like that address from her dying couch. You can never quite forget it, or shake yourself free from its power. Beware how you trifle with it. To Pilate his wife's message was God's ultimatum; he warned him never again, and even Jesus stood silent before him. O my friend, to you it may be that your child, your mother, or your affectionate wife may be God's last messenger, the final effort of the warning angel to bring you to a better mind. A loving relative pleading with tears is often the forlorn hope of mercy. An attack so skilfully planned and wisely conducted may be regarded as the last assault of love upon a stubborn spirit, and after this it will be left to its own devices. The selection of the wife was no doubt made by infinite wisdom and tenderness, that if possible Pilate might be arrested in his career of crime and strengthened to the performance of an act of justice by which he would have avoided the most terrible of crimes.

So, then, we may safely conclude that the Lord has his missionaries where the city missionary cannot enter; he sends the little children to sing and pray where the preacher is never heard; he moves the godly woman to proclaim the gospel by her lip and life where the Bible is not read. He sends a sweet girl to grow up and win a brother or a father where no other voice would be allowed to tell of Jesus and his love. We thank God it is so; it gives hope for the households of this godless city – it gives us hope even for those for whom the Sabbath-bell rings out in vain. They will hear, they must hear these home preachers, these messengers who tug at their hearts.

Ay, and let me add that where God does not employ a dream, nor use a wife, yet he can get at men's conscience by no visible means but *by thoughts which come unbidden and abide upon the soul.* Truths long buried suddenly rise up, and when the man is in the very act of sin he is stopped in the way, as Balaam was when the angel met him. How often it has happened that conscience has met a guilty man even in the moment when he meant to enjoy the pleasure bought with wrong, even as Elijah met Ahab at the gate of Naboth's vineyard! How the king starts back as he beholds the prophet: he would sooner have seen the very fiend than Elijah. Angrily he cries, 'Hast thou found me, O mine enemy?' Though, indeed, Elijah was his best friend, had he known it. Often does conscience pounce upon a man when the sweet morsel of sin has just been rolled under his tongue, and he is sitting down to enjoy it: the visitation of conscience turns the stolen honey into bitterness, and the forbidden joy into anguish. Conscience often lies like a lion in a thicket, and when the sinner comes along the broad road it leaps upon him, and for a while he is sorely put to it. The bad man is comparable to leviathan, of whom we read that his scales are his pride, shut up together as with a close seal; so that the sword of him that layeth at him cannot hold, the spear, the dart, nor the javelin; and yet the Lord hath a way of coming at him and of sore wounding him. Let us, therefore, both hope and pray for the very worst of men.

Brothers and sisters, use for the good of men anything which comes in your way. Use not only sober argument and sound doctrine, but even if a dream has touched your heart, do not hesitate to repeat it where it may have effect. Any weapon may he used in this war. But see to it that you do seek the souls of men, all of you. You who are wives should be especially stirred up to this sacred work. Remember Pilate's wife, and think of her as affectionately giving the warning to her husband, and go and do likewise. Never keep back from an ungodly husband the word which may convert him from the error of his ways. And you, dear children, you sisters, you of the gentler sort, do not hesitate, in your own quiet way, to be heralds for Jesus wherever your lot is cast. As for us all, let us take care that we use every occasion for repressing sin and creating holiness. Let us warn the ungodly at once; for perhaps the man to whom we are sent has not yet performed the fatal deed. Let us stand in the gap while yet there is space for repentance. Pilate is even now sitting on the judgment-seat. Time is precious. Make haste! Make haste, ere yet he commits the deed of blood! Send the messenger to him! Stop him ere the deed is done; even though he should complain of your interference. Say to him, 'Have thou nothing to do with this just person: for I have suffered many things because of him, and I pray thee do nothing against him.'

That is our second point. God bless it; although I cannot preach upon it as I would, the Spirit of God can put power into it.

III. Thirdly, we have now the lamentable task of observing THE FREQUENT FAILURE EVEN OF THE BEST MEANS. I have ventured to say that, humanly speaking, it was the best means of reaching Pilate's conscience for his wife to be led to expostulate with him. He would hear but few, but her he would hear; and yet even her warning was in vain. What was the reason?

First, *self-interest* was involved in the matter, and that is a powerful factor. Pilate was afraid of losing his governorship. The Jews would he angry if he did not obey their cruel bidding; they might complain to Tiberius, and he would lose his lucrative position. Alas, such things as these are holding some of you captives to sin at this moment. You cannot afford to be true and right, for it would cost too much. You know the will of the Lord; you know what is right; but you renounce Christ by putting him off, and by abiding in the ways of sin that you may gain the wages thereof. You are afraid that to be a true Christian would involve the loss of a friend's goodwill, or the patronage of an ungodly person, or the smile of an influential worldling, and this you cannot afford. You count the cost, and reckon that it is too high. You resolve to gain the world, even though you lose your soul! What then? You will go to hell rich! A sorry result this! Do you see anything desirable in such an attainment? Oh that you would consider your ways and listen to the voice of wisdom!

The next reason why his wife's appeal was ineffectual was the fact that Pilate was *a coward*. A man with legions at his back, and yet afraid of a Jewish mob – afraid to let one poor prisoner go whom he knew to be innocent; afraid because he knew his conduct would not bear inspection! He was, morally, a coward! Multitudes of people go to hell because they have not the courage to fight their way to heaven. 'The fearful and unbelieving shall have their portion in the lake which burneth with fire and brimstone, which is the second death.' So saith the word of God. They are afraid of encountering a fool's laugh, and so rush upon everlasting contempt. They could not bear to tear themselves away from old companions, and excite remarks and sarcasm among ungodly wits, and so they keep their companions and perish with them. They have not the pluck to say 'No,' and swim against the stream; they are such cowardly creatures that they will sooner be for ever lost than face a little scorn.

Yet while there was cowardice in Pilate, there was *presumption* too. He who was afraid of man and afraid to do right, yet dared to incur the guilt of innocent blood. Oh, the cowardice of Pilate to take water and wash his hands, as if he could wash off blood with water; and then to say, 'I am innocent of his blood' – which was a lie – 'see ye to it.' By those last words he brought the blood upon himself, for he consigned his prisoner to their tender mercies, and they could not have laid a hand upon him unless he had given them leave. Oh, the daring of Pilate thus in the sight of God to commit murder and disclaim it. There is a strange mingling of cowardliness and courage about many men; they are afraid of a man, but not afraid of the eternal God who can destroy both body and soul in hell. This is why men are not saved, even when the best of means are used, because they are presumptuous, and dare defy the Lord.

Besides this, Pilate was *double-minded:* he had a heart and a heart. He had a heart after that which was right, for he sought to release Jesus; but he had another heart after that which was gainful, for he would not run the risk of losing his post by incurring the displeasure of the Jews. We have plenty around us who are double-minded. Such are here this morning; but where were they last night? You will be touched by today's sermon! How will you be affected tomorrow by a lewd speech or a lascivious song? Many men run two ways; they seem earnest about their souls, but they are far more eager after gain or pleasure. Strange perversity of man that he should tear himself in two. We have heard of tyrants tying men to wild horses and dragging them asunder, but these people do this with themselves. They have too much conscience to neglect the Sabbath, and to forego attendance at the house of prayer; too much conscience to be utterly irreligious, to be honestly infidel; and yet at the same time they have not enough conscience to keep them from being hypocrites. They let 'I dare not' wait upon 'I would'. They want to do justly, but it would be too costly. They dare not run risks, and yet, meanwhile, they run the awful risk of being driven for ever from the presence of God to the place where hope can never come. Oh that my words were shot as from a culverin! Oh that they would hurl a cannon-shot at indecision! Oh that I could speak like God's own thunder, which maketh the hinds to calve, and breaketh the rocks in pieces: even so would I warn men against these desperate evils which thwart the efforts of mercy, so that, even when the man's own wife, with tenderest love, bids him escape from the wrath to come, he still chooses his own destruction.

IV. Lastly, we have a point which is yet more terrible, THE OVERWHELMING CONDEMNATION OF THOSE WHO THUS TRANSGRESS. This Pilate was guilty beyond all excuse. He deliberately and of his own free will condemned the just Son of God to die, being informed that he was the Son of God, and knowing both from his own examination and from his wife that he was a 'just person'.

Observe that the message which he received was most distinct. It was suggested by a dream; but there is nothing dreamy about it. It is as plain as words can be put: 'Have thou nothing to do with that just man: for I have suffered many things this day in a dream because of him.' He condemned the Lord with his eyes open, and that is an awful way of sinning. Oh, my dear friends, am I addressing any here who are purposing to do some very sinful thing, but have lately received a warning from God? I would add one more caution. I pray you by the blessed God, and by the bleeding Saviour, and as you love yourself, and as you love her from whom the warning may have come to you, do stop, and hold your hand! Do not this abominable thing! You know better. The warning is not put to you in some mysterious and obscure way; but it comes point blank to you in unmistakable terms. God has sent conscience to you, and he has enlightened that conscience, so that it speaks very plain English to you. This morning's discourse stops you on the highway of sin, puts its pistol to your ear, and demands that you 'Stand and deliver.' Stir an inch, and it will be at your own soul's peril. Do you hear me? Will you regard the heaven-sent expostulation? Oh, that you would stand still awhile and hear what God shall speak while he bids you yield yourself to Christ today.

It may be *now or never* with you, as it was with Pilate that day. He had the evil thing which he was about to do fully described to him, and therefore if he ventured on it, his presumption would be great. His wife had not said, 'Have nothing to do with this man,' but 'with this just man,' and that word rang in his ears, and again and again repeated itself till he repeated it too. Read the twenty-fourth verse. When he was washing his wicked hands he said, 'I am innocent of the blood of this just person' – the very name his wife had given to our Lord. The arrows stuck in him! He could not shake them off! Like a wild beast, he had the javelin sticking in his side, and though he rushed into the forest of his sin, it was evidently rankling in him still – 'that just person' haunted him. Sometimes God makes a man see sin as sin, and makes him see the blackness of it; and if he then perseveres in it, he becomes doubly guilty, and pulls down upon himself a doom intolerable beyond that of Sodom of old.

Beside that, Pilate was sinning not only after distinct warning, and a warning which set out the blackness of the sin, but he was sinning after his conscience had been touched and moved through his affections. It is a dreadful thing to sin against a mother's prayer. She stands in your way; she stretches out her arms, with tears she declares that she will block your road to perdition. Will you force your way to ruin over her prostrate form? She kneels! She grasps your knees, she begs you not to be lost. Are you so brutal as to trample on her love? Your little child entreats you; will you disregard her tears? Alas, she was yours, but death has removed her, and ere she departed she entreated you to follow her to heaven and she sang her little hymn – 'Yes, we'll gather at the river.' Will you fling your babe aside us though you were another Herod that would slay the innocents, and all in order that you may curse yourself for ever and be your own destroyer? It is hard for me to talk to you thus. If it is coming home to any of you it will be very hard for you to hear it; indeed, I hope it will be so hard that you will end it by saying, 'I will yield to love which assails me by such tender entreaties.'

It will not be a piece of mere imagination if I conceive that at the last great day, when Jesus sits upon the judgment-seat, and Pilate stands there to be judged for the deeds done in the body, that his wife will be a swift witness against him to condemn him. I can imagine that at the last great day there will be many such scenes as that, wherein those who loved us best will bring the most weighty evidences against us, if we are still in our sins. I know how it affected me as a lad when my mother, after setting before her children the way of salvation, said to us, 'If you refuse Christ and perish, I cannot plead in your favour and say that you were ignorant. No, but I must say Amen to your condemnation.' I could not *bear* that! Would my mother say 'Amen' to my condemnation? And yet, Pilate's wife, what canst thou do otherwise? When all must speak the truth, what canst thou say but that thy husband was tenderly and earnestly warned by thee and yet consigned the Saviour to his enemies?

Oh, my ungodly hearers, my soul goes out after you. 'Turn ye, turn ye, why will ye die?' Why will ye sin against the Saviour? God grant you may not reject your own salvation, but may turn to Christ and find eternal redemption in him. 'Whosoever believeth in him hath everlasting life.'

16

PILATE AND OURSELVES GUILTY OF THE SAVIOUR'S DEATH[1]

> When Pilate saw that he could prevail nothing, but that rather a tumult was made, he took water, and washed his hands before the multitude, saying, I am innocent of the blood of this just person: see ye to it. Then answered all the people, and said, His blood be on us, and on our children.
>
> MATTHEW 27:24–25

THE CRUCIFIXION OF CHRIST was the crowning sin of our race. In his death we shall find all the sins of mankind uniting in foul conspiracy. Envy and pride and hate are there, with covetousness, falsehood, and blasphemy, eager to rush on to cruelty, revenge, and murder. The devil roused around the seed of the woman the iniquities of us all: they compassed the Lord about, yea, they compassed him about like bees. All the evils of human hearts of all ages were concentrated around the cross: even as all the rivers run into the sea, and as all the clouds empty themselves upon the earth, so did all the crimes of man gather to the slaying of the Son of God. It seemed as if hell held a *levée*, and all the various forms of sin came flocking to the rendezvous; army upon army, they hastened to the battle. As the vultures hasten to the body, so came the flocks of sins to make the Lord their prey. By all the assembled troops of sins there was consummated the foulest

---

[1] Sermon No. 1,648. Preached at the Metropolitan Tabernacle on Sunday morning, 5 March 1882.

crime which the sun has ever beheld. By wicked hands they did crucify and slay the Saviour of the world.

We have been singing two hymns in which we took to ourselves a share of the guilt of our Lord's death. We sang —

> Oh, the sharp pangs of smarting pain
>   My dear Redeemer bore,
> When knotty whips and rugged thorns
>   His sacred body tore.
>
> But knotty whips and rugged thorns
>   In vain do I accuse;
> In vain I blame the Roman bands,
>   And the more spiteful Jews.
>
> 'Twas you, my sins, my cruel sins,
>   His chief tormentors were;
> Each of my crimes became a nail,
>   And unbelief the spear.

And then after the same manner we sorrowfully asked a question, and sang a penitential reply:

> My Jesus! who with spittle vile
>   Profaned thy sacred brow?
> Or whose unpitying scourge has made
>   Thy precious blood to flow?
>
> 'Tis I have thus ungrateful been,
>   Yet, Jesus, pity take!
> Oh, spare and pardon me, my Lord,
>   For thy sweet mercy's sake!

Perhaps some of you hardly understand what you have been singing; but others of us have sincerely and intelligently pleaded guilty of the death of our Lord Jesus Christ. We know that he not only suffered for our transgressions, but by our iniquities. This is not clear to a great many; and I would not have them pretend that it is. They cannot see that they have anything to do with the matter of Jesus' death, and therefore they are not moved to repentance by hearing thereof; indeed, they imitate the example of Pilate in our text, when he took water and washed his hands before the multitude, and said, 'I am innocent of the blood of this just person.' The object of our present discourse will be to arouse slumbering consciences. Without going into any metaphysical questions as to whether such a man did or did not actually have a share in the particular action by which Jesus died, I shall show you that in many ways men practically commit a like crime, and so prove that they have similar dispositions to those ancient Kill-Christs. Though they repudiate the crucifixion, they repeat it, if not in form, yet in spirit. Though Jesus is not here in flesh and blood, yet the cause of holiness and truth and his divine Spirit are still among us, and men act towards the kingdom of Christ, which is set up among them, in the same way as the Jews and Romans acted towards the incarnate God. True, all men are not alike inveterate against him; for the Lord spoke of some who have 'the greater sin'; and few are as guilty as the traitor Judas, that son of perdition; but in every form of it the rejection of Christ is a great sin, and it will be a great gospel blessing if it be repented of after the fashion of the prophet when he said, 'They shall look upon me whom they have pierced, and they shall mourn for him, as one mourneth for his only son, and shall be in bitterness for him, as one that is in bitterness for his firstborn.'

I shall now take up the story of our Lord's appearance before Pilate, from the moment of his being sent back to Herod to the time when he was delivered to the Jews to be led away for crucifixion, and I shall try to exhibit by this narrative several ways in which men virtually put the Christ to death, and therefore become partakers of the ancient transgression which was committed at Jerusalem.

I. First, there are some – and these are they who have the greater sin who are DETERMINEDLY AND AVOWEDLY THE OPPONENTS OF THE LORD JESUS. These are the men who are represented by the chief priests and elders of the Jews, who of old sought the Saviour's blood, because they could not endure his teaching. Nothing else would satisfy them but that he should be removed from the earth, for he was a standing protest against their evil deeds. They hated him because by his light their wicked lives were reproved. These were the true murderers of Christ, who gloried in their shame and defied the punishment of it, crying, 'His blood be on us, and on our children.' We have still among us those who cannot endure the teaching of our Lord Jesus. His very name seems to excite their worst passions; they rave at the mention of it. Oh, the atrocious things that some have said of late of the Christ of God. They have gone out of their way to insult him. If anyone else had been slandered as he has been, society would not have tolerated the loathsome tongues. Accusations against Jehovah and his Son would seem to be delectable morsels to modern blasphemers, dainties upon which they feed greedily. My flesh trembles when I think of the hard speeches which the ungodly still utter against him who in the day of his humiliation endured such contradiction of sinners against himself.

Absurd many of these calumnies would have been, and to be dismissed with uttermost contempt, if it were not for the guilt of the men themselves; for in these speeches we see that the poison of asps is under their lips; their mouth is full of cursing and bitterness. They treat not so the heroes of war, the philosophers of antiquity, nor even the notorious scourges of the race to all of these they show some candour, and often award honours which are doubtfully due; but when they touch upon the person and life of our blessed Lord, candour and honesty are dismissed: anything like an attempt to understand him is refused, and he and his are treated with ridicule, misrepresentation, and falsehood. They heap up their coarsest epithets, they put the worst interpretation upon his words, they give the vilest misrepresentations of his deeds, and attribute to him motives to which he was an utter stranger. Such men are among us, clamouring to be heard. There have been unbelievers and deriders of Jesus in all time; but just now the race is of fouler speech than usual. Once infidelity was philosophical and thoughtful, and great names were to be found upon her roll; but now her noisiest advocates are bullies after the manner of Tom Paine, men who seem to delight in wounding the feelings of the godly and crushing every sacred thing under their feet. These are the true followers of the men whose mouths were full of 'Crucify him! Crucify him!' They cannot endure that Jesus should be remembered, much less revered. They claim to be 'liberal', and to be large-hearted towards all religions; but their unmitigated scorn of the faith of Jesus is displayed on every possible occasion, proving that the spirit of persecution burns within them. It would be idle for these to say that they would not crucify Christ, for they do crucify him to the utmost of their power by their profane speeches against him.

By a certain number their main attack is aimed against the royal authority and reigning power of the Lord Jesus. They exclaim against him because he claims universal sovereignty. They might not object so much to Christianity as one of various creeds; but as it claims to be supreme they will have nothing to do with it. The Roman Senate was willing to set up Jesus in the Pantheon, among other gods, but when they learned that the Christ claimed to be worshipped alone, then he was denied a place in the circle of adoration. If the gospel claims to be truth, and judges other systems to be false, straightway it arouses the opposition of the broad school. We have men among us today who say, 'Yes, there is something good in Christianity as there is in Buddhism.' Of this precious Buddhism they seem of late to be wonderfully fond; any idol will suit men so long as they can be rid of the living God. A Christ who will be everything or nothing is not to their taste. When he saith that the idols he will utterly demolish, and break his enemies in pieces as with a rod of iron, they give him the cold shoulder, for they are distinctly the enemies of Jesus Christ if he be set forth as Lord of all.

And we have some of milder cast who, nevertheless, join with this band; for their opposition is to the deity of Christ. These in effect cry, 'We have a law, and by our law he ought to die, because he made himself the Son of God.' They grow indignant over the claims which Christians advance for their God and Saviour. Christ the best of men, Christ the noblest of prophets, Christ near akin to deity, possibly a delegated God, they will go as far as that, but further they will not stir. 'That all men should honour the Son even as they honour the Father' is not to their mind. If Jesus be

253

preached as 'very God of very God', straightway we hear from them the cry, 'Away with him! away with him!' When we proclaim Jesus as King upon God's holy hill of Zion, and say of him, 'Thy throne, O God, is for ever and ever,' they refuse to bow before his divine majesty. They do, so far as they are able, destroy the divinity of Christ and reduce him to a mere man. How can such people blame the Jews and the Romans? They could but slay his manhood, but these would destroy his deity. Is not their guilt as great? I charge all deniers of the godhead of our Lord with being, as far as they can be, his murderers; for they strike at his noblest nature by assailing his divine power and godhead. May the Spirit of God be here to convince them of their error and lead them to worship Jesus, who is exalted at the right hand of the Father.

I must charge home the accusation in the name of God and truth. Avowed opposers of Christ, had they been alive in the days of his flesh, would have wished him to be put to death, for, so far as they are concerned, he is either dead to them in his true character, or else they are doing their best in their own conscience and upon the conscience of others to sweep him out of existence. If they say they would not have put Jesus to a literal death on the cross, I say they are putting him to a death which he would deprecate even more, namely, the destruction of all his influence over the minds of men. By decrying his atonement by which he reconciles men to God, by setting men's hearts against him and causing them to refuse his salvation, these men do as far as they can rob him of the joy that was set before him, for which he endured the cross, despising the shame. Is this nothing? Put me to death if you will, for I shall live when I am dead by the words which I have spoken: I should count it a far worse murder if you could sweep out of men's minds all that I have taught, and overthrow all the good which I have attempted to do. And if it be so of a mere man, much more must it be so of Jesus – that merely to murder him upon a cross is comparatively little compared with declaring, 'We will not be influenced by him, nor believe in him as Saviour and God, and to the best of our power we will prevent others from believing in him.' What a wretched object for a man to live for, what a horrible fame for a man to seek after – to stamp out the gospel of Jesus. Terrible will be the punishment of this sin. Oh opponent of Jesus, instead of being less guilty than the Jews of our Lord's day, you are even more culpable. You are not slaying him in one way, but you are doing it in another, and the crime is the same in spirit. I see a mystic cross to which your cruel words do nail my Lord; I see before my mental eye a Calvary whereon the Lord Jesus is crucified afresh and put to an open shame by infidel sarcasms and sceptical insinuations; I see him derided and made nothing of by those who deny his deity and refuse to believe in his sacrifice Enough of this. May conscience be present here, and the Spirit of God be present too, that men may not dare to wash their hands in innocency if they have been the open antagonists of Jesus and are so still, Oh that you would turn to him, and become his disciples. His beauties are such that they might well charm every honest heart: his teaching is so tenderly reasonable, so full of sweetness and of light, that it is marvellous that men do not receive it with joy. His cross is unique – a bleeding sufferer, bearing offences that were not his own, that his own enemies might live! The conception is so strange that it could never have originated in the selfish mind of fallen man. It bears its own witness on its brow. Woe unto those that fight against it, for it shall cost them dear. He that stumbleth upon this stone shall be broken, but upon whomsoever this stone shall fall it shall grind him to powder. See what came to these Jewish people: they were themselves crucified by Titus in such numbers that they could no longer find wood enough for their execution. Jerusalem destroyed is the result of Jesus crucified. Beware, ye that fight against him, for the omnipotent Father will take up his quarrel, and all the forces of creation and of providence will be at his command to wage war for truth and righteousness. The Nazarene has triumphed, and he will triumph even to the end, when he shall have all his enemies under his feet. O ye that hate him, be wise betimes, and close the hopeless contest in which you chiefly fight against your own souls.

II. I hope there are not many here to whom this first part of my sermon applies; we will advance to a second point. Pilate having a conscience which troubled him was exceedingly anxious not to put Jesus to death, and yet could not see how he could avoid doing so, seeing that the Jews threatened to accuse him of want of loyalty to Caesar, and that Caesar the gloomy tyrant Tiberius, who was unrelenting in his fury. After first sending his prisoner to Herod, he finds that he cannot escape in that way, and therefore he catches at a second hope. He tells the mob that the custom of the feast required that one prisoner should be released, and that the choice remained with them. He hopes that they will choose Jesus of Nazareth. A vain hope indeed! It so happened that there was another Jesus in prison at the time, namely, Jesus Barabbas, who had been a murderer, and was guilty both of sedition and robbery. Pilate brings out the two, and he gives the Jews their choice, It would make a wonderful picture if it were really so, as a writer on the Life of Christ suggests, that Pilate actually set the two individuals before the crowd. See there the dark-browed, scowling assassin, with fierce looks, and every mark of fury and hate upon his face, the man taken red-handed, familiar with blood, the brigand whose very profession was strife! There he stands like a wolf, and by his side is set the gentle Lamb of God. See there in his face and bearing all that is good, tender, benevolent, heroic. The incarnations of hate and love are before them; and Pilate gives the crowd their choice. Without hesitation they cry, 'Not this man, but Barabbas. Now Barabbas was a robber.' The murderer walks away free, and the innocent Jesus is left to die. In this I shall have to impeach a second class of men IN THE MATTER OF THEIR CHOICE. Many among us have by divine grace chosen Jesus to be our Saviour, King, and Lord. He is the groundwork of our eternal hope, and the spring of our present joy: we have selected Christ to be the guide and leader of our lives, and we are not ashamed of the choice. It has been made deliberately and solemnly, and we renew it from day to day.

> High heaven that heard the solemn vow,
> That vow renewed shall daily hear,
> Till in life's latest hour we bow,
> And bless in death a bond so dear.

I fear that some among you have not chosen Christ; but what have you chosen? Let me mention two or three objects of human choice, worthy to be ranked with Barabbas of old. Too many have chosen *lust* to be their delight: I will not paint the hideous monster; I have no colours. It is a foul and bestial thing: the cheek of modesty crimsons at the very mention of it. Yet, for the pleasures of wantonness, Christ is set aside. For the strange woman many a man has thrown away his soul, and chosen infamy instead of glory. I half excuse the Jews for choosing Barabbas when I see a man obeying the lusts of the flesh instead of Christ; and yet I am probably addressing individuals who secretly indulge their baser passions, and are thereby held back from becoming decided Christians. They know they cannot be followers of Christ and yet indulge in wantonness and chambering, and therefore for this vile self-indulgence they let Jesus go. Very frequently I meet with persons who have chosen another Barabbas instead of Jesus. What if, to borrow from heathenism, I call it Bacchus? Drink is the demon which enthrals millions. It is a vice which degrades men, and defaces the image of God in them. We insult the brutes when we say that a drunken man sinks to the level of the beasts; for the cattle never go so low as that. Alas, I have known men – ay, and women, too – who have been hearers of the gospel, and have in a measure felt its power, and yet for this sin they have sold their souls and given up their Saviour. No drunkard hath eternal life abiding in him; and, to speak plain English, there are professing Christians who deserve to be called by that name. I say that they prefer the drink-demon to the holy Lord Jesus. You condemn the Jews for choosing Barabbas: where will you find a counsellor to plead for you when you choose drunkenness? If it was sinful for them to choose a murderer, what must it be for you to choose this cursed vice, which murders its hundreds of thousands? Oh, this national vice of ours, the vice which makes this nation a byword and a proverb among the nations of the earth! What shall I say of it? And is this to be set in rivalry with my Lord? Oh, shame, cruel shame that this should be selected in preference to him who loved us and gave himself for us!

'Well, well,' says one, 'I do not fall into that sin.' No, my friend, but what is it that you do choose instead of Christ, for if you do not set him on the throne of your heart, you are choosing something else. Is it that you do not want to be a Christian because you wish to save yourself trouble and would be happy and comfortable and enjoy yourself? You do not choose any openly vicious way in particular, but you prefer to be moderately sinful and to take care of yourself, and save all care, thought, and anxiety about death and heaven and hell. You think that by leading a careless life you are happier than if you yielded yourself to Jesus. You are labouring under a mistake; but one thing is clear, self is your god, and that is a deity as grovelling as any other. The idolater who worships a god of gold or silver, or even of stone or mud, is not quite so degraded as the man who worships himself. Self-worship is coming very low indeed. When I am my own god, or my belly is my god, can there be a lower depth? If I live merely to be easy and comfortable, and have no care for God, or Christ, or heavenly things; what a choice I am making. Think of it, and be ashamed. Oh, I say again, in many a man's choice of what should be the object of his life, he sins precisely as they sinned who put away Jesus and chose Barabbas. I say no more. May the Holy Spirit send home this sadly convicting truth.

III. Thirdly. Pilate, seeing that he cannot thus set his prisoner free, gives him over into the hands of the soldiers, who straightway make merry over him and treat him as an object of contempt. The words are cruel, and are enough to draw tears from all eyes as we read them: 'Then Pilate therefore took Jesus, and scourged him. And the soldiers platted a crown of thorns, and put it on his head, and they put on him a purple robe.' 'I am innocent here,' cries one of my hearers. What! are you quite sure that you are free from THE SIN OF CONTEMPT AND OF CAUSING PAIN TO JESUS? Listen a while. When you have been so busy about the world that you could not think of him; when you have been so eager to be rich that you laughed at the true riches, do you not know that you were plaiting a crown of thorns to put upon his head? Your folly in despising your own soul sorely wounds him. He pities you, and cannot bear to see that the thorns of this world should be the harvest which you sow and reap. If he were not so loving of heart and tender of spirit it would not matter, but this unkindness to yourself is unkindness to him, and virtually when you have been full of cares and anxieties concerning the world, and have had no care and no anxiety about him or about your own soul, you have put a crown of thorns upon his head. Is this nothing?

Let me ask you when you have gone up to the place of worship on the Sunday, as you always do, and have pretended to adore him, though you do not love him, do you know what you have done? You have mocked him by a feigned worship, and thus you have put the purple robe upon him. For that purple robe meant that they made him a nominal king, a king who was not in truth a king, but a mere show. Your Sunday religion, which has been forgotten in the week, has been a sceptre of reed, a powerless ensign, a mere sham. You have mocked and insulted him even in your hymns and prayers, for your religion is a pretence, with no heart in it; you brought him an adoration that was no adoration, a confession that was no confession, and a prayer that was no prayer.

Is it not so? I pray you be honest with yourselves. Is it not so? And then all the week long have you not preferred anyone to Jesus? any book to the Bible? any exercise to prayer? any enjoyment to communion with himself? Political objects have aroused you, but not the Lord's glory nor the spread of his kingdom. Is not this despising Jesus? Is not this mocking him?

Are there not among you some who are weary of the Lord? weary of the Sabbath? weary of sermons about Jesus? weary of atoning blood? weary of praising the Redeemer? What is this but contempt of him?

Too many have even jested about the holiest of things: if they have not mocked Jesus personally they have ridiculed his people for his sake, and made mirth of his gospel. By some religion is set up as a scarecrow, and piety is treated as a byword, conscientious scruples are laughed at as old-fashioned absurdities, and devotion to Christ is set down as next of kin to insanity. We know it is so, even among some who are hearers of the gospel, and outwardly its upholders.

There is contempt for the life and power of it: they know and honour its name, but the reality of vital godliness they do not value. At times their conscience thunders heavily at them, and then they are compelled to wish they had what at other times they disdain. They do despite to the blood of Jesus, and yet would fain be partakers in its pardoning power.

I fear me none of us dare wash our hands of this as a sin of our fallen estate. Time was when those of us who love Jesus now, and could kiss every wound of his, yet thought so little of him that anything was better than he. The story of his sufferings was as wearisome as a worn-out tale; and as for giving our whole selves to him, we deemed it a fanatical expression or an enthusiastic dream. Blessed Saviour, thou hast forgiven us: forgive others who are doing the same.

IV. I have but a minute to spare for each point; so now I mast turn to another sin of which many are guilty, namely, THE SIN OF HEARTLESSNESS WITH REGARD TO THE SUFFERINGS OF OUR LORD. Pilate thought he had another way of letting his prisoner go, and this he tried. He scourged him. I will not tell you how dreadful Roman scourging was. It could not now be equalled except it be by the Russian knout. It was the most terrible of tortures. Many died under it, and almost all the victims fainted after a few blows: by it the human frame was reduced to a mass of bruised, bleeding, quivering flesh. When the Saviour was all a mass of wounds and bruises, Pilate brought him forth and said, 'Behold the man,' appealing to what little humanity he hoped there still might be in the chief priests and elders. 'Behold the man!' said he. 'Is not that enough? He is crashed and battered and bleeding all over, is not that enough?' But they had no feeling for him whatever, and only cried, 'Away with him.' If the spectacle of woe which our Lord presented on this occasion does not touch you, it is a lamentable proof of hardness of heart. Do not many read the story of his sufferings without emotion?

Despised, reviled, thorn-crowned, and scourged, our Lord stands alone as the Man of sorrows, the Monarch of miseries. Griefs without parallel! Woes unique and by themselves! Have you no tears to shed for him whom soldiers mocked and Jews derided? No? Is it possible that you answer 'No'? Have you heard the story till it has less effect than an idle romance? For shame! For shame! And the worst of it is that it should not affect men when they recollect that these griefs were voluntarily borne out of love, and neither of necessity nor from any selfish motive. His woes were borne for his enemies. He bade his disciples begin to preach at

Jerusalem that the men who spat in his face might know that they had a share in his compassion, and that he who drove the lance into his heart was one for whom he tasted death. He dies praying for his murderers. Ah me! that it should be so. A man dying for his friend is a noble sight; but a man dying for those who put him to death is the most extraordinary sight that angels ever beheld.

There is this about it too, which touches believers most tenderly: our Lord suffered thus on our account. In his death is our hope, or else we are lost for ever. If we have not part and lot in the merits of the agony, then for us there remains nothing but a fearful looking for of judgment and of fiery indignation. Do we not mourn when we see Jesus dying for us. O feeling, thou art fled to brutish beasts, and men have lost their reason. Surely our hearts will be like the rock in Horeb. Stricken by the rod of the cross, our souls will gush with rivers of penitential grief. But herein is a marvellous proof of our guiltiness, that we have compassion for everybody but the Saviour; that we can cry over a lapdog, and yet can hear of Christ with utter indifference. There are multitudes of persons of this kind, and I pray God's Spirit to touch their conscience upon this matter of heartlessness toward Jesus.

But I must hasten on, though I might wish to linger, leaving with meditations the enlargement of these charges.

V. There is another crime of which many are guilty which was seen in Pilate himself, and that was the crime of COWARDICE. No less than three times did Pilate say of our Lord, 'I find no fault in him,' and yet he did not let him go. He himself owned, 'I have power to crucify thee, and have power to release thee,' and yet he dared not exercise the power to deliver. Through cowardice he dared not let his perfectly innocent prisoner go free. He knew, but he did not act up to his knowledge. Have I none before me whose knowledge of good things far outruns their practice? This, surely, will be one of the never-dying worms of hell – the gnawing of an instructed and disregarded conscience. Over the door of their prison-house the lost shall read this inscription – Ye knew your duty but ye did it not. The knowledge which makes men responsible for their deeds increases that responsibility as it is itself increased, and with it their guilt and their punishment. Moreover,

Pilate did not only know the right, but after his own fashion he wished to do it. One almost pities the vacillating coward. See how he struggles to release Jesus in some indirect fashion which may cost him nothing. He wishes, he resolves, and then hangs back. Like a vessel tossed with contrary winds, he is at one time almost in harbour, and anon he is far out at sea. Oh, the quantities of dead wishes that one might gather in this Tabernacle, as men gather untimely fruit which the wind has shaken from the tree. Men wish to repent, wish to believe, wish to decide, wish to be holy, wish to be right with God; but their wishing leads to no practical decision, and so they perish at the threshold of mercy. Their goodness ends in empty desires, which do but evidence their responsibility, and so secure their condemnation. Yet, to be just, we must admit that Pilate did more than wish; he spoke for Christ. But having spoken in his favour he did not proceed to action, as he was bound to have done. It is possible for a man to say with his tongue, 'I find no fault in him,' and then by his actions to condemn Jesus by giving him up to die.

Words are a poor homage to the Saviour. Not by words does he save mankind, and not by lip-service is he to be repaid. Pilate spake boldly enough, and then retreated before the clamours of the crowd; and yet Pilate could be firm sometimes. When Jesus was nailed to the cross, the priests begged Pilate to change the accusation which was written over his head, and he would not, but replied, 'What I have written I have written.' Why could he not have shown a little backbone when Jesus yet lived? He was not altogether such a weak, effeminate being as to be incapable of putting his foot down firmly; if he did so once he might have done it before, and so have saved himself from this great transgression. Are there no Pilates here – persons who would long ago have been Christians if they had possessed enough moral courage? Some foolish companion would laugh at them if they became religious, and this they could not bear. Poor dastards! I heard the other day of a lad who dared not pray in the room where two or three others slept; and so, like a craven, he crept into bed and succumbed to the fear of others. I fear that some men would sooner be damned than be laughed at. Another person has a wicked companion, and he knows that he must cut his acquaintance if he becomes a follower of Jesus: this he would do, but he lacks courage. O ye, who shrink back from that which Christ's service involves, because of the fear of men, know ye not the portion of the fearful? O ye trembling ones, is Jesus covered with wounds and shame for you, and are you ashamed of him? Death is coming upon him speedily, and do you hide your faces from him? This is cruelty, indeed, both to Christ and to yourself. Can you not leave his enemies? 'Come ye out from among them, and be ye separate: touch not the unclean thing.' Will you not espouse his cause? 'If any man will serve me let him follow me.' By this cowardice you do as much as in you lies to put the Christ to death. 'How?' say you. Well, suppose everybody acted as you do, would there be any Christianity in the world? If everybody was cowardly, would there be a church at all? Are you not killing Christ and burying Christ as far as ever you can? Are you not destroying his influence and weakening his church by refusing to own him? Is it not so? Look at it. Whatever influence you have in the world you refuse to use for Jesus. Though multitudes are active in despising and opposing him, you do not lift a hand in his favour.

Why do you not come out and say, 'I am on his side'? By your supposed neutrality you act as his foe. You must be on one side or the other now that you have heard the gospel; for Jesus has said, 'He that is not with me is against me: he that gathereth not with me scattereth abroad.' You are against him, and you are scattering abroad. Suppose others follow your example? 'Well,' say you, 'there is nothing bad in my example, except that I am not a Christian.' Just so, and under some aspects the very goodness of your example makes it operate all the more powerfully for evil. I do not think that the example of a thoroughly drunken man, for instance, leads many young people into intemperance; on the contrary, many take warning from the spectacle, and fly to total abstinence for security. I have often had young men and women coming to join the church who have been total abstainers of the most intense kind because a drunken father made their childhood so wretched, and kept the home so poor that they abhorred the accursed thing. See, then, how an ill example may lose its evil power by very excess. Yours is another case; your example is in some respects admirable, and then you throw it on the side of the devil. The better man you are the more mischief you are doing by siding with evil. Inasmuch as you are that which is moral, excellent, amiable, you are the very man whose influence Christ ought to have on his side, and if you cause it to go against him the fact is all the more deplorable. If the weight of your character goes to make men ignore the claims of the Son of God, what is this but spiritually to bring about his death?

Lastly, and oh that the Spirit of God may bless this sharp medicine to some heart that it may feel the pangs of penitence this morning – there is the sin of SELF-RIGHTEOUS HYPOCRISY. This Pilate committed in set form. He took water and washed his hands, and said, 'I am innocent of the blood of this just person: see ye to it.' What a contradiction! He is innocent, but he gives them permission to be guilty. They could not murder the Lord without his permission; he gives the necessary permit, and yet he says, 'I am innocent.' Do I not see another of the same class over yonder? He says, 'I do not despise Christ, or speak a word against him. I am perfectly innocent of any ill-will towards him. Of course, if others oppose him they may, for it is a free country: let them do as they like, but I am perfectly clear of it.' It is not thus that a man acts if he sees another being murdered. He does not look on and say that he would rather not interfere. You say you cannot help other people's opinions. Have you no opinion of Jesus of your own? Do you say, 'No; I never think of him?' Is not that contempt? Do you decline to hold any opinion about one who claims to be your God? about one who must be your Saviour, or you must perish for ever? You cannot sheer off in that way. Now that rebellion is afoot you must either be loyal or be a traitor. The standard is unfurled, and each man must take his side. Your negligence of Jesus contradicts your claim to be neutral. You pretend to let him alone, but that letting alone is fatal. A man is yonder in the upper room of a burning house, and you can save him. You refuse to touch the matter, for it is no concern of yours either way, and so you leave it to the firemen and their helpers. Meanwhile, the man perishes because you will not help him. I say that you are inexcusable: that man's blood lies at your door. It was your duty to have rescued him. So the Lord Jesus Christ comes here among men and he is persecuted. You quietly say, 'No doubt it is a pity, but I cannot help it.' Just so; but by your inaction you side with his foes.

Do you say that you are so righteous that you do not want a Saviour? That, indeed, is smiting him on the face. He comes to be a Saviour, and you tell him that he is superfluous; that you are so good that you can do without being washed in his blood. That is spitting in his face, and telling him that he was a fool to die for you. Why should he shed his blood if you are innocent enough without it? In effect you charge God with folly for providing a great propitiation when such good people as you are need nothing of the kind. I do not believe anybody can more grossly insult the Son of the Highest! This is crucifying him indeed! The self-righteous man who says, 'I am clean,' deprives Christ's sacrifice of its glory, his life of its end, his person of its dignity, his whole work of its wisdom. The very heart of God is set upon the object for which Christ died, and yet the self-righteous man counts this a folly.

Come, my hearers, there is no room for any one of us to accuse his fellow: let us all come with humble confessions to the feet of Jesus, now risen from the dead, and let us each say to him right sorrowfully –

> 'Tis I to whom these pains belong,
> 'Tis I should suffer for my wrong,
> Bound hand and foot in heavy chains;
> Thy scourge, thy fetters, whatsoe'er
> Thou bearest, 'tis my soul should bear,
> For she hath well deserved such pains.
>
> Yet thou dost even for my sake
> On thee, in love, the burdens take
> That weighed my spirit to the ground:
> Yes; thou art made a curse for me,
> That I might yet be blest through thee:
> My healing in thy wounds is found.

17

THE WHOLE BAND
AGAINST CHRIST[1]

Then the soldiers of the governor took Jesus into
the common hall, and gathered unto him the
whole band of soldiers.
MATTHEW 27:27

I HAVE NOT OBSERVED that anyone has turned to account the
fact that 'the whole band of soldiers' gathered in the Praetorium,
or common hall, for the purpose of mocking our Lord. That they
did mock him, has often been noticed, and preached upon; but
that they should have gathered unto him the whole cohort, that
all should have been there, is mentioned both by Matthew and by
Mark, and this being twice recorded cannot have been without
some meaning and some lesson for us.

To begin then, our blessed Lord, being condemned to die, was
given over to the brutal soldiery who garrisoned Jerusalem. They
lived in quarters round about the palace of the governor; and when
the Saviour was delivered to them to be put to death, they must
needs make him the centre of their mockery and derision before
they executed the terrible sentence upon him. Does it not strike
you that any man condemned to die ought to be protected against
such usage as that? If he must die, some respect should be paid to
one who is about to endure the death penalty. I think that there
should be great indulgence shown in such a case; at any rate,

---

[1] Sermon No. 2,333. Preached at the Metropolitan Tabernacle on Sunday evening,
15 September 1889.

nothing should be done or said to hurt the feelings, or to wound the sensibilities. Pity seems to say, 'If the man must die, then so be it; but let us not for a single moment jest at him. Far hence be mirth; that is a brutality not to be thought of at such a time as this; and to make a man, about to die, the subject of scorn, is a superfluity of cruelty and wickedness.' Methinks that even a devil might be ashamed of such savagery as this. But there was no law to protect the Saviour from these soldiers. Every man's heart seems to have been steeled against him; the common dictates of the most ignorant humanity appear to have been violated. They said by their actions, if not in words, 'He shall not only die, but he shall be stripped of all his honour; he shall be robbed of every comfort; he shall become the butt and target of all the cruel arrows of contempt that we can shoot at him.'

Still, why is it said that, in order to make him the object of derision, they gathered together 'the whole band'? I do not know how many soldiers constituted the garrison, or how many were barracked round about the governor's palace; but they gathered together 'the whole band'; not merely a few of them who were on duty that day, but all were summoned to make a mock of Christ. It was not because he needed to be guarded lest he should escape, for he had no desire to be set free. It was not because the soldiers would be wanted to keep him securely lest the people should attempt to rescue him, for the Jews did not want him to be rescued. On the contrary, it was by their clamour that he was doomed to die. They had cried, 'Crucify him! Crucify him!' He had no friends to stand up for him, no band of disciples to come and force the soldiery away, and set him free. Therefore these legionaries did not guard him with the whole strength of the band on that account.

Nor were they all wanted to execute the death sentence. With a people eager for his death, four soldiers, a single quaternion, sufficed. He carried his own cross, and they had but to drive the nails into his hands and feet, and fasten him to the tree. That could be soon done to a victim so defenceless, so inoffensive; it did not need that they should gather together 'the whole band', and so we are told it, as a remarkable circumstance which did not rise necessarily out of the narrative. It must have a meaning of its own, 'They gathered unto him the whole band of soldiers.'

I shall speak thus upon it. First, it would appear that *the soldiers were unanimous in mocking their Prisoner;* secondly, *so are men united in opposing Christ;* and, thirdly, *what shall we say of both the facts whereof we are to speak tonight?*

I. First, then, it is clear that THE SOLDIERS WERE UNANIMOUS IN MOCKING THEIR PRISONER.

Upon this, I remark, first, that *men are very apt to go together when they go wrong.* You notice, in a workshop, how the religion of Christ will be despised, and how certain men will lead the way in uttering calumnies against it, and then the rest will follow. When men go astray, they are like a flock of sheep; one gets through the hedge, and all the rest go after it. We have heard of one sheep leaping the parapet of a bridge into a river, and the whole flock went after it, and all were destroyed. Men are such curious beings, not only the creatures of their own habits, but the imitators of other men's example. I know not how it is, but persons who, alone and apart, would seem to have some good inclinations, will shake them all off when they get into evil company. At home, they will talk reasonably; but, in the crowd, they speak, madly. At home and alone, they are amenable to rebuke and conviction; but when they get with other men, they will not hear a word of it; they shut their ears to anything like good teaching, and they run greedily to do mischief. I do not, therefore, so much wonder that, when our Lord was given over to the soldiers, they gathered together the whole band, for it is so usual for men to go together when they go wrong.

Frequently, too, it will happen that *there is not one man to bear his protest.* Would you not have expected that, in a large band of soldiers, there would have been at least one man of noble spirit, who would have said, 'Nay, do not torture him; he is about to die'? Would it have been at all wonderful if one man had stood forward, and said, 'This Man has done nothing amiss; our governor has said that he finds no fault in him. Why, therefore, do you set him in that chair, and robe him, and bow the knee in mockery, and spit upon him?' It would not have been very surprising if there had been amongst the Roman soldiery some one or two who had espoused Christ's cause; for, truth to tell, those valiant men, although they grew brutalized by living amidst scenes of blood, were capable of deeds of high virtue. One has but to read the old Roman story, to stand amazed sometimes that such fair flowers of virtue and benevolence could grow on such a dunghill as the Roman State then was. Yet you see that not one out of the whole band of soldiery would say a word for Christ, or absent himself from the ring, when their comrades mocked him.

Peradventure, I address some men here who work together, and who are in the habit of scoffing at the cross of Christ. I hope that there is not a workshop in London without one man, at least, who will stand forward, and defend his Master's cause; but if I speak to one to whom that thought has occurred, and yet he has said, 'I dare not; I should be myself the subject of so much persecution, that I could not stand forth alone;' now, listen, sir, if a Gaius, or a Fabius, or a Julius, had stood forth alone to defend the Lord's cause, we should have had his name here, and if he had even suffered death for it, he would have been amongst the brightest of the martyr host. And you know not what honour you lose if you conceal your testimony. If you allow the whole drift of the talk to be infidel and atheistic, and never put in your good word for him whom you call Master and Lord, you dishonour yourself; but if you could have the courage, and I hope that you may, to say, 'He, of whom you speak thus ill, has saved my soul, snatched me from habits of vice, and renewed my character,' if you could stand forward, and bear such testimony for him, I know that it were a short road to glory, and honour, and immortality. It is not likely that you would have to suffer as the martyrs did; but suppose that you did, the more of suffering, the brighter that ruby crown which would be set upon your head in the day of your Lord's appearing. I hope that Christian men are still made of that grand old stuff which defied the Roman emperors, and made them weary of slaughter, for they could not mow down the crops of the church so fast as they grew. The blood of the martyrs was the seed of the church; and the more copiously it was shed, the more the church multiplied.

But, once more, *the number of those who thus mocked Christ made their conduct all the baser.* When you, young fellow, get in with fifty more, and in the workshop you mock at some solitary Christian youth, when you each one have your jibe, when you give him what you call 'chaff', which is sport to you, but cruel enough to be death to him, did it never occur to you that it was a most cowardly thing, and altogether unworthy of you, that ten, twenty, thirty, forty, fifty, should all set upon one? What if a man does believe in religion? Has he not a right to do so if he likes? Some of you who talk so much about freedom are the biggest bullies in the world; you boast loudly of religious liberty, but to you it means liberty to be irreligious. Surely I have as much right to worship Christ as you have to despise him; and if my views of religion should seem to you to be peculiar, yet, if peculiar, have I not as good reason to hold them as you have to reject them? I speak thus plainly because I know of many, many cases where, if men were men at all, they would cease to persecute Christians, seeing that they persecute one or two wherever they can if they themselves happen to be in the majority. Think of this lot of howling dogs around this one gentle Lamb of God, the Christ who had never even a hard word for them, whose mightiest weapon was silence and patience; think of him surrounded by all these men of war from their youth up, these Roman legionaries with their imperial eagles. It was a cruel shame. The more there were of them, the meaner it was of them thus, as a whole band, to gather together to mock the Saviour.

But I suppose that *their number accounted for the excess to which they went.* If there had only been two or three of them, they would not have thought of all the cruel things that they did to our Lord. To put an old cloak upon him, and to call him the purpled Caesar, is commonplace enough; but one cries, 'Let us make a crown for him,' and they plait the thorns with cruel hands, piercing his temples with the sharp spines. Another says, 'Fetch a sceptre, and put it in his hand. Set him in that chair, and let us bow before him, let us cry, "Hail, King of the Jews!"' They would have stopped at that point had there not been so many of them; but, being so large a band, one coarse fellow must go further still, and he spits into that blessed face!

> See how the patient Jesus stands,
> Insulted in his lowest case!
> Sinners have bound the Almighty's hands!
> And spit in their Creator's face!

I hardly think that one, two, three, or even half-a-dozen by themselves could have been guilty of such detestable, loathsome conduct to Christ; but the whole band being together, they thought of fresh insults.

Take heed of sinning in a crowd. Young man, abandon the idea that you may sin in a crowd. Beware of the notion that, because many do it, it is less a guilt to any one of them. Remember that the broad way always was the wrong road, and that it leads to destruction none the less because many walk in it. 'Though hand join in hand, the wicked shall not be unpunished.' Though you finish up the day's work of sin with three cheers for your noble selves, you shall find yourselves arraigned each one before the judgment seat of God, each one to give account for the deeds done in his body according to what he hath done, whether it be good or whether it be evil. Oh, the pitiful story, a whole company of soldiers united against Christ, with not one to quit the ranks, and say, 'No, comrades; do not so;' but all wallowing in their cruelty, like swine in the mire!

II. That leads me to talk to you, secondly, about another point. As these soldiers were unanimous in mocking their illustrious prisoner, so ARE MEN UNITED IN OPPOSING CHRIST.

Like these soldiers, *many do not pass Christ by with neglect*. I should have thought that many a brave man of that Roman legion would have said, 'Pshaw! I shall not go to taunt the poor Jew who has been hunted down by the priests. Nobody gives him a good word; even his own followers have fled from him. I heard one of them declare that he did not know him, though I knew that man was a liar, for I saw him in the garden with his Master. My comrades are going to the Praetorium to mock him, but I shall not go; such mirth is unworthy of a man, especially of a Roman.' Instead thereof, they were all there. Curiosity fetched them up, they must all come to see this man of whom they had heard so much; and an evil conscience made them bitter against him, for, because they were evil, his being good was a protest against their wicked deeds.

So they were all united against him, and *they came up, every one of them, to show their scorn*. It is a strange thing; but if Christ is fully preached, somehow men cannot be indifferent to him. If they can be right away, and never hear of him, they may be indifferent; but the true gospel either offends men, or else it charms them. I believe that you may preach a certain sort of gospel, from the first of January to the end of December, and everybody will say, 'Yes, that is very good, very, very good, perfectly harmless.' Yes, a chip in the porridge, with no flavour in it; but if it is the real out-and-out gospel of a crucified Saviour, there will be someone who will say, 'Ah, that is what I want! I like that;' but there will be others who will grind their teeth, and say, 'I will never hear that man again; I cannot bear his talk; I hate it.' Do not be surprised when I say that, if I hear that So-and-so was very angry at one of my sermons, I state as my belief, 'That man will go to heaven. I have the hook in that fish, and I shall catch him yet.' But when I hear people simply say, 'Oh, yes; we heard the sermon!' and they make some trifling remark about it and go their way, nothing good comes of it. It is better that a man should be in a downright rage against Christ than be utterly indifferent to him; and where he really comes so that men are obliged to see him, they cannot long be indifferent. 'That the thoughts of many hearts may be revealed,' is one of the objects of his death. The cross of Christ is the great detector of men. Fix it up, and men straightway go to the right or to the left of it. It is the parter and divider of the ways. Jesus himself said, 'He that is not with me is against me; and he that gathereth not with me scattereth abroad.' Men cannot pass by utterly with neglect after once hearing the story of the cross. They must gather up for Christ or against him, and alas! many of them do gather up to pour their scorn upon him.

Many ungodly men *feel an inward contempt for Christ's claims.* No, says one, 'I have no such contempt for Christ.' I would not wish to charge you wrongfully; but if you are not a believer in him, if you have never accepted him to be your Saviour and your Lord, I venture to repeat the charge, you have an inward contempt for his claims, my hearers. Whether you are Christians or not, you are the subjects of King Jesus. God has put you into his hand, and you will have to stand before his judgment seat at the last. The Man Christ Jesus, who died on Calvary, and rose again, and went to heaven, will judge every one of you at the last great day; and he claims that you now should become his servants, and yield obedience to him. Now, I know that you will say in your hearts, 'We shall not do anything of the kind.' Just so, and have I not proved what I said? 'The carnal mind is enmity against God,' and that carnal mind may be in a man who always goes to church, or to chapel. If he has not been renewed, he does not believe in Christ as King; and as far as his heart is concerned, he mocks at the idea of his being a servant of Christ, and Christ being Lord over him. In his very soul he thinks this to be a preposterous claim, that he should be obedient to Christ in everything. Besides, the mass of men do not seek to know what Christ's claims are. They are ignorant of his royalty and sovereignty, and it is in this way that their minds are filled with an indistinctly expressed, but still very powerful, contempt for him.

And so it happens, in the next place, that *men invent different ways of showing their derision.* It is very curious that you find very learned men opposed to Christ, and they go to work usually by destructive criticism, trying to get rid of this part of the Bible and that; but an ignorant man cannot do that, so he says that he does not believe in the Bible at all. Here you find a rich man despising Christ, sneering at 'the common people', as he calls Christ's followers, and there you see another man, who is very poor, despising Christ by wishing to overthrow all the rules of his sacred kingdom. Herod and Pilate hate one another till Christ comes, and then they join together in reviling him.

These Roman soldiers, having all come together, found employment in mocking Christ. First, some of them stripped him. Oh, have I not seen men at it in these days, stripping Christ of his deity, stripping him of his priesthood, stripping him of his sovereignty, stripping him of his righteousness, stripping Christ of everything that makes him Christ? Is not that the way with many of the rich, and the great, and the 'advanced' theologians of the present day? They show their hatred of Christ by stripping him.

There are others who go to work the other way; they put on him a scarlet robe. I have seen them do it; put other men's garments upon him, make him out to be what he never was, travesty the doctrines of grace, caricature the gospel, and hold it all up to contempt, imputing to Christ the faults of all his followers, and even laying at his door the sin of men who, like Judas, have betrayed him. That is another method of showing enmity to Christ.

Then we see all around us men who mock at Christ's royalty. They crown him with a crown of thorns by their harsh speeches against his people. By their persecutions of those who love him, Christ is often crowned again with thorns. The husband has done it in his unkindness to his believing wife; parents have done it in their objection to their children following Christ; the man or woman who has given the cold shoulder to a pious friend has thus put another crown of thorns upon the Saviour's head. And have we not seen them put the reed into his hand by representing Christ as being a mere myth, and his doctrine as a dream, a holy fancy, a proper thing to keep the people quiet, but with no matter of fact or truth in it?

So they put into his hand the reed-sceptre to mock him, and he regards it as mockery. And thus, around the Christ today, I seem to see, with eyes closed, but by the vision of faith, a multitude kneeling before him, and pretending to worship him, hypocritical worshippers, those who even by their bedsides are hypocrites, repeating a form of prayer, and yet never really praying, drawing near to him with their lips, while their hearts are far from him. Oh, how do sinners thus prove their unanimity of enmity to Christ! Even in their pretended worship, they do but show the opposition of their hearts to him.

Here and there, also, I see one coarser than other men, who spits upon Jesus, and smites him. You cannot live long in London without hearing from men who are opposed to the cross of Christ expressions that disgust you. I have given up all idea now that we are living in a Christian country. Believers, in England, are a band of Christ's soldiers who are holding the fort against deadly odds. Ours is a heathen country, with an admixture of Christian people, and a smear, a varnish, of pretended religion, but a heathen country still. And every now and then, some outspoken heathen, by his awful profanity, makes us wish that we could not hear at all. This is how they spit on Christ. One does it very politely with a bow; another comes forward, and abuses both the Christ and his cross. He has spat in his face, and honestly let us know where he stands. One will undermine the truth; another brings the battering ram, in open day, to beat down the citadel; but they are so united together that, with one accord, the whole band of soldiers is gathered against Christ.

Dear friends, if men attacked any one doctrine, you would find only one band of men opposing it; but when Christ himself is the object of mockery, the whole band gathers round him. If I preach some of the doctrines of Calvinism, I shall find men, who are fatalists, and necessitarians, and the like, who will agree with me; but if I preach the whole gospel of Christ, these very men, who might have been my friends under one form of doctrine, will be my enemies against the whole of it. Only let Jesus appear, and Jews and Gentiles, rich and poor, learned and unlearned, until they are renewed by grace, count his cross to be a stumbling block and his doctrine to be foolishness.

Now notice that *men who could mock Christ like this were capable of doing anything evil*. If they could revile Christ, it was no wonder that they cast lots for his vesture just at his feet when he hung on the cross. I am often astounded at things that I read about gamblers, and what they have been known to do. It is fifty years ago since there was a story told by a policeman, and I do not doubt its truth, of two men at Hampstead who, having bet with one another all that they had, at last had a wager as to which should hang the other, and one of them did hang the other. The policeman came along just in time to save him; and when the man was cut down, what do you think he said? Why, he said that he would have hung the other man, if he could, to win the bet!

That was thought to be very extraordinary; but it is not so very long ago since, at the laying of the first stone of a chapel, a friend of mine stood behind two gentlemen from Newmarket; and when one whom I know stood up to pray over the first stone, these two made a bet about how long he would be praying! Men will do anything for a wager. That mischievous vice, which is becoming so common nowadays, leads to an extraordinary hardness of heart beyond anything else; and I cannot so much wonder that men, who were brought up as these Roman soldiers were, were capable of mockery of Christ, and of anything else that was evil.

III. I have finished when I have asked and answered this question, WHAT SHALL WE SAY OF BOTH THE FACTS WHEREOF WE HAVE SPOKEN TONIGHT?

These cruel soldiers unanimously came together to see Christ as a prisoner, and to put him to extraordinary scorn; *yet out of this band Christ found witnesses.* Their chief officer, 'the centurion, and they that were with him,' as they stood and saw Christ die, said, 'Truly this was the Son of God;' and some of these soldiers, being appointed to watch the tomb of Christ, came and declared that he had risen from the dead. They were fine witnesses, were they not? men who were too rough to lie to help a sect. They came forward to bear testimony to the Christ. O God, if there be any here who have blasphemed thee, who have cursed Christ to his face, who have persecuted Christ's people, save them tonight, and make them witnesses of thy power to bless! When such a man gets saved, he is a good witness for Christ. He says, 'I know what Christ can do, for he has changed my heart, he has appeared to me by the way, and manifested himself to me; and I know and am sure of that which I testify, that verily this is the Son of God.'

Next, learn another lesson. *All this mockery should rebuke the backwardness among Christ's friends.* When he was to be mocked, all the soldiers came up. Some of them were down in the canteen, but they left their wine, and came up to mock him. Some of the soldiery, perhaps, had furlough for that day; but they gave up their holiday to go to mock Christ. Now, then, brethren and sisters, if his enemies could gather together the whole band against him, let us gather together the whole band for him. Why, just look at some of you on the Lord's day! There are a few drops of rain, that might spoil your best bonnets, or wet your new clothes, so you cannot go to chapel. You would have gone to market, you know, rain or shine. How many there are who will not be able to come to the prayer meeting tomorrow night! One pleaded, some time ago, at the prayer meeting, 'Lord, bless those that are at home on beds of sickness!' 'Yes,' said the preacher, 'and, Lord, bless those that are at home on sofas of wellness!' There are plenty of that kind, who stay at home because they have not enough of the hearty spirit that ought to be in them to let the whole band gather together to confess Christ. Do you love Jesus Christ, my dear sister? Then, come and confess it. Do you love Jesus Christ, my brother? Then out with your avowal of it. Do not try to go to heaven behind the hedges. Get into the King's high road, and travel in broad daylight as a soldier of Christ should. Say –

> I'm not ashamed to own my Lord,
> Or to defend his cause.

Next, I think that *these mockers chide the uninventiveness of many Christians*. See how they brought out the old red cloak, and plaited the crown of thorns, and cried, 'Put them on him.' Then they brought the sceptre of reed, saying 'Stick it in his hand, and shout, "Hail, King of the Jews!"' Then came the spitting and the smiting; they could not have made the mockery more complete. They soon rigged up all that mimicry of royalty. Come, then, brethren and sisters, let us be inventive in honouring Christ.

> Bring forth the royal diadem,
> And crown him Lord of all.

See, is there not some new plan to be tried, some method that you have not yet attempted by which you could make Jesus loved and honoured in the soul of somebody, be it only a poor child, a servant girl, or the humblest man in the street? Surely, if enmity was so quick to deride him, love ought to be equally alert and inventive to find out ways by which to honour him.

But, once more, *all this mockery should excite our admiration of our patient Lord*. Remember that, as he sat there, flouted and made a jest of, he might with one glance of his eyes have flashed hell into their souls, and slain every one of them. Had he only opened those lips, he could have spoken thunderbolts that would have destroyed them at once; but he sat there, and patiently bore it all. As a sheep before her shearers, he was dumb; he opened not his mouth, because he was bearing all this to save you and to save me. Blessed Saviour! Oh, come, let us worship and adore and love him!

The last lesson is, *let us summon all our faculties to honour Christ tonight*. Gather together the whole band, your memory of all his goodness, your judgment of all his greatness, all your hopes, and all your fears, your quieted conscience, your soul at rest, come, and with the whole band of faculties that God has given you, from the highest to the lowest, bow down in grateful adoration before him who bowed so low that he might lift us up to be with him for ever.

Dear hearers, are you trusting Christ? There is no other trust that will do for a soul for time and for eternity. On a dying bed, it must be none but Jesus; let it be none but Jesus on your bed tonight before you fall asleep. Do not dare to close your eyes till you have committed your soul into the keeping of him who holds out his hands still, as he did upon the cross, that he may receive you with open arms, and save you with an everlasting salvation. Amen.

18

THE CROWN OF THORNS[1]

'And when they had platted a crown of thorns,
they put it upon his head.'
MATTHEW 27:29

BEFORE we enter the common hall of the soldiers, and gaze upon 'the sacred head once wounded,' it will be well to consider who and what he was who was thus cruelly put to shame. Forget not the intrinsic excellence of his person; for he is the brightness of the Father's glory, and the express image of his person; he is in himself God over all, blessed for ever, the eternal Word by whom all things were made, and by whom all things consist. Though heir of all things, the Prince of the kings of the earth, he was despised and rejected of men, 'a man of sorrows and acquainted with grief'; his head was scornfully surrounded with thorns for a crown, his body was bedecked with a faded purple robe, a poor reed was put into his hand for a sceptre, and then the ribald soldiery dared to stare into his face, and worry him with their filthy jests –

> The soldiers also spit upon that face
> Which angels did desire to have the grace,
> And prophets once to see, but found no place.
> Was ever grief like mine?

Forget not the glory to which he had been accustomed aforetime, for ere he came to earth he had been in the bosom of the Father,

[1] Sermon No. 1,168. Preached at the Metropolitan Tabernacle on Sunday morning, 13 April 1874.

adored of cherubim and seraphim, obeyed by every angel, worshipped by every principality and power in the heavenly places; yet here he sits, treated worse than a felon, made the centre of a comedy before he became the victim of a tragedy. They sat him down in some broken chair, covered him with an old soldier's cloak, and then insulted him as a mimic monarch –

> They bow their knees to me, and cry, Hail king;
> Whatever scoffs and scornfulness can bring,
> I am the floor, the sink, where they'd fling.
>   Was ever grief like mine?

What a descent his love to us compelled him to make! See how he fell to lift us from our fall! Do not also fail to remember that at the very time when they were thus mocking him, he was still the Lord of all, and could have summoned twelve legions of angels to his rescue. There was majesty in his misery; he had laid aside, it is true, the glorious pomp imperial of his Father's courts, and he was now the lowly man of Nazareth, but for all that, had he willed it, one glance of those eyes would have withered up the Roman cohorts; one word from those silent lips would have shaken Pilate's palace from roof to foundation; and had he willed it, the vacillating governor and the malicious crowd would together have gone down alive into the pit, even as Korah, Dathan, and Abiram of old. Lo, God's own Son, heaven's darling, and earth's prince, sits there and wears the cruel thorn-crown which wounds both mind and body at once, the mind with insult, and the body with piercing smart. His royal face was marred with 'wounds which could not cease to bleed, trickling faint and slow', yet that 'noblest brow and dearest' had once been fairer than the children of men, and was even then the countenance of Immanuel, God with us. Remember these things, and you will gaze upon him with enlightened eyes and tender hearts, and you will be able the more fully to enter into fellowship with him in his griefs. Remember whence he came, and it will the more astound you that he should have stooped so low. Remember what he was, and it will be the more marvellous that he should become our substitute.

And now let us press into the guardroom, and look at our Saviour wearing his crown of thorns. I will not detain you long with any guesses as to what kind of thorns he wore. According to the Rabbis and the botanists there would seem to have been from twenty to twenty-five different species of thorny plants growing in Palestine; and different writers have, according to their own judgments or fancies, selected one and another of these plants as the peculiar thorns which were used upon this occasion. But why select one thorn out of many? He bore not one grief, but all; any and every thorn will suffice; the very dubiousness as to the peculiar species yields us instruction. It may well be that more than one kind of thorn was platted in that crown: at any rate sin has so thickly strewn the earth with thorns and thistles that there was no difficulty in finding the materials, even as there was no scarcity of griefs wherewith to chasten him every morning and make him a mourner all his days.

The soldiers may have used pliant boughs of the acacia, or shittim tree, that unrotting wood of which many of the sacred tables and vessels of the sanctuary were made; and, therefore, significantly used if such was the case. It may have been true, as the old writers generally consider, that the plant was the *spina Christi,* for it has many small and sharp spines, and its green leaves would have made a wreath such as those with which generals and emperors were crowned after a battle. But we will leave the matter; it was a crown of thorns which pierced his head, and caused him suffering as well as shame, and that suffices us. Our inquiry now is, what do we see when our eyes behold Jesus Christ crowned with thorns? There are six things which strike me most, and as I lift the curtain I pray you watch with me, and may the Holy Spirit pour forth his divine illumination and light up the scene before our wondering souls.

I. The first thing which is seen by the most casual observer, before he looks beneath the surface, is A SORROWFUL SPECTACLE. Here is the Christ, the generous, loving, tender Christ, treated with indignity and scorn; here is the Prince of life and glory made an object of derision by a ribald soldiery. Behold today the lily among thorns, purity lifting up itself in the midst of opposing sin. See here the sacrifice caught in the thicket, and held fast there, as a victim in our stead to fulfil the ancient type of the ram held by the bushes, which Abraham slew instead of Isaac. Three things are to be carefully noted in this spectacle of sorrow.

Here is Christ's *lowliness and weakness triumphed over* by the lusty legionaries. When they brought Jesus into the guardroom they felt that he was entirely in their power, and that his claims to be a king were so absurd as to be only a theme for contemptuous jest. He was but meanly dressed, for he wore only the smock frock of a peasant – was he a claimant of the purple? He held his peace – was he the man to stir a nation to sedition? He was all wounds and bruises, fresh from the scourger's lash – was he the hero to inspire an army's enthusiasm and overturn old Rome? It seemed rare mirth for them, and as wild beasts sport with their victims, so did they. Many, I warrant you, were the jibes and jeers of the Roman soldiery at his expense, and loud was the laughter amid their ranks. Look at his face, how meek he appears! How different from the haughty countenances of tyrants! To mock his royal claims seemed but natural to a rough soldiery. He was gentle as a child, tender as a woman; his dignity was that of calm quiet endurance, and this was not a dignity whose force these semi-barbarous men could feel, therefore did they pour contempt upon him. Let us remember that our Lord's weakness was undertaken for our sakes: for us he became a lamb, for us he laid aside his glory, and therefore it is the more painful for us to see that this voluntary humiliation of himself must be made the object of so much derision and scorn, though worthy of the utmost praise. He stoops to save us, and we laugh at him as he stoops, he leaves the throne that he may lift us up to it, but while he is graciously descending, the hoarse laughter of an ungodly world is his only reward. Ah me! was ever love treated after so unlovely a sort? Surely the cruelty it received was proportioned to the honour it deserved, so perverse are the sons of men.

> O head so full of bruises!
> Brow that its lifeblood loses!
> Oh great humility.
> Upon his face are falling
> Indignities most galling;
> He bears them all for me.

It was not merely that they mocked his humility, but *they mocked his claims to be a king*. 'Aha,' they seemed to say, 'is this a king? It must be after some uncouth Jewish fashion, surely, that this poor peasant claims to wear a crown. Is this the Son of David? When will he drive Caesar and his armies into the sea, and set up a new state, and reign at Rome. This Jew, this peasant, is he to fulfil his nation's dream, and rule over all mankind? Wonderfully did they ridicule this idea, and we do not wonder that they did, for they could not perceive his true glory. But, beloved, my point lies here, *he was a king* in the truest and most emphatic sense. If he had not been a king, then he would as an impostor have deserved the scorn, but would not have keenly felt it; but being truly and really a king, every word must have stung his royal soul, and every syllable must have cut to the quick his kingly spirit. When the impostor's claims are exposed and held up to scorn, he himself must well know that he deserves all the contempt he receives, and what can he say? But if the real heir to all the estates of heaven and earth has his claims denied and his person mocked at, then is his heart wounded, and rebuke and reproach fill him with many sorrows. Is it not sad that the Son of God, the blessed and only Potentate, should have been thus disgraced?

Nor was it merely mockery, but *cruelty added pain to insult*. If they had only intended to mock him they might have platted a crown of straw, but they meant to pain him, and therefore they fashioned a crown of thorns. Look ye, I pray you, at his person as he suffers under their hands. They had scourged him till probably there was no part of his body which was not bleeding beneath their blows except his head, and now that head must be made to suffer too. Alas, our whole head was sick, and our whole heart faint, and so he must be made in his chastisement like to us in our transgression. There was no part of our humanity without sin, and there must be no part of his humanity without suffering. If we had escaped in some measure from iniquity, so might he have escaped from pain, but as we had worn the foul garment of transgression, and it covered us from head to foot, even so must he wear the garments of shame and derision from the crown of his head even to the sole of his foot.

> O Love, too boundless to be shown
> By any but the Lord alone!

> O Love offended, which sustains
> The bold offender's curse and pains!
> O Love, which could no motive have,
> But mere benignity to save.

Beloved, I always feel as if my tongue were tied when I come to talk of the sufferings of my Master. I can think of them, I can picture them to myself, I can sit down and weep over them, but I know not how to paint them to others. Did you ever know pen or pencil that could? A Michael Angelo or a Raphael might well shrink back from attempting to paint this picture; and the tongue of an archangel might be consumed in the effort to sing the griefs of him who was loaded with shame because of our shameful transgressions. I ask you rather to meditate than to listen, and to sit down and view your Lord with your own loving eyes rather than to have regard to words of mine. I can only sketch the picture, roughly outlining it as with charcoal; I must leave you to put in the colours, and then to sit and study it, but you will fail as I do. Dive we may, but we cannot reach the depths of this abyss of woe and shame. Mount we may, but these storm swept hills of agony are still above us.

II. Removing the curtain again from this sorrowful spectacle, I see here a SOLEMN WARNING which speaks softly and meltingly to us out of the spectacle of sorrow. Do you ask me what is that warning? It is a warning against our ever committing the same crime as the soldiers did. 'The same!' say you; 'why, we should never plat a crown of thorns for that dear head.' I pray you never may; but there are many who have done, and are doing it. Those are guilty of this crime who, as these soldiers did, *deny his claims.* Busy are the wise men of this world at this very time all over the world, busy in gathering thorns and twisting them, that they may afflict the Lord's Anointed. Some of them cry, 'Yes, he was a good man, but not the Son of God;' others even deny his superlative excellence in life and teaching; they cavil at his perfection, and imagine flaws where none exist. Never are they happier than when impugning his character. I may be addressing some avowed infidel here, some sceptic as to the Redeemer's person and doctrine, and

I charge him with crowning the Christ of God with thorns every time that he invents bitter charges against the Lord Jesus, and utters railing words against his cause and his people. Your denial of his claims, and especially your ridicule of them, is a repetition of the unhappy scene before us. There are some who ply all their wit, and tax their utmost skill for nothing else but to discover discrepancies in the gospel narratives, or to conjure up differences between their supposed scientific discoveries and the declarations of the word of God. Full often have they torn their own hands in weaving crowns of thorns for him, and I fear some of them will have to lie upon a bed of thorns when they come to die, as the result of their displays of scientific research after briers with which to afflict the Lover of mankind. It will be well if they have not to lie on worse than thorns for ever, when Christ shall come to judge them and condemn them and cast them into the lake of fire for all their impieties concerning him.

Oh, that they would cease this useless and malicious trade of weaving crowns of thorns for him who is the world's only hope, whose religion is the lone star that gilds the midnight of human sorrow, and guides mortal man to the port of peace! Even for the temporal benefits of Christianity the good Jesus should be treated with respect; he has emancipated the slave, and uplifted the downtrodden; his gospel is the charter of liberty, the scourge of tyrants, and the death of priests. Spread it and you spread peace, freedom, order, love, and joy. He is the greatest of philanthropists, the truest friend of man, wherefore then array yourselves against him, ye who talk of progress and enlightenment? If men did but know him they would crown him with diadems of reverent love, more precious than the pearls of India, for his reign will usher in the golden age, and even now it softens the rigour of the present, as it has removed the miseries of the past. It is an ill business, this carping and cavilling, and I beseech those engaged in it to cease their ungenerous labours, unworthy of rational beings and destructive to their immortal souls.

This crowning with thorns is wrought in another fashion by *hypocritical professions of allegiance to him*. These soldiers put a crown on Christ's head, but they did not mean that he should be king; they put a sceptre in his hand, but it was not the substantial ivory rod which signifies real power, it was only a weak and slender reed. Therein they remind us that Christ is mocked by insincere professors. O ye who love him not in your inmost souls, ye are those who mock him: but you say, 'Wherein have I failed to crown him? Did I not join the church? Have I not said that I am a believer?' Oh, but if your hearts are not right within you, you have only crowned him with thorns, if you have not given him your very soul, you have in awful mockery thrust a sceptre of reed into his hand. Your very religion mocks him. Your lying professions mock him. Who hath required this at your hands, to tread his courts? You insult him at his table! You insult him on your knees! How can you say you love him, when your hearts are not with him? If you have never believed in him and repented of sin, and yielded obedience to his command, if you do not own him in your daily life to be both Lord and King, I charge you lay down the profession which is so dishonouring to him. If he be God, serve him; if he be King, obey him; if he be neither, then do not profess to be Christians. Be honest and bring no crown if you do not accept him as King. What need again to insult him with nominal dominion, mimic homage, and pretended service? O ye hypocrites, consider your ways, lest soon the Lord whom ye provoke should ease him of his adversaries.

In a measure the same thing may be done by those who are sincere, but through want of watchfulness *walk so as to dishonour their profession.* Here, if I speak rightly, I shall compel every one of you to confess it in your spirits that you stand condemned; for every time that we act according to our sinful flesh we crown the Saviour's head with thorns. Which of us has not done this? Dear head, every hair of which is more precious than fine gold, when we gave our hearts to thee we thought we should always adore thee, that our whole lives would be one long psalm, praising and blessing and crowning thee. Alas, how far have we fallen short of our own ideal! We have hedged thee about with the briers of our sin. We have been betrayed into angry tempers, so that we have spoken unadvisedly with our lips; or we have been worldly, and loved that which thou abhorrest, or we have yielded to our passions, and indulged our evil desires. Our vanities, follies, forgetfulnesses, omissions, and offences have set upon thy head a coronet of dishonour, and we tremble to think of it. Oh, cruel hearts and hands to have so maltreated the Well-beloved, whom it should have been our daily care to glorify! Do I speak to any backslider whose open sin has dishonoured the cross of Christ? I fear I must be addressing some who once had a name to live, but now are numbered with the dead in sin. Surely if there be a spark of grace in you, what I am now saying must cut you to the quick, and act like salt upon a raw wound to make your very soul to smart. Do not your ears tingle as I accuse you deliberately of acts of inconsistency which have twisted a thorny crown for our dear Master's head? It is assuredly so, for you have opened the mouths of blasphemers, taught gainsayers to revile him, grieved the generation of his people, and made many to stumble. Ungodly men have laid your faults at the door of the innocent Saviour; they have said 'This is your religion.' You have grown the thorns, but he has had to wear them. *We* call your offences inconsistencies, but worldly men regard them as the fruit of Christianity, and condemn the vine because of your sour clusters. They charge the holy Jesus with the faults of his erring followers. Dear friends, is there not room to look at home in the case of each one of us? As we do so, let us come with the sorrowful and loving penitent, and wash his dear feet with tears of repentance, because we have crowned his head with thorns.

Thus our thorn-crowned Lord and Master stands before us as a sorrowful spectacle, conveying to us a solemn warning.

III. Lifting the veil again, in the person of our tortured and insulted Lord we see TRIUMPHANT ENDURANCE. He could not be conquered, he was victorious even in the hour of deepest shame.

> He with unflinching heart
> Bore all disgrace and shame,
> And 'mid the keenest smart
> Lov'd on, yea lov'd the same:

He was bearing at that moment, first, the *substitutionary griefs* which were due to him because he stood in our place, and from bearing them he did not turn aside. We were sinners, and the reward of sin is pain and death, therefore he bore the chastisement of our peace. He was enduring at that time what we ought to have endured, and draining the cup which justice had mingled for us. Did he start back from it? Oh, no. When first he came to drink of that wormwood and gall in the garden he put it to his lips, and the draught seemed for an instant to stagger even his strong spirit. His soul was exceeding sorrowful, even unto death. He was like one demented, tossed to and fro with inward agony. 'My Father,' said he, 'if it be possible, let this cup pass from me.' Thrice did he utter that prayer, while every portion of his manhood was the battlefield of legions of griefs. His soul rushed out at every pore to find a vent for its swelling woes, his whole body being covered with gory sweat. After that tremendous struggle the strength of love mastered the weakness of manhood; he put that cup to his lips and never shrank, but he drank right on till not a dreg was left; and now the cup of wrath is empty, no trace of the terrible wine of the wrath of God can be found within it. At one tremendous draught of love the Lord for ever drank destruction dry for all his people. 'Who is he that condemneth? It is Christ that died, yea, rather, that hath risen again,' and 'there is therefore now no condemnation to them that are in Christ Jesus, who walk not after the flesh but after the Spirit.' Now surely endurance had reached a very high point when he was made to endure the painful mockery which our text describes, yet he quailed not, nor removed from his settled purpose. He had undertaken, and he would go through. Look at him, and see there a miracle of patient endurance of griefs which would have sent a world to hell had he not borne them on our behalf.

Besides the shame and suffering due for sin, with which it pleased the Father to bruise him, he was enduring *a superfluity of malice from the hate of men*. Why did men need to concentrate all their scorn and cruelty into his execution? Was it not enough that he must die? Did it give pleasure to their iron hearts to rack his tenderest sensibilities? Wherefore these inventions for deepening his woe? Had any of us been thus derided we should have resented it. There is not a man or woman here who could have been silent under such indignities, but Jesus sat in omnipotence of patience, possessing his soul right royally. Glorious pattern of patience, we adore thee as we see how malice could not conquer thine almighty love! The pain which he had endured from the scourges caused him to throb with exquisite anguish, but we read neither of tears nor groans, much less of angry complaints or revengeful threats. He does not seek for pity, or make one appeal for clemency. He does not ask wherefore they torture or why they mock. Brave witness! Courageous martyr! Suffering exquisitely thou dost also suffer calmly. Such a perfect frame as his, his body being conceived without sin, must have been capable of tortures which our bodies, unstrung by sin, cannot feel. His delicate purity felt a horror of ribald jests which our more hardened spirits cannot estimate, yet Jesus bore all, as only the Son of God could bear it. They might heap on the load as they would, he would only put forth more endurance, and bear it all, but shrink or quail he would not.

I venture to suggest that such was the picture of patience which our blessed Lord exhibited that it may have moved some even of the soldiery themselves. Has it ever occurred to you to ask how Matthew came to know all about that mockery? Matthew was not there. Mark also gives an account of it, but he would not have been tolerated in the guardroom. The Praetorians were far too proud and rough to tolerate Jews, much less disciples of Jesus, in their common hall. Since there could have been nobody there except the legionaries themselves, it is well to inquire – Who told this tale? It must have been an eye-witness. May it not have been that centurion who in the same chapter is reported to have said, 'Certainly this was the Son of God'? May not that scene as well as the Lord's death have led him to that conclusion? We do not know, but this much is very evident, the story must have been told by an eye-witness, and also by one who sympathized with the sufferer, for to my ear it does not read like the description of an unconcerned spectator. I should not wonder – I would almost venture to assert – that our Lord's marred but patient visage preached such a sermon that one at least who gazed upon it felt its mysterious power, felt that such patience was more than human, and accepted the thorn-crowned Saviour as henceforth his Lord and his King. This I do know, that if you and I want to conquer human hearts for Jesus we must be patient too; and if, when they ridicule and persecute us, we can but endure without repining or retaliation, we shall exercise an influence which even the most brutal will feel, and to which chosen minds will submit themselves.

IV. Drawing up the veil again, I think we have before us, in the fourth place, in the person of the triumphant sufferer, a SACRED MEDICINE. I can only hint at the diseases which it will cure. These blood-besprinkled thorns are plants of renown, precious in heavenly surgery if they be rightly used. Take but a thorn out of this crown and use it as a lancet, and it will let out the hot blood of passion and abate the fever of pride; it is a wonderful remedy for swelling flesh and grievous boils of sin. He who sees Jesus crowned with thorns will loathe to look on self, except it be through tears of contrition. This thorn at the breast will make men sing, but not with notes of self-congratulation, the notes will be those of a dove moaning for her mate. Gideon taught the men of Succoth with thorns, but the lessons were not so salutary as those which we learn from the thorns of Jesus. The sacred medicine which the good Physician brings to us in his thorny crown acts as a tonic, and strengthens us to endure without depression whatever shame or loss his service may bring upon us –

> Who defeats my fiercest foes?
> Who consoles my saddest woes?
> Who revives my fainting heart,
> Healing all its hidden smart?
> Jesus crowned with thorns.

When you begin to serve God, and for his sake endeavour to benefit your fellow-mortals, do not expect any reward from men, except to be misunderstood, suspected, and abused. The best men in the world are usually the worst spoken of. An evil world cannot speak well of holy lives. The sweetest fruit is most pecked at by the birds, the most heaven-nearing mountain is most beaten by the storms, and the loveliest character is the most assailed. Those whom you would save will not thank you for your anxiety, but blame you for your interference. If you rebuke their sins they will frequently resent your warnings, if you invite them to Jesus, they will make light of your entreaties. Are you prepared for this? If not, consider him who endured such contradiction of sinners against himself lest ye be weary and faint in your minds. If you succeed in bringing many to Christ, you must not reckon upon universal honour, you will be charged with self-seeking, popularity-hunting, or some such crime; you will be misrepresented, belied, caricatured, and counted as a fool or a knave by the ungodly world. The probabilities are that the crown you will win in this world, if you serve God, will contain more spikes than sapphires, more briers than beryls. When it is put upon your head pray for grace to wear it right gladly, counting it all joy to be like your Lord. Say in your heart, 'I feel no dishonour in this dishonour. Men may impute shameful things to me, but I am not ashamed. They may degrade me, but I am not degraded. They may cast contempt upon me, but I am not contemptible.' The Master of the house was called Beelzebub and spit upon, they cannot do worse to his household, therefore we scorn their scorn. Thus are we nerved to patience by the patience of the despised Nazarene.

The thorn crown is also a remedy for discontent and affliction. When enduring bodily pain we are apt to wince and fret, but if we remember Jesus crowned with thorns, we say –

> His way was much rougher and darker and mine;
> Did Christ my Lord suffer, and shall I repine?

And so our complaints grow dumb; for very shame we dare not compare our maladies with his woes. Resignation is learned at Jesus' feet, when we see our great Exemplar made perfect through suffering.

The thorn crown is a cure for care. We would cheerfully wear any array which our Lord may prepare for us, but it is a great folly to plat needless thorn crowns for ourselves. Yet I have seen some who are, I hope, true believers take much trouble to trouble themselves, and labour to increase their own labours. They haste to be rich, they fret, they toil, they worry, and torment themselves to load themselves with the burden of wealth; they wound themselves to wear the thorny crown of worldly greatness. Many are the ways of making rods for our own backs. I have known mothers make thorn crowns out of their children whom they could not trust with God, they have been worn with family anxieties when they might have rejoiced in God. I have known others make thorn crowns out of silly fears, for which there were no grounds whatever; but they seemed ambitious to be fretful, eager to prick themselves with briers. O believer, say to thyself, 'My Lord wore my crown of thorns for me; why should I wear it too?' He took our griefs and carried our sorrows that we might be a happy people, and be able to obey the command, 'Take no thought for the morrow, for the morrow shall take thought for the things of itself.' Ours is the crown of loving kindness and tender mercies, and we wear it when we cast all our care on him who careth for us.

That thorn crown cures us of desire for the vainglories of the world, it dims all human pomp and glory till it turns to smoke. Could we fetch hither the Pope's triple crown, or the imperial diadem of Germany, or the regalia of the Czar of All the Russias, what of them all compared with Jesus' crown of thorns? Let us set some great one on his throne, and see how little he looks when Jesus sits beside him. What is there kingly in being able to tax men, and live upon their labours, giving little in return? The royalest thing is to lay them all under obligations to our disinterested love, and be the fountain of blessing to them. Oh, it takes the glitter from your gold, and the lustre from your gems, and the beauty from all your fancy baubles, to see that no imperial purple can equal the glory of his blood, no gems can rival his thorns. Show and parade cease to attract the soul when once the superlative excellencies of the dying Saviour have been discerned by the enlightened eye.

Who seeks for ease when he has seen the Lord Christ? If Christ wears a crown of thorns, shall we covet a crown of laurel? Even the fierce Crusader when he entered into Jerusalem, and was elected king, had sense enough to say, 'I will not wear a crown of gold in the same city where my Saviour wore a crown of thorns.' Why should we desire, like feather-bed soldiers, to have everything arranged for our ease and pleasure? Why this reclining upon couches when Jesus hangs on a cross? Why this soft raiment when he is naked? Why these luxuries when he is barbarously entreated? Thus the thorn crown cures us at once of the vainglory of the world, and of our own selfish love of ease. The world's minstrel may cry, 'Ho, boy, come hither, and crown me with rose buds!' but the hedonist's request is not for us. For us neither delights of the flesh nor the pride of life can have charms while the Man of Sorrows is in view. For us it remains to suffer, and to labour, till the King shall bid us share his rest.

V. I must notice in the fifth place that there is before us a MYSTIC CORONATION. Bear with my many divisions. The coronation of Christ with thorns was symbolical, and had great meaning in it, for, first, it was to him *a triumphal crown*. Christ had fought with sin from the day when he first stood foot to foot with it in the wilderness up to the time when he entered Pilate's hall, and he had conquered it. As a witness that he had gained the victory behold sin's crown seized as a trophy! What was the crown of sin? Thorns. These sprang from the curse. 'Thorns also and thistles shall it bring forth to thee,' was the coronation of sin, and now Christ has taken away its crown, and put it on his own head. He has spoiled sin of its richest regalia, and he wears it himself. Glorious champion, all hail! What if I say that the thorns constituted a mural crown?

Paradise was set round with a hedge of thorns so sharp that none could enter it, but our champion leaped first upon the bristling rampart, and bore the blood-red banner of his cross into the heart of that better new Eden, which thus he won for us never to be lost again. Jesus wears the mural crown which denotes that he has opened Paradise. It was a wrestler's crown he wore, for he wrestled not with flesh and blood, but with principalities and powers, and he overthrew his foe. It was a racer's crown he wore, for he had run with the mighty and outstripped them in the race. He had well-nigh finished his course, and had but a step or two more to take to reach the goal. Here is a marvellous field for enlargement, and we must stay at once lest we go too far. It was a crown rich with glory, despite the shame which was intended by it. We see in Jesus the monarch of the realms of misery, the chief among ten thousand sufferers. Never say, 'I am a great sufferer.' What are our griefs compared with his? As the poet stood upon the Palatine Mount and thought of Rome's dire ruin, he exclaimed, 'What are our woes and sufferings?' even so I ask, What are our shallow griefs compared with the infinite sorrows of Immanuel? Well may we 'control in our close breasts our petty misery'. Jesus is, moreover, the prince of martyrs. He leads the van among the noble army of suffering witnesses and confessors of the truth. Though they died at the stake, or pined in dungeons, or were cast to wild beasts, they none of them claim the first rank; but he, the faithful and the true witness, with the thorn crown and the cross, stands at the head of them all. It may never be our lot to join the august band, but if there be an honour for which we might legitimately envy saints of former times, it is this, that they were born in those brave days when the ruby crown was within human grasp, and when the supreme sacrifice might have been made. We are cravens, indeed, if in these softer days we are ashamed to confess our Master, and are afraid of a little scorn, or tremble at the criticisms of the would-be wise. Rather let us follow the Lamb whithersoever he goeth, content to wear his crown of thorns that we may in his kingdom behold his glory.

VI. The last word is this. In the thorn crown I see a MIGHTY STIMULUS. A mighty stimulus to what? Why, first, to fervent love of him. Can you see him crowned with thorns and not be drawn to him? Methinks, if he could come among us this morning, and we could see him, there would be a loving press around him to touch the hem of his garment or to kiss his feet. Saviour, thou art very precious to us. Dearest of all the names above, my Saviour and my God, thou art always glorious, but in these eyes thou art never more lovely than when arrayed in shameful mockery. The Lily of the Valley, and the Rose of Sharon, both in one is he, fair in the perfection of his character, and blood-red in the greatness of his sufferings. Worship him! Adore him! Bless him! And let your voices sing 'Worthy the Lamb.'

This sight is a stimulus, next, to repentance. Did our sins put thorns around his head? Oh, my poor fallen nature, I will scourge thee for scourging him, and make thee feel the thorns for causing him to endure them. What, can you see your best Beloved put to such shame, and yet hold truce or parley with the sins which pierced him? It cannot be. Let us declare before God our soul's keen grief that we should make the Saviour suffer so; then let us pray for grace to hedge our lives around with thorns that from this very day sin may not approach us.

I thought this day of how ofttimes I have seen the blackthorn growing in the hedge all bristling with a thousand prickles, but right in the centre of the bush have I seen the pretty nest of a little bird. Why did the creature place its habitation there? Because the thorns become a protection to it, and shelter it from harm. As I meditated last night upon this blessed subject, I thought I would bid you build your nests within the thorns of Christ. It is a safe place for sinners. Neither Satan, sin, nor death can reach you there. Gaze on your Saviour's sufferings, and you will see sin atoned for. Fly into his wounds! fly, ye timid trembling doves! there is no resting-place so safe for you. Build your nests, I say again, among these thorns, and when you have done so, and trusted Jesus, and counted him to be all in all to you, then come and crown his sacred head with other crowns. What glory does he deserve? What is good enough for him? If we could take all the precious things from all the treasuries of monarchs, they would not be worthy to be pebbles beneath his feet. If we could bring him all the sceptres, mitres, tiaras, diadems, and all other pomp on earth, they would be altogether unworthy to be thrown in the dust before him. Wherewith shall we crown him? Come let us weave our praises together and set our tears for pearls, our love for gold. They will sparkle like so many diamonds in his esteem, for he loves repentance, and he loves faith. Let us make a crown this morning with our praises, and crown him as the laureate of grace. This day on which he rose from the dead, let us extol him. Oh, for grace to do it in the heart, and then in the life, and then with the tongue, that we may praise him for ever who bowed his head to shame for us.

19

MOCKED OF THE SOLDIERS[1]

And when they had platted a crown of thorns, they put
it upon his head, and a reed in his right hand: and they
bowed the knee before him, and mocked him,
saying, Hail, King of the Jews!
MATTHEW 27:29

IT IS A SHAMEFUL SPECTACLE where cruelty uses its keenest
instrument to cut, not into the flesh, but into the very spirit, for
scorn, contempt, insult, and ridicule, are as painful to the mind
and heart as a scourge is to the body, and they cut like the sharpest
lance. These Roman soldiers were a rough body of men, – fierce,
courageous, terrible in fight, uncouth, untaught, uncivilized, little
better than barbarians; and when they had this unique King in
their power, they made the most of their opportunity to torment
him. Oh, how they laughed to think that he should call himself a
King – this poor, emaciated creature, who looked as if he would
faint and die in their hands, whose blessed visage was marred more
than that of any of the sons of men! It must have seemed to them
a sorry jest that he should be a rival to imperial Caesar, so they
said, 'If he is a King, let us clothe him with royal purple,' so they
flung over his shoulders a soldier's tunic. 'As he is a King, let us
plait him a crown;' and they made it of thorns. Then they bowed
the knee in mock homage to the man whom his own people
despised, whom even the mob rejected, and whom the chief men

[1] Sermon No. 2,824. Preached at the Metropolitan Tabernacle on Sunday evening,
3 June 1883.

of the nation abhorred. It seemed to them that he was such a poor, miserable, dejected creature that all they could do was to make scorn of him, and treat him as the butt for their utmost ridicule.

These Roman soldiers had in them, as men, a spirit which I sometimes grieve to see in boys at this present day. That same cruel spirit that will torture a bird or a cockchafer, or hunt a dog or cat simply because it looks miserable, and because it is in their power, that was the sort of spirit, that was in these soldiers. They had never been taught to avoid cruelty; nay, cruelty was the element in which they lived. It was worked into their very being; it was their recreation. Their grandest holiday was to go and sit in those tiers of seats at the Coliseum, or at some provincial amphitheatre, and see lions contending with men, or wild beasts tearing one another in pieces. They were trained and inured to cruelty; they seemed to have been suckled upon blood, and to have been fed on such food as made them capable of the utmost cruelty; and, therefore, when Christ was in their hands, he was in a sorry case indeed. They called together the whole band, and put upon him a purple robe, and a crown of thorns upon his head, and a reed in his right hand; and they bowed the knee before him, and mocked him, saying, 'Hail, King of the Jews! Then they spat upon him, and took the reed from his hand, and smote him on the head.

Now we will leave those Roman soldiers, and the Jews that had a hand in persecuting him, for he that delivered him unto them had committed even greater sin. Neither Pilate nor his legionaries were the chief criminals at that time, as we well know. From this incident in our Lord's life, I think we may learn, first, *lessons for the heart;* and, secondly, *lessons for the conscience.*

I. First, we have here A SET OF LESSONS FOR OUR HEART.

Beloved, we begin with this one. Where I see the great Substitute for sinners put to such shame, scorn, and ridicule, my heart says to itself, *'See what sin deserves.'* There, is nothing in the world that more richly deserves to be despised, abhorred, condemned, than sin. If we look at it aright, we shall see that it is the most abominable thing, the most shameful thing in the whole universe. Of all the things that ever were, this is the thing which most of all deserves to be loathed and spurned. It is not a thing of God's creating, remember. It is a misshapen being – a monster abortion; a spectre of the night, which plucked a host of angels from their thrones in heaven, drove our first parents out of paradise, and brought upon us unnumbered miseries.

Think, for a minute, what sin is, and you will see that it deserves ridicule for its folly. What is sin? It is rebellion against the Omnipotent, a revolt against the Almighty. What utter folly that is! Who shall hurl himself against the bosses of Jehovah's buckler, and not be dashed in pieces? Who shall rush upon the point of his spear, and hope to vanquish him? Laugh to scorn such folly as that. Under that aspect, sin is the apex of folly, the climax of absurdity; for what power can ever stand up against God, and win the day?

But, further, sin deserves to be scorned because it is a wanton attack upon One who is full of goodness, and justice, and truth. Note that evil thing that assails the Most High, and brand it so that the mark of the iron shall abide on it for ever. Set it up in the public pillory, and let all true hearts and hands hurl scorn upon it for having disobeyed the perfect law of God, angered the generous Creator and Preserver of men, done despite to eternal love, and infinite damage to the best interests of the human race. It is a ridiculous thing, because it is fruitless, and must end in being defeated. It is a shameful thing, because of its wanton, malicious, unprovoked attack upon God. If you will look back a little, and consider what sin attempted to do, you will see the reason why it should be shamed for its audacity. 'Ye shall be as gods,' said he who was the mouthpiece of sin; but are we, by nature, like gods? Are we not more like devils? And he who uttered that lie – even Satan – did he succeed as he expected when he dared to rebel against his Creator? See how his former glory has vanished! How art thou fallen from heaven, O Lucifer, son of the morning, and how is thy brightness quenched in everlasting night! Yet sin, speaking through the lips of Satan, talked about being a king, and of making all of us kings; but it has degraded us to the dunghill, and to utter beggary; ay, to worse than that, to death and hell. What spitting sin deserves! If it is to be crowned, let it be crowned with thorns. Bow not your knee to it, but pour upon it all the scorn you can. Every true and honest heart, in heaven, among the angels and the glorified spirits, and on earth, among sanctified men and women, must look upon sin as a thing worthy of unspeakable contempt. May God make sin as contemptible in our sight as Christ appeared to be to the Roman soldiers! May we scoff at its temptations; may we scorn its proffered rewards; and may we never bow our hearts to it in any degree whatsoever, since God has set us free from its accursed thraldom!

That is the first lesson for our hearts to learn from the mockery of our Saviour by the soldiers – see what a contemptible thing sin is.

Learn, next, my dear brethren and sisters, *how low our glorious Substitute stooped for our sake.* In him was no sin either of nature or of act. He was pure, entirely without spot before God himself; yet, as our Representative, he took our sin upon himself. 'He was made sin for us,' says the Scripture most emphatically; and inasmuch as he was regarded as being the sinner, though in him was no sin, it naturally followed that he should become the object of contempt. But what a wonder that it should be so! He, who created all things by the word of his power, and by whom all things consist – he, who counted it not robbery (not a thing to be grasped) to be equal with God – sits in an old chair to be made a mimic king, and to be mocked and spat upon! All other miracles put together are not equal to this miracle; this one rises above them all, and out-miracles all miracles – that God himself, having espoused our cause, and assumed our nature, should deign to stoop to such a depth of scorn as this. Though myriads of holy angels adored him, though they would have gladly left their high estate in heaven, to smite his foes, and set him free, he voluntarily subjected himself to all the ignominy that I have described, and much more which is utterly indescribable – for who knows what things were said and done, in that rough guardroom, which holy pens could not record, or what foul jests were made, and what obscene remarks were uttered, which were even more shocking to Christ than the filthy spittle which ran down his blessed cheeks in that time of shameful mockery? Ah, my brothers and sisters; you cannot imagine how low your Lord stooped on your account! When I hear any say that they have been so slandered for his sake that they cannot endure it, I have wished that they knew what he endured on their account. If we stood in the pillory, and all mankind hooted at us for a million, million years, it would be as nothing compared with the wondrous condescension of him who is God over all, blessed for ever, stooping as he did for our sake.

That is the second lesson for our hearts to learn.

Then let me say to you very tenderly, wishing that some other voice could speak of it more effectively, *see how your Redeemer loved you.* You know that, when Christ stood by the grave of Lazarus, and wept, the Jews said, 'Behold how he loved him!' Ah! but look at him there among those Roman soldiers – despised, rejected, insulted, ridiculed; and then let me say to you, 'Behold how he loved us – you, and me, and all his people!' In such a case, I might quote the words of John, 'Behold, what manner of love!' But this love of Jesus is beyond all manner and measure of which we can have any conception. If I were to take all your love to him, and heap it up like a vast mountain; if I were to gather all the members of the one Church of Christ on earth, and bid them empty their hearts, and then fetched out of heaven the myriads of redeemed and perfected spirits before the throne, and they added all their heart's love; and if I could collect all the love that ever has been and that ever shall be throughout eternity in all the saints – all that would be but as a drop of a bucket compared with the boundless, fathomless love of Christ to us, that brought him down so low as to be the object of the scorn and derision of these wicked men for our sake. So, beloved, from this sad scene let us learn how greatly Jesus loved us, and let each one of us, in return, love him with all our heart.

I cannot leave this set of lessons for your heart without giving you one more; that is, *see the grand facts behind the scorn.* I do believe – I cannot help believing – that our blessed Master, when he was in the hands of those cruel soldiers, and they crowned him with thorns, and bowed before him in mock reverence, and insulted him in every possible way, all the while looked behind the curtain of the visible circumstances, and saw that the heartless pantomime – nay, tragedy – only partially hid the divine reality, for he was a King even then, and he had a throne, and that thorn crown was the emblem of the diadem of universal sovereignty that shall, in due season, adorn his blessed brow; that reed was to him a type of the sceptre which he shall yet wield as King of kings and Lord of lords; and when they said, 'Hail, King of the Jews!' he heard, behind that mocking cry, the triumphant note of his future glory, 'Hallelujah! Hallelujah! Hallelujah! the Lord God omnipotent reigneth; and he shall reign for ever and ever!' for when they mockingly bowed the knee to him, he saw all nations really bowing before him, and his enemies licking the dust at his feet. Our Saviour knew that these ribald soldiers, unconsciously to themselves, were setting before him pictures of the great reward of his soul-travail. Let us not be discouraged if we have to endure anything of the same sort as our Lord suffered. He was not discouraged, but remained steadfast through it all. Mockery is the unintentional homage which falsehood pays to truth. Scorn is the unconscious praise which sin gives to holiness. What higher tribute could these soldiers give to Christ than to spit upon him? If Christ had received honour from such men, there would have been no honour in it to him. You know how even a heathen moralist, when they said to him, 'So-and-so spoke well of you yesterday in the market,' asked, 'What have I done amiss that such a wretch as that should speak well of me?' He rightly counted it a disgrace to be praised by a bad man; and because our Lord had done nothing amiss, all that these men could do was to speak ill of him, and treat him with contumely, for their nature and character were the very opposite of his.

Representing, as these soldiers did, the unregenerate, God-hating world, I say that their scorn was the truest reverence that they could offer to Christ while they continued as they were; and so, at the back of persecution, at the back of heresy, at the back of the hatred of ungodly men to the cross of Christ, I see his everlasting kingdom advancing, and I believe that 'the mountain of the Lord's house shall be exalted above the hills,' and that 'all nations shall flow unto it,' even as Isaiah foretold; that Jesus shall sit upon the throne of David, and that of the increase of his kingdom there shall be no end, for the kings of the earth shall bring their glory and honour unto him, 'and he shall reign for ever and ever. Hallelujah!' Glory be to his holy name!

Have all our hearts truly learned these four grand lessons – the shamefulness of sin – the condescension of our Lord – the immeasurable love which made him so condescending – and the ineffable glory which hides behind the skirts of all this shame and sorrow? If not, let us beseech the Holy Spirit to teach them to us.

II. Now I want to give you, from this same incident, A SET OF LESSONS FOR YOUR CONSCIENCE.

And, first, it is a very painful reflection – let your conscience feel the pain of it – that *Jesus Christ can still be mocked*. He has gone into the heavens, and he sits there in glory; but yet, spiritually, so as to bring great guilt upon him who does it, the glorious Christ of God can still be mocked, and he is mocked by those who deride his people. Now, men of the world, if you see faults and failings in us, we do not wish you to screen us. Because we are the servants of God, we do not ask for exemption from honest criticism, we do not desire that our sins should be treated with more leniency than those of other men; but, at the same time, we bid you beware that you do not slander, and scandalize, and persecute those who are the true followers of Christ; for, if you do, you are mocking and persecuting him.

I believe that, if it be the poorest of his people, the least gifted and the most faulty, yet, if they are evil spoken of for Christ's sake, our Lord takes it all as done to himself. You remember how Saul of Tarsus, when he lay smitten to the ground, heard a voice which said to him, 'Saul, Saul, why persecutest thou me?' 'Well, but,' he might have said, 'I have never persecuted thee, Lord.' No; but he dragged Christian men and women to prison, and scourged them, and compelled them to blaspheme; and because he had done this to Christ's people, Christ could truly say to him, 'Inasmuch as thou hast done it unto one of the least of these my brethren, thou hast done it unto me.' If you persecutors want to amuse yourselves, you can find much cheaper sport than that of slandering the servants of Christ. Remember that the Lord has said concerning them, 'He that toucheth you toucheth the apple of his eye.' If you were to touch the apple of a man's eye, you would be provoking him to defend himself; so do not arouse Christ's righteous anger by scoffing at any of his people. I say no more upon that point; if the message is meant for any man here, let him give heed to the warning.

Next, Christ may be mocked by despising his doctrine. It seems to me a fearful thing that men should ever hold up Christianity to scorn; yet, nowadays, there is scarcely any portion of the truth of God which is not ridiculed and caricatured. It is stripped of its own clothes, and dressed up in somebody else's old purple cloak, and then it is set in a chair, while men pretend great homage for it, and salute it, saying that they have great reverence for Christ's teaching; but, before long, they spit in its face, and treat it with the utmost disdain. There are some who deny the deity of Christ, others who hate the central doctrine of his atoning sacrifice, while many rail at justification by faith, which is the very heart of the gospel. Is there any doctrine – I scarcely know one – which has escaped the mockery and scorn of ungodly men. In the present day, if a man wants to make himself a name, he does not write upon something which he understands, and which is for the public good, but he straightway begins to assail some doctrine of Scripture of which he does not know the meaning; he misrepresents it, and sets up some notion of his own in opposition to it, for he is a 'modern thought' man, a person of much importance. It is easy work to scoff at the Bible, and to deny the truth. I think that I could myself pose as a learned man, in that way, if ever the devil should sufficiently control me to make me feel any ambition of that sort. In fact, there is scarcely a fool in Christendom who cannot make himself a name among modern thinkers if he will but blaspheme loudly enough, for that seems to be the road to fame, nowadays, among the great mass of mankind. They are dubbed 'thoughtful' who thus insult the truth of God as the soldiers, with their spittle, insulted the Christ of God.

I shall come closely home to some of you, who attend here regularly, when I say that Christ can still be mocked by resolves which never lead to obedience. Let me speak very softly upon this solemn truth. Give me your hand, my friend; let me look into your eyes; I would fain look into your soul if I could, while I put this matter very personally to you. Several times, ere leaving this house, you have said, 'I will repent of my sin; I will seek the Lord; I will believe in Jesus.' You meant these words when you uttered them; why, then, have you not fulfilled your promises? I do not care what excuse you give, because any reason which you give will be most unreasonable, for it will only amount to this – that there was something better than to do what Christ bids you, something better for you than to be saved by him, something better than the forgiveness of your sins, something better than regeneration, something better than Christ's eternal love. You would have chosen Christ, but Barabbas came across your path, so you said, 'Not this Man, but Barabbas.' You would have thought seriously about the salvation of your soul, but you had promised to go to a certain place of amusement, so you put off seeking the Saviour till a more convenient season. Possibly, you said, 'My trade is of such a character that I shall have to give it up if I become a Christian, and I cannot afford to do that.' I heard of one who listened to a sermon which impressed him – and he did not often hear sermons – and he wished that he could be a Christian; but he had made various bets for large amounts, and he felt that he could not think of other things till they were ended.

There are many such things that keep men from Christ. I do not care what it is that you prefer to the Saviour; you have insulted him if you prefer anything to him. If it were the whole world, and all that it contains, that you had chosen, these things are but trifles when compared with the sovereignty of Christ, his crown rights to every man's heart, and the immeasurable riches that he is prepared to give to every soul that comes and trusts in him. Do you prefer a harlot to the Lord Jesus Christ? Then tell me not that you do not spit in his face; you do what is worse even than that. Do you prefer profits wrongly gained to accepting Jesus as your Saviour? Do not tell me, sir, that you have never bowed the knee before him in scorn; for you have done far worse than that. Or was it a little paltry pleasure – mere trifling laughter and folly of an hour – that you preferred to your Lord? Oh, what must he feel when he sees these contemptible things preferred to him, knowing that eternal damnation is at the back of your foolish choice? Yet men choose a moment's folly and hell, instead of Christ and heaven! Was ever such an insult as that paid to Christ by Roman soldiers? Go, legionaries; you are not the worst of men! There are some who, being pricked in their conscience, make a promise of repentance, and then, for the world's sake, and for their flesh's sake, and for the devil's sake, break that promise; the soldiers did not sin against Christ so grossly as that!

Listen once more. I must again come very closely home to some of you. Was it not a shameful thing that they should call Christ King, and yet not mean it; and, apparently, give him a crown, a sceptre, a royal robe, the bowing of the knee, and the salutation of the lips, but not to mean any of it? It cuts me to the heart to think of what I am going to say, yet I must say it. There are some professors – members of Christian churches – members of this church – who call Christ Master and Lord, yet they do not the things which he says. They profess to believe the truth, yet it is not like the truth to them, for they never yield to its power, and they act as if what they call truth were fiction and human invention. There are still some, like those of whom the apostle wrote, and I can say as he did – 'of whom I have told you often, and now tell you even weeping, that they are the enemies of the cross of Christ' – though in the nominal church. Their God is their belly, they glory in their shame, and they mind earthly things; yet they bow the knee before Christ, they sing, 'Crown him! Crown him!' and they eat the bread and drink the wine which set forth his broken body and shed blood, yet they have no part nor lot in him. It has always been so in the nominal church, and it will be so, I suppose, till Christ comes to separate the chaff from the wheat. But, oh, how dreadful it is! To insult Christ in the Roman guardroom, was bad enough; but to insult him at the communion table, is far worse. For a Roman soldier to spit in his face, was bad enough; but to come and mingle with his people, and call yourself his servant, and then to go deliberately to drink with the drunkard, or to be unchaste in your life, or dishonest in your trade, or false in your talk, or foul in your heart, is even more abominable. I know no milder word that can express the truth. To call Christ Master, and yet never to do his bidding – this is mockery and scorn of the worst possible kind, for it wounds him at the very heart.

I was reading, today, part of a Welsh sermon which struck me much. The preacher said, 'Let all who are in this congregation avow their real master. I will first call upon the servants of the devil to own him. He is a fine master, and a glorious one to serve, and his service is joy and delight; now all of you who are serving him say, "Amen. Glory be to the devil!" Say it.' But nobody spoke. 'Now,' said he, 'don't be ashamed to own him whom you serve every day of your life; speak out, and say, "Glory be to my master, the devil!" or else hold your tongues for ever.' And still nobody spoke, so the minister said, 'Then, I hope that, when I ask you to glorify Christ, you will speak.' And they did speak, till the chapel seemed to ring again as they cried, 'Glory be to Christ!' That was good; but if I were to test you in a similar fashion, I feel tolerably certain that nobody here would own his master if his master is the devil, and I am afraid that some of the devil's servants would join us in our hallelujahs to Christ. That is the mischief of it; the devil himself can use self-denial, and he can teach his servants to deny their master, and in that very way to do him the most honour. O dear friends, be true to Christ; and, whatever you do, never mock him! There are many other things, which you can do, that will be much more profitable to you than mocking Christ. If God be God, serve him; if Christ be your Master and Lord, honour him; but if you do not mean to honour him, do not call him Master; for, if you do, all your faults and sins will be laid at his door, and he will be dishonoured through you.

Now I think that I hear somebody say, 'I am afraid, sir, that I have mocked Christ; what am I to do?' Well, my answer is – Do not despair, because that would be mocking him, in another way by doubting his power to save you. 'I am inclined to throw it all away.' Do not act so, for that would be to insult your Maker by another sin; namely, open revolt against him. 'What shall I do, then?' Well, go and tell him your grief and sorrow. He told his disciples to preach the gospel first at Jerusalem, because that was where those soldiers lived, the very men who had mocked him; and he prayed for his murderers, 'Father, forgive them, for they know not what they do.' In a like manner, he presents his mercy to you, first. Come to him, then; and if you are conscious that you have mocked him in any one of these ways that I have mentioned, say to yourself, 'Then, if he will but forgive me, I will henceforth live all the more to his praise. I cannot wipe out my sin, but he can; and if he will do so, I will love him much because I shall have had much forgiven; and I will spend and be spent to glorify his holy name.'

My time has almost gone, so this must be my last remark. Whether we have mocked Christ or not, come, dear brothers and sisters, *let us now glorify him.* This very hour, let us crown him with our heart's love and trust. Bring forth that royal crown – the crown of your love, of your trust, of your complete consecration to him – and put it upon his head now, saying, 'My Lord, my God, my King.' Now put the sceptre into his hand by yielding absolute obedience to his will. Is there anything he bids you do? Do it. Is there anything he bids you give? Give it. Is there anything he bids you abstain from? Abstain from it. Put not a reed sceptre into his hand, but give him the entire control of your whole being. Let him be your real Lord, reigning over your spirit, soul, and body. What next? Bow before him, and worship in the quiet of your inmost heart. You need not bow your bodies, but let your spirits fall down before him that sitteth upon the throne, and cry, 'Unto him that loved us, and washed us from our sins in his own blood, and hath made us kings and priests unto God and his Father; to him be glory and dominion for ever and ever. Amen.'

And when you have worshipped him, then proclaim him King. As those soldiers said in mockery, 'Hail, King of the Jews!' so now do you in real earnestness proclaim him King of Jews and Gentiles, too. Go home, and tell your friends that Jesus is King. Tell it out among the nations that 'the Lord reigneth,' as the old version has it, 'reigneth from the tree.' He has made his cross to be his throne, and there he reigns in majesty and in mercy. Tell it to your children, tell it to your servants, tell it to your neighbours, tell it in every place wherever you can be heard – that the Lord, even Jesus, reigns as King of kings and Lord of lords. Say to them, 'Kiss the Son, lest he be angry, and ye perish from the way, when his wrath is kindled but a little.'

And then, when you have proclaimed him, kiss him yourself. As the rough soldiers spat upon him, so do you give to him the kiss of homage and affection, saying, 'Lord Jesus, thou art mine for ever and ever.' Say, with the spouse, 'I am my Beloved's, and my Beloved is mine.' I suggest to you that each individual here, who loves his Lord much, should think of something fresh that he can do for Christ during this week – some special gift that you can bestow upon him – some special action that you can do, which shall be quite new; and shall be only for Jesus, and altogether for Jesus, as an act of homage to his name. I often wish that God's people were more inventive, like that woman who wanted greatly to honour him, so she brought out her alabaster box, and broke it, and poured the precious ointment upon his head. Think of something special that you can do for Christ, or give to him.

A dear friend, now in heaven, but who used to worship in this place, had a son who had been a great scapegrace, and was, in fact, living a vicious life. He had been long away from his father, and his father did not know what to do about getting him home, for he had treated him very badly, marred his comfort, and spoiled his home But, as I was preaching, one night, this thought came to him, 'I will find out, tomorrow morning, where my son is, and I will go to him.' The father knew that the son was very angry with him, and very bitter against him, so he thought of a certain fruit, of which his son was very fond, and he sent him a basketful of it next morning; and when the son received it, he said, 'Then, my father has still some affection for me.' And the next day the father called, and the day after he had him at home again, and that was the means of bringing the son to the Saviour. He had worn himself out with vice, and he soon died but his father told me that it was a great joy to his heart to think that he could have a good hope concerning his son. Had the son died away from home, had the father not sought him out, he would never have forgiven himself.

Now, he did that for Christ's sake; cannot some of you do a similar deed for the same reason? Is there any skeleton in your house? Is there any mischief you could set right; or have you anything you can give to your Lord and Master? Think, each one of you for himself or herself, what you can do and, inasmuch as Christ was so shamefully despised and rejected, seek to honour and glorify him in the best way that you can, and he will accept your homage and your offering for his love's sake.

May he help you so to do! Amen.